NEOLIBERALISM AND INSECURITY IN ADVANCED CAPITALISM

This book examines the relationship between neoliberalism and insecurity, beginning with the post-World War II period and continuing up through the present. Neoliberalism – the dominant political economic perspective that elevates competition above all else at both the structural and individual levels – has increased the amount of insecurity (e.g., food, energy, job) across the world. It provides a theoretical and empirical analysis of how and why neoliberalism and insecurity have become intertwined over the last half century.

The book takes a novel approach to the study of neoliberalism, insecurity, and their intersection. First, in addition to examining specific types of insecurity, the overall concept of insecurity is defined and theorized as a fundamental part of neoliberal capitalism. Second, to help bypass the structural versus individual binary that has come to characterize much of the neoliberalism literature, a field-theoretic framework, heavily influenced by the work of Pierre Bourdieu, is employed.

As such, it will be of great interest for researchers in neoliberalism, insecurity, and Bourdieu's theory of practice, including advanced undergraduate students and graduate scholars from sociology, anthropology, geography, political science, and public health.

Michael A. Long is Professor of Sociology and Director of the Center for Insecurity and Inequality Research at Oklahoma State University. He has written widely on food insecurity, environmental sociology, sustainability, public health, and quantitative methodology. His most recent book is *Applying Benford's Law for Assessing the Validity of Social Science Data* (with P. Stretesky, K. Berry, J. Johnston, M. Lynch, 2023).

Andrew S. Fullerton is Professor of Sociology at Oklahoma State University. He has written widely on job insecurity, quantitative methodology, social stratification, and political sociology. He has published several articles on regression models for ordinal outcomes and a book titled *Ordered Regression Models: Parallel, Partial, and Non-Parallel Alternatives* (with J. Xu, 2016).

Paul B. Stretesky is Professor of Criminology and Director of Teaching and Learning in the School of Social and Political Sciences at the University of Lincoln, UK. His research interests include food insecurity, environmental crime and justice, quantitative methods, and violence. His most recent book, *Applying Benford's Law for Assessing the Validity of Social Science Data* (2023), was co-authored with M. Long, K. Berry, J. Johnston, and M. Lynch.

Routledge Advances in Sociology

402 **Doubting Ghosts**
Paranormal Investigation and the Paradoxes of Belief
Michele Hanks

403 **A Sociology of Awkwardness**
On Social Interactions Going Wrong
Pauwke Berkers and Yosha Wijngaarden

404 **Migration, Mobility and Transformation**
Examining the Role of Family and Schooling
Kate Hoskins and Bernard Barker

405 **Avoiding Retirement in Chile**
Extending Working Lives in an Uncertain and Precarious Context
Ignacio Cabib

406 **Citizenship in Crisis in Athens**
Migration, Media and Identity
Afroditi-Maria Koulaxi

407 **Neoliberalism and Insecurity in Advanced Capitalism**
Michael A. Long, Andrew S. Fullerton, Paul B. Stretesky

For more information about this series, please visit: https://www.routledge.com/Routledge-Advances-in-Sociology/book-series/SE0511

NEOLIBERALISM AND INSECURITY IN ADVANCED CAPITALISM

Michael A. Long, Andrew S. Fullerton,
Paul B. Stretesky

Routledge
Taylor & Francis Group
LONDON AND NEW YORK

Designed cover image: Shutterstock

First published 2025
by Routledge
4 Park Square, Milton Park, Abingdon, Oxon OX14 4RN

and by Routledge
605 Third Avenue, New York, NY 10158

Routledge is an imprint of the Taylor & Francis Group, an informa business

British Library Cataloguing-in-Publication Data
A catalogue record for this book is available from the British Library

Library of Congress Cataloging-in-Publication Data
Names: Long, Michael A., author. | Fullerton, Andrew S., author. | Stretesky, Paul B., author.
Title: Neoliberalism and insecurity in advanced capitalism / Michael A. Long, Andrew S. Fullerton, Paul B. Stretesky.
Description: Abingdon, Oxon ; New York, NY : Routledge, 2025. | Series: Routledge advances in sociology | Includes bibliographical references and index.
Identifiers: LCCN 2024060352 (print) | LCCN 2024060353 (ebook) | ISBN 9781032354392 (hardback) | ISBN 9781032354378 (paperback) | ISBN 9781003326892 (ebook)
Subjects: LCSH: Neoliberalism—History. | Food supply—History. | Power resources—History. | Competition—History. | Capitalism—History.
Classification: LCC HB95 .L66 2025 (print) | LCC HB95 (ebook) | DDC 330.12/2—dc23/eng/20250214
LC record available at https://lccn.loc.gov/2024060352
LC ebook record available at https://lccn.loc.gov/2024060353

ISBN: 978-1-032-35439-2 (hbk)
ISBN: 978-1-032-35437-8 (pbk)
ISBN: 978-1-003-32689-2 (ebk)

DOI: 10.4324/9781003326892

Typeset in Sabon
by codeMantra

CONTENTS

FIGURES

TABLES

ACKNOWLEDGMENTS

We would like to thank some people that have been integral in helping us complete this book. First, we would like to acknowledge Emily Briggs and Lakshita Joshi at Routledge for providing us the opportunity to write this book and for their guidance throughout the process. Second, the research assistance of Lara Gonçalves and Madison Scott was invaluable and helped make the final product what it is. We would also like to acknowledge Jeff Dixon for lending us his expertise and providing feedback on drafts of various chapters. Most importantly, we want to thank our families, especially, Kelsey, Archie, Christine, Denver, and Mason. We do this for you. Finally, we dedicate this book to everyone who suffers from insecurities daily and to those people who have devoted their lives to helping reduce the insecurities of others.

1

INTRODUCTION

This book is about two concepts – "neoliberalism" and "insecurity." These two concepts are multifaceted, mean different things to different people in different contexts, have been independently studied a great deal by academics, and have profound implications for human life in what we refer to as "advanced capitalism." To add an additional layer of complexity, the term "advanced capitalism" has been conceptualized in different ways. For us, advanced capitalism signifies a time period. In this book, when we discuss advanced capitalism, we are referring to the period of time when capitalism has been established and well developed throughout the world. Critical theorist Jürgen Habermas (1988), who studied advanced capitalism extensively, suggested that there are several characteristics of advanced capitalist societies, including industrial concentration, use of the State to keep the economy stable, and democratic governments. We generally agree with Habermas' conception of advanced capitalism and suggest that, for our purposes, it begins with the post-World War II (WWII) period. We focus primarily on the current phase of advanced capitalism, characterized by the rise and establishment of neoliberalism as the dominant political economic organization across the world. To capture the downfall of the previous era of advanced capitalism, which was highlighted by the role of State intervention and its replacement with neoliberal policies to solve the current economic problems, for us, the "neoliberal era" of advanced capitalism begins in the latter half of the 1970s and runs through the present.

What we suggest theoretically and then examine empirically throughout this book is that during this time, as neoliberalism has become the dominant economic philosophy beginning in the late 1970s and arguably continuing until the present, insecurity has become one of the defining features of life

DOI: 10.4324/9781003326892-1

for people living today in a world organized by neoliberal capitalism. In this introductory chapter, we first provide a definition and brief discussion of neoliberalism, then define several types of insecurity (food, energy, and job), and finally make the case that we need to investigate the broader concept of "insecurity," rather than just specific types of insecurity, if we want a fuller understanding of how it operates in neoliberal capitalism. We then review Pierre Bourdieu's theory of practice, highlighting his concepts of field, habitus, and capital. This is a necessary step as we employ a field-theoretic approach to our study of neoliberalism and insecurity. We discuss how we plan on examining what we refer to as the "global neoliberal capitalist field," and then end the chapter with a plan for the remainder of this book.

What Is Neoliberalism?

Chapter 2 provides a detailed description of neoliberalism and related topics. Here, we briefly define neoliberalism so that readers have an idea about what we are referring to as we layout our rationale and plan for this book. Like many social science concepts, neoliberalism can be tough to define, and to be sure, there are many definitions of neoliberalism throughout the extant literature. Some have argued that there is no one pure form of neoliberalism (e.g., Peck and Tickell 2007). However, we can turn to perhaps the definitive political economic treatment of neoliberalism for a theoretical definition. Geographer David Harvey, in *A Brief History of Neoliberalism*, suggests that

> [n]eoliberalism is in the first instance a theory of political economic practices that proposes that human well-being can best be advanced by liberating individual entrepreneurial freedoms and skills within an institutional framework characterized by strong private property rights, free markets, and trade. The role of the state is to create and preserve an institutional framework appropriate for such practices.
>
> *(2005:2)*

The theory of neoliberal economics was then often implemented in national contexts with specific types of policy measures, including, privatization, marketization, state deregulation (and market-friendly re-regulation), and the desire to create self-sufficient individuals and communities (Castree 2010; Liverman and Vilas 2006; Mansfield 2004). These processes can be thought of as typical policy measures influenced by neoliberal economics (Kopnina 2015; Mudge 2008; Parr 2013).

Further, as we will see in subsequent chapters, many definitions and applications of the neoliberalism concept focus on either the structural level or the individual level. Indeed, both these approaches to understanding the impacts of neoliberalism are very important. Sparke (2016:238) summarizes the usefulness of both approaches:

> At a macro scale these developments [neoliberal reforms] can be seen as comprising 'neoliberal governance,' a set of governmental norms including the privatization, business deregulation, and trade liberalization, that reconstitute policies in the shape of the market and repurpose the state as an entrepreneurial actor that governs through proliferating public-private partnerships in the interests of business classes and global investors...At a more intimate scale of personal behaviour it becomes 'neoliberal governmentality', a suite of practices in which individuals across a much wider set of social classes are enlisted into becoming competitive agents who invest in their human capital as entrepreneurs and who reimagine the meaning of their lives, citizenship and individuality – including their personal health – as calculating consumers constantly comparing metrics of ownership, mobility and social ranking.

The macro and micro (or structural and individualistic) perspectives on neoliberalism have drastically increased our understanding of advanced capitalism. However, little effort has been made to bridge the gaps between these approaches, with some scholars even suggesting that they may be incompatible (e.g., Barnett 2005; Dardot and Laval 2014). We believe that a more complete understanding of neoliberalism and the relationship between neoliberalism and insecurity can emerge from a perspective that integrates (and some might say, transcends) macro-level political economic analyses of neoliberalism and micro-level analysis of neoliberalism in the Foucauldian biopolitics and governmentality tradition (Foucault 2008).

We take a Bourdieusian approach in this book for a number of reasons. One main reason is to problematize the dualism between structural/individual explanations of neoliberalism's impact on life in advanced capitalism. As we just noted, researchers have suggested that there are difficulties in bridging these two schools of neoliberalism scholarship (Barnett 2005; Dardot and Laval 2014). Bourdieu was an ardent critic of dualistic thinking and used his approach to attempt to bypass them, especially the structure/agency and macro/micro dualisms. Rather than conceptualize explanations of neoliberalism's impacts in an either/or (structural or individual), Bourdieu argues that the two are interwoven in the form of a habitus and its relation to a field. Agency is past structure, and structures are remade and reproduced through agency. Bourdieu's theory of practice has been designed to account for this relationship between agency and structure – or between individual and structural explanations. Therefore, we take this approach in our examination of neoliberalism and insecurity.

We suggest that neoliberalism has created an environment where insecurity is a fundamental aspect of life for individuals during advanced capitalism. To comprehensively examine and understand the relationship between neoliberalism and insecurity during advanced capitalism, we believe it is necessary to undertake a theoretical and empirical analysis of the relationship between these concepts that bridges the dichotomy found throughout the neoliberalism literature. We therefore undertake our study of neoliberalism and insecurity using an approach heavily influenced by Bourdieu's theory of practice (Bourdieu 1977, 1984, 1990). To begin, we start with a discussion of several specific types of insecurity (food, energy, and job) and then demonstrate how our overall concept and definition of the more general condition of insecurity is built to include the various types of insecurity that exist. While types of insecurity share characteristics and often affect the same individuals, that is not always the case. Therefore, our definition of insecurity needs to be broad enough that it can be used as an umbrella definition that covers specific types of insecurity, but not too broad that it loses analytic utility.

Insecurity during Advanced Capitalism

In this book, we argue that "insecurity" is a fundamental aspect of neoliberalism. Below we provide our definition of the general conception of insecurity. However, we first would like to highlight that there are many specific forms of insecurity in advanced capitalism. For example, throughout the world, there is substantial food, energy, housing, job, medical, and water insecurity (in addition to many other forms). Scholars often study one type of (in)security at a time, which makes analytical sense since each form of insecurity is complicated, has its own tradition of scholarship, and is often viewed by policymakers as a separate problem. However, we argue that the broader concept of insecurity needs to be investigated for a more complete understanding of neoliberal capitalism. In other words, the *intersection of insecurities* is an important area of study.

Food, Energy, and Job Insecurity

We cannot dedicate a full chapter to each form of insecurity that exists in the world. We therefore focus on three forms of insecurity – food, energy, and job insecurity – that are well known, exist extensively throughout the world, and have been studied by academics (including ourselves). Here, we will simply define the individual concepts, using accepted definitions of each type of insecurity. We will then dedicate a chapter to each form of insecurity (Chapter 3, food insecurity; Chapter 4, energy insecurity; and Chapter 5, job insecurity), where we review the development of and data on that type of insecurity.

At this juncture, we need to draw attention to an important point. When we talk about insecurity, we are also talking about "security." Regardless of the type of insecurity in question (including general insecurity), insecurity is the absence of security. To aid in readability and comprehension, we sometimes refer to insecurity, while at other times, we refer to security. For example, below we define food *security*, and then define job *in*security. This difference is simply because the broadly accepted definitions of these concepts are usually defined in those ways. Our argument in this book is that insecurity is a fundamental element of neoliberal capitalism – we could just as easily say that this book is about the absence of security and neoliberal capitalism.

We now briefly define food, energy, and job insecurity, leaving an extended discussion of each to their respective chapters. It is useful to define these individual types of security/insecurity now, as we can highlight how we bring types of insecurity together in our overall definition of insecurity that we present in the following subsection. First, *food security* is a condition that is met "when all people, at all times, have physical, social and economic access to sufficient, safe and nutritious food that meets their dietary needs and food preferences for an active and healthy life" (FAO 2000:26). *Food insecurity*, then, is the absence of food security. Second, *energy insecurity* can be defined as "an inability to adequately meet basic household energy needs" (Hernández 2016:2) for things like "cooking, boiling water, lighting and heating" World Health Organization (2006:6). And third, in the case of *job insecurity*, scholars traditionally conceptualize it in two ways: "cognitive job insecurity" and "affective job insecurity." According to Anderson and Pontusson (2007:214), "'cognitive job insecurity' is an individual's estimate of the probability that he or she will lose their job in the near future, while 'affective job insecurity' refers to worry or anxiety about losing one's job."[1]

A quick examination of the definitions of food, energy, and job security/insecurity reveals similarities and differences between the three forms of insecurity. For example, all three forms of insecurity highlight the absence of a vital component of life in advanced capitalism – food, energy, and employment. However, while food insecurity and energy insecurity are primarily objective conditions (though people certainly worry about future access to food and energy), it is clear from the definition of job insecurity that while there is some underlying objective probability of job security for each worker, this is unknown to the worker. As a result, job insecurity is primarily conceived in the literature as a subjective experience based on an unknown objective condition. We take a different approach in this book that highlights the interdependence of purportedly objective and subjective forms of job insecurity, which is consistent with our field-theoretic perspective (see Chapter 5). Despite some differences between the individual types of insecurity, we see more similarities between them, especially in the way that neoliberal capitalism has arguably increased all types of insecurity. Therefore, we now turn to a discussion about the broader concept of insecurity.

Insecurity as a General Concept

As noted, while each of these individual types of insecurity that we defined and outlined above has been the subject of extensive multidisciplinary research, less scholarship has looked at the overall concept of insecurity. That is not to say that a more general argument about how intertwined insecurity is with life under contemporary capitalism has not been made at all. In fact, Astra Taylor's *The Age of Insecurity: Coming Together as Things Fall Apart*, published in 2023, is fantastic. Written from the perspective of a community organizer (among other vocations), who took part in the Occupy Wall Street social movement and founded the world's first union for debtors called "The Debt Collective," Taylor highlights how the myriad forms of insecurity dominate people's lives under capitalism. Further, the argument we will make is that the general concept of "insecurity" is necessary to investigate as it is a fundamental element of life during neoliberalism.

Taylor (2023) makes a number of interesting observations about insecurity (including its relationship with neoliberalism). She notes that, "insecurity plays a unique role in the liberal capitalist order that dominates today – a role underscored by the fact that the modern word *insecurity* entered into common usage in the seventeenth century, just as our market-driven society was coming into being" (Taylor 2023:8).[2] In other words, as human life was beginning to be framed in free-market terms, the word (and material conditions of) "insecurity" became commonplace. This was not coincidental.

It is also important to note that "insecurity" is not solely a problem for people of limited economic resources. Oftentimes, we hear the word "insecurity," and we think of two of the topics of this book: food insecurity and energy insecurity. These are primarily problems for people of lower social classes. However, other forms of insecurity, such as job and housing insecurity, can affect people across the social-class spectrum. As Taylor (2023:11) notes, "you do not have to be at rock bottom to feel insecure, because insecurity results as much from expectation as from deprivation. This is why insecurity impacts the well-being of people on every rung of the economic ladder, from the impecunious to the privileged (albeit in very different ways)." Taylor makes an important point here when she highlights two distinct causes of insecurity – expectation and deprivation. The links between deprivation and insecurity are obvious, as demonstrated above with food and energy insecurity. The relationship between expectation and insecurity may be less obvious. When peoples' reality does not meet their expectations, they may become insecure. Even though their basic needs (e.g., food, shelter, water) may be met, people may feel insecure if they are less well-off relative to others or if their conception of what their lives should be like does not match their reality. In other words, insecurity can be both relative and absolute. Insecurity has become ubiquitous with neoliberalism. Why? Taylor (2023:48) suggests,

> [t]he command to live life according to market priorities is so persuasive precisely because it is coupled with threats – threats of unemployment, destitution, shame, loss of status, and respect. Rapid economic changes and new technologies have multiplied our insecurities while also raising our expectations, increasing the risks of failure as a result.

In other words, people in a world structured by neoliberal capitalism are afraid of many types of failure.

At this point, we need our own working definition of general insecurity during advanced capitalism. Taylor (2023:64–65) notes that "[w]hen we talk about insecurity and security, we are often talking about the future; we anticipate what might occur beyond the here and now...Security means having some assurance of future stability and the ability to plan ahead." Further, she notes that "[t]oday, we understand the future in terms of probabilities" (Taylor 2023:236). Similarly, Lorey (2015:1) suggests that "[p]recarization [insecurity] means living with the unforeseeable, with contingency." We agree that insecurity has to do with the probability of correctly predicting the future. Bourdieu made a similar argument in his work on the uprooted Algerian peasants he studied during the Algerian war for independence. The forced resettlement of Algerians during the war created an unstable and divided habitus (Bourdieu 1962:142; Bourdieu and Sayad 2020:118; Steinmetz 2023:329). The state of "mens momentanea" (Bourdieu 2013:154) is one in which the individual is trapped in the current moment, struggling to adjust to rapidly changing social conditions. A hyper-focus on the present, coupled with the resulting inability to plan for and predict the future, is a defining aspect of insecurity that Bourdieu considered in the context of jobs (Bourdieu 1998:83), and one that we apply to all types of insecurity.

Building off this scholarship, we argue that at its core, *insecurity reflects the inability to successfully predict a stable and secure future.* Conversely, *security is the ability to successfully predict a stable and secure future.* If you cannot count on consistent, reliable access to sufficient food, have your energy needs met, and have consistent, reliable paid employment (in addition to other material needs), then you qualify as "insecure."

Now that we have provided a definition of neoliberalism and overviewed the specific types of insecurity and the general concept of insecurity that we employ in this book, we turn to an overview of the framework we use – Pierre Bourdieu's theory of practice.

Bourdieu's Theory of Practice: A Brief Outline and Review

In this section, we review Bourdieu's theory of practice (Bourdieu 1977, 1984, 1990). A solid comprehension of his concepts of (1) field, (2) capital, and (3) habitus – and how they fit together into a coherent theoretical perspective – is vital to understand the arguments we make in subsequent chapters. We then discuss the concepts of social space and symbolic power, which are critical for understanding his relational approach and understanding of how power operates in fields. Bourdieu's theory of practice attempts to explain social practices through a combination of conscious and unconscious decisions and actions that are determined by individual and structural factors. Therefore, the theory of practice attempts to bridge the dualism of structure and agency (Bourdieu and Wacquant 1992). In this work, Bourdieu frequently refers to the "dispositions" of individuals. While there are numerous definitions of disposition throughout Bourdieu's oeuvre, a simple one will suffice here. According to Bourdieu (2020:132), dispositions are "lasting manners of being that are the product of the conditions of existence." Dispositions are patterns of behavior that individuals learn (consciously or unconsciously) and internalize based on their experiences throughout the course of their lives.

In this section, we explicate Bourdieu's concepts of field, capital, and habitus. We then discuss how these three components come together to form his "theory of practice." We end this section with a discussion of another of Bourdieu's central concepts, symbolic power, which will become important in our analysis.

Field

We begin our overview of Bourdieu's theory of practice with a discussion of his concept of "field." Fields are social spaces that are simultaneously sites of forces exerted on agents (i.e., individuals) with varying amounts of capital (i.e., resources) and sites of struggle in which agents struggle to preserve or transform the structure of power and improve their position in the space (Bourdieu 2020). The idea of a social field derives from the electromagnetic field developed by Faraday and Maxwell in physics (Cassirer 1953 [1923]). As with physical fields, social fields are only observable through their effects on individuals in the space (Martin 2003). Bourdieu and other field theorists use the energy metaphor to explain how capital operates within a field and is used as a marker of relative position (Bourdieu 2020). Fields operate on multiple scales or levels (Emirbayer and Desmond 2015), and they may be nested in a manner like a Russian doll (Fligstein and McAdam 2012). However, fields are also relatively autonomous spaces. According to Bourdieu's approach, fields are organized based on the volume and composition of different forms of capital that serve as principles of hierarchization in the space (Bourdieu 2020). The ability to define the most important forms of capital is one of the key stakes in the field. Wacquant (2019) argues that "social space" is the more generic concept and is defined as a multidimensional distribution of "socially efficient properties (capitals) which stipulate a set of patterned positions from which one can intelligibly predict strategies." Fields are a special type of social space "arising when a domain of action and authority becomes sufficiently demarcated, autonomized, and monopolized" (Wacquant 2019:17). The global neoliberal capitalist field is one such example and serves as the focus of this book. It is a meta-field connecting national spaces of neoliberal capitalism.[3]

Each field has its own "doxa," or shared set of beliefs that are often unstated (Bourdieu 1977; Husserl 1973 [1948]). Adherence to the doxa is a requirement for membership in the field (Bourdieu 2000). The doxa exists primarily in a practical, unconscious state. It is the "common sense" shared by members of a field that does not require expression and is evident primarily in negative terms. Those who violate the unspoken but shared view of the order of things are deemed heretics or incompetent. Thus, fields impose limits on thought by silently conveying what is thinkable (Bourdieu 2023:209). Agents within a field may not even notice these limits as adherence to the doxa is a requirement for membership in the field (Bourdieu 2014:91). Relatedly, autonomous fields require members to believe in the value of the rewards offered in the field ("illusio") and impose their own rules ("nomos").

While fields are autonomous spaces, Bourdieu often discussed similarities between separate fields. He used the term "homology" to indicate that one field had aspects that correspond to aspects of a second field (what Bourdieu often referred to as "structural and functional homologies" [Bourdieu and Wacquant 1992: 105–106]). "Fields are homologous to the extent that they develop isomorphic properties, such as positions of dominance and subordination, strategies of exclusion and usurpation, and mechanisms of reproduction and change" (Swartz 1997:129). The homology property of fields allows researchers to compare fields and unpack where overlapping forms of domination occur.

Capital

Field members accumulate capital, hold positions in the field based on their volume and composition of capital, and struggle over the power to define the importance of types of capital (or the "dominant principle of hierarchization" [Bourdieu 2020]). The two primary forms of capital in Bourdieu's work are economic capital and cultural capital. Economic capital is an individual's wealth, property, etc. The concept of cultural capital is a bit more complicated. Swartz (1997:75) provides a useful overview of Bourdieu's concept of cultural capital.

> A form of power as capital in the differentiated societies that Bourdieu conceptualizes by extending the logic of economic analysis to ostensibly noneconomic goods and services is *cultural capital*. His concept of cultural capital covers a wide variety of resources including such things as verbal facility, general cultural awareness, aesthetic preferences, information about the school system, and educational credentials. His point is to suggest that culture (in the broadest sense of the term) can become a power resource. This occurs when cultural markets emerge where investors exchange currencies, strive for profits, and, in the case of educational credentials in recent years, suffer from inflation.

Bourdieu (2021:243) generalizes cultural capital as a type of information capital, which exists in three forms: embodied, objectified, and institutionalized (i.e., in bodies, objects, and institutions). Access to this information about "legitimate culture" is a powerful resource that along with economic capital defines one's position in the social space (Bourdieu 1984).

Habitus

Fields require agents operating in the space to have the appropriate set of dispositions, which are the incorporation of previous experiences and social structures in the body (Bourdieu 1984, 1990). The habitus is a potentiality for action that operates as a spring triggered by a field (Wacquant 2016:69). It is the bodily incorporation of previous social structures acquired in the multidimensional "family field" (Bourdieu 2000:166), which is first formed in childhood (the "primary habitus") and then refined in adulthood as individuals enter new fields and acquire the secondary habitus required of participants. The habitus is a generative formula for action operating below the level of consciousness that guides tastes, preferences, attitudes, and bodily comportment in an intentional yet unconscious way because of how deeply embedded it is (Bourdieu 2020). The habitus remains only a potential for action, however, until it is sprung into action by a field. Entrance into a field is contingent upon the individual having a habitus prior to entry that is consistent with the specific habitus required within the field. In this sense, the field and the individual simultaneously choose one another (e.g., the idea of an occupational "calling").

The class habitus is so central to the original or "primary" habitus developed in childhood (Bourdieu and Passeron 1977:42) that it is common in the literature to equate the two forms of habitus. However, class is merely one dimension of several comprising the primary habitus, which one could reasonably label the "family habitus," given that it originates within the "family field" during childhood (Bourdieu 2000:166; Wacquant 2014:7). The family field is a meta-field comprising several fields impacting child development, including class, gender, sexuality, race, ethnicity, nationality, and rurality.

The key difference between the family field (and its subfields) and a field like the global neoliberal capitalist field is that the former shapes the primary or generic habitus, while the latter shapes the secondary or specific habitus (Bourdieu and Passeron 1977:43). An individual's habitus is a combination of a primary habitus formed in the family field during early childhood and several specific habitus developed in various fields later in life (e.g., educational, occupational, neoliberal). The primary habitus plays a decisive role in the decisions (and ability to) enter subsequent fields and thus develops each new, specific habitus.

The concept of the habitus calls into question traditional dualisms such as structure vs. agency and macro vs. micro because it is a purportedly individual-level phenomenon constructed out of previous social structures. It is the past social structures that constitute the habitus. It is true as Faulkner wrote in *Requiem for a Nun* that "the past is never dead. It is not even past." Social agents are "history incorporated" (Bourdieu 2023:61). The implication of this is that the actions of individuals, such as statements regarding experiences with food, energy, and job insecurity, are always simultaneously expressions of human agency and evidence of structural constraint. One may feel free to make choices without constraint when one's habitus is perfectly attuned to a field, but the habitus producing the choices is not of one's choosing (Bourdieu 2023:101).

Theory of Practice

The theory of practice integrates the concepts of field, capital, and habitus to generate a science of "practices" – that is, human action and behavior. While Bourdieu described his theory of practices in his 1977 book, *Outline of a Theory of Practice* (Bourdieu 1977), and his 1990 book, *The Logic of Practice* (Bourdieu 1990), perhaps the most well-known descriptions and applications of his theory of practice are in *Distinction: A Social Critique of the Judgement of Taste* (Bourdieu 1984). In *Distinction*, Bourdieu posits the following equation in relation to the theory of practice: [(habitus)(capital)] + field = practice (Bourdieu 1984:95). This is a conceptual model, not something that can solved directly to get a value for practice. Rather, what Bourdieu was describing was that an individual's habitus and capital interact with each other within the confines of a specific field to produce practices.

There have also been visual interpretations of the theory of practice, especially in terms of field and capital. In a 1983 article in *Poetics*, Bourdieu

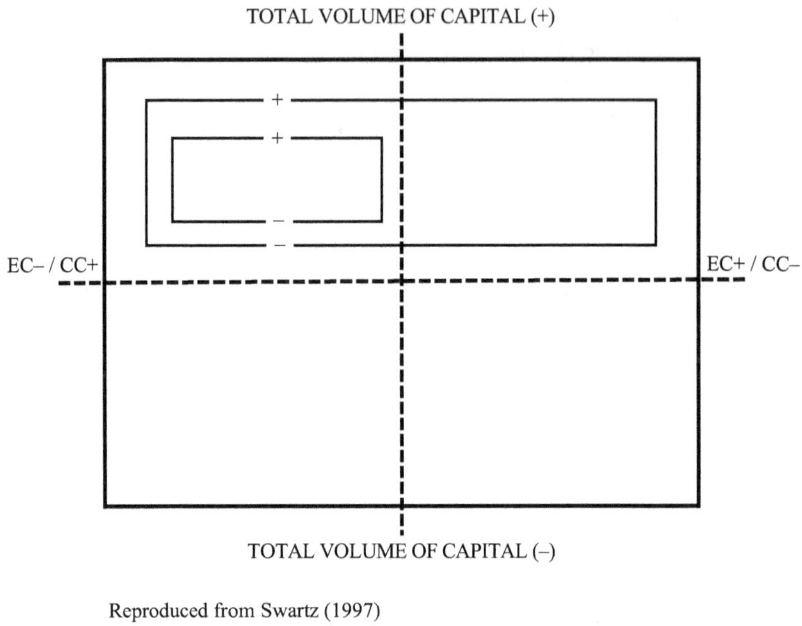

FIGURE 1.1 Example of Fields

Source: Reproduced from Swartz (1997)

introduced a rather rudimentary, but useful, description of the artistic field, nested within the field of power, which is itself nested within the field of class relations (Bourdieu 1983:319).[4] Recognizing the usefulness of this figure in the *Poetics* article, David Swartz (1997:139) produced a more detailed version of the figure, which appears in his excellent treatment of Bourdieu's canon in *Culture & Power: The Sociology of Pierre Bourdieu*. We have reproduced Swartz's figure here (Figure 1.1) to help aid our description of the theory of practice.

Figure 1.1 enables researchers to map individuals within the fields under investigation. It also allows for the comparison of field homologies, as some fields are nested within others; however, the dominant and dominated poles remain the same and are organized around the same criteria – an individual's composition of economic and cultural capital. We anticipate that national spaces of neoliberal capitalism will deviate somewhat from the first two axes in the social space given that the correspondence analyses used to inform the construction of the space were based on data from a single country (France) approximately 60 years ago (see Bourdieu 1984). The space of US neoliberal capitalism, as presented in Chapter 7, is structured by the volume and composition of capital, but in a somewhat different manner than described in this chapter.

Symbolic Power

Those with enough economic or cultural capital to exert influence on the functioning of the field have what Bourdieu (2023:3) termed "symbolic capital," which is a type of prestige or recognition of the value of one's capital that allows the bearer of this form of capital to define the legitimate categories of perception (Bourdieu 1991). These categories or classification schemes derive from the structure of power within fields and become incorporated within the specific habitus requirement of field members in the form of mental structures or schemes of perception. The ability of holders of symbolic capital to impose these categories of perception on social agents without having the act interpreted as an exercise of power is the ultimate source of its efficacy. This misrecognition of the arbitrary nature of the classificatory schemes of perception and their political roots is an essential component of what Bourdieu (1991, 2023) referred to as symbolic power. The State has a monopoly over the exercise of symbolic power (i.e., symbolic violence) (Bourdieu 2014, 2024). The complicity of social agents in this process is the ultimate source of its power. Categories of perception are accepted as natural rather than arbitrary and recognized as legitimate, which is simultaneously a misrecognition of their arbitrary nature and the political struggle that produced them.

We now proceed to a discussion of how we use Bourdieu's perspective to help us understand the relationship between neoliberalism and insecurity in advanced capitalism.

A Theory of Practices in Advanced Capitalism

Now that we have outlined Bourdieu's theory of practice, generally, we turn to a discussion of what we call the "global neoliberal capitalist field." Understanding the global neoliberal capitalist field is essential to an understanding of practices and, more generally, life in advanced capitalism. We are not the first to refer to neoliberal capitalism in field-theoretic terms (Mudge 2008, 2016); however, to our knowledge, we are the first to conduct a comprehensive analysis of neoliberal capitalism through a theory of practice approach.

We argue that there is a global neoliberal capitalist field (however, our empirical example in Chapter 7 focuses on the US neoliberal capitalist space, which is nested within the global neoliberal capitalist field). Bourdieu did not discuss transnational (or global) fields. Rather, subsequent scholars have delved into the conceptualization and development of transnational fields. An important advancement in this scholarship is a special issue of the journal *The Sociological Review* (volume 64, issue 2) on "Fielding Transnationalism," co-edited by Julian Go and Monika Krause (see Go and Krause 2016, for overview of the special issue). Of particular interest to us is Buchholz

(2016), who works to expand field theorizing beyond the nation-state to a potentially global field by introducing the concept of "relative vertical autonomy" to unpack the relations between national and global fields. As she notes,

> [t]he idea of relative vertical autonomy offers a conceptual basis from which it is possible to theorize relations between global and national levels in ways that avoid simple dualisms…As the 'relativity' of field autonomy suggest that national and global field levels are only *partially* independent, we must approach them, by the same token, as still *relatively interdependent.* Thus, the concept permits us to grasp global and national field levels as simultaneously distinct and entangled, as independent and interdependent – beyond any dualistic or even zero-sum terms.
>
> *(Buchholz 2016:48)*

As Buchholz notes, it is crucial not to fall back into dualism when examining the existence of a global field, with national fields or social spaces nested within it. She suggests that applying the relative vertical autonomy principle, which she posits, helps researchers theorize the emergence of global fields, how those global fields interact with national fields, and reformulate Bourdieu's typically nation-specific forms of capital. Given that we are positing the existence of a global neoliberal capitalist field, which suggests the existence of national neoliberal capitalist spaces, we need to ensure that our theorizing reflects the relationships between global and national neoliberal capitalist fields/spaces. We will expand on this further in Chapter 8 when we discuss the implications and findings of our empirical investigation of the US neoliberal capitalist space, which is nested within the larger global neoliberal capitalist field.

While Bourdieu did not write about or refer to a neoliberal capitalist field, he did discuss what he called the "economic field" (Bourdieu 2005:196) and a "global economic field," with global subfields nested within it (Bourdieu 2005:229). And, during the time of his later writings, the economic field he was discussing was heavily influenced by neoliberalism. In *The Social Structures of the Economy*, Bourdieu highlights the benefits of a field-theoretic approach to understanding neoliberal capitalism,

> field theory stands opposed to the atomistic, mechanistic vision [neoliberal economic theory] which hypostasizes the price effect and which, like Newtonian physics, reduces agents (shareholders, managers or firms) to interchangeable material points, whose preferences, inscribed in an exogenous utility function or even, in the most extreme variant (formulated by Gary Becker, among others), an immutable one, determine actions mechanically. It also stands opposed, through in a different way, to the

> interactionist vision, which is, by virtue of the representation of the agent as a calculating, able to cohabit with the mechanistic vision, and according to which the economic and social order can be reduced to a host of interacting individuals, most often interacting on a contractual basis.
>
> *(2005:97)*

Here, Bourdieu is suggesting that field theory is a useful approach for examining neoliberal capitalism, as it avoids the traps of assuming individuals (agents) operate in mechanistic ways, while also sidestepping the pitfalls of a purely interactional approach. We agree with Bourdieu that a field-based approach to neoliberal capitalism helps us avoid these traps as well as the other dualistic concerns that characterize the neoliberalism literature.

Economic and Security Capital in Advanced Capitalism

In the global (and national) neoliberal capitalist field, we argue that one of the primary forms of capital that organize the field and therefore delineate spaces within the field is based on (in)security. We refer to this as "security capital." We view security capital as a type of cultural capital. While economic capital and cultural capital are the primary types of capital for Bourdieu, he notes that other forms of capital operate in different fields. In one of his lectures captured in the five volumes on "General Sociology," Bourdieu remarked on this, when he noted,

> I indicated at the outset that a species of capital is always specific. To put it simply, we could say that the specific capital of a field is what works in that field. Even more basically, it is what 'works' in that field, what you need in order to really belong to a field.
>
> *(Bourdieu 2021:156)*

We argue, then, that the two organizing aspects of the global neoliberal capitalist field are economic capital and security capital. We define "security capital" as a variant of cultural capital consisting of information or knowledge pertaining to the successful navigation of uncertain work, family, and economic environments. As with all types of cultural capital, it takes one of three forms (Bourdieu 2021:161): incorporated (e.g., neoliberal habitus), objectified (e.g., a pension plan or a house), and institutionalized (e.g., the tenure system in higher education or the financial planning industry). The different forms of security capital promote a sense of *confidence in one's future*. It involves having trust in oneself to produce positive (secure) outcomes for the future. Security capital is necessary to operate effectively in a neoliberal space. The legitimate culture of neoliberalism is one of self-reliance and self-promotion, which forms the basis of the entrepreneurial view of the self that is dominant under neoliberalism (Foucault 2008; see also Dardot and Laval 2014; Lemke 2002; Larner 2000). As Larner (2000:13) suggests, people view "themselves as individualized and active subjects responsible for enhancing their own well-being." Generalizing this into a type of information, we conceptualize this as a stock of confidence in oneself and one's future, which we term security capital. Misrecognition is a process of taking the social structures in a field and the mental structures they condition in the habitus as a given rather than a political outcome of field struggles (Bourdieu 2020, 2022), and it is key to understanding security capital as well. To embody the entrepreneurial self and maintain a large stock of security capital, one must misrecognize this view of the self as natural, rather than as the outcome of struggles within the bureaucratic and economic fields, promoting a view of the self that denies the fundamentally social nature of the self as one rooted in social relations (Mead 1934), for political and economic gains. Although security capital, rather than the more general category of cultural capital, organizes the global neoliberal capitalist field, we suggest that there are structural homologies between the global neoliberal capitalist field, the field of social classes, and the field of power.

Security capital includes those things that help individuals navigate the global neoliberal capitalist field or - in other words – reduce insecurity. Some examples include forms of job security (e.g., tenure in the US education field, labor union membership), current and future financial security (e.g., requisite knowledge of the financialized neoliberal field to successfully participate in it, investments, pensions, and retirement saving such as IRAs and 401ks – especially when employers make substantial contributions), medical security (e.g., health, dental, vision, and other medical insurance), residential (housing) security (e.g., home owners and renters insurance, more specialized insurance forms such as flood, earthquake, and other security threats that vary by geography and climate), food security (e.g., planting a garden/converting a small piece of land to food production, raising small livestock [e.g., chickens, goats, pigs]), and energy security (installing a backup generator in the home for when the power [provided by the State] goes offline). While there are other examples, we believe these examples of security capital help us explain the concept of security capital. Accumulating security capital helps reduce insecurity and therefore move toward the dominant pole of the global neoliberal capitalist field.

The global neoliberal capitalist field is a meta-field connecting national-level spaces of neoliberal capitalism. We expect the volume and composition of capital (along with social trajectory) to play important roles in the structuring of the space, but national differences in institutions and the country's neoliberal trajectory are likely to matter for the structure of the space. The features of any field or social space are revealed by the underlying empirical structures in the data rather than determined a priori, which is why geometric data analysis techniques are also referred to as exploratory or inductive data analysis (Le Roux and Rouanet 2010). Therefore, we do not offer a generic representation of the field of neoliberal capitalism. In Chapter 7, we map the neoliberal capitalist space in the US based on data from a survey we administered in the summer of 2024. The two dimensions organizing the space are the volume of economic and security capital (first axis) and the composition of security capital (second axis) (for more details, see Chapter 7).

The Neoliberal Habitus

In a theory of practice approach, understanding the habitus of the individuals in the field is important to bridge dualisms such as structure/agency and macro/micro. Bourdieu used the concept of habitus to avoid dualism. The habitus is both agentic and structural given that it is a generative formula operating below the level of individual consciousness, but it is also the embodiment of past social structures. If there is a global neoliberal capitalist field, then there must be a neoliberal habitus of agents within that field. As we noted above, Bourdieu wrote of an economic field, one which was highly neoliberal in nature. Similarly, he described an "economic habitus" to bridge the dualism of mechanistic/individualistic (rational) approaches to the economy. Specifically, Bourdieu (2005:211) noted that

> [t]he economic behaviour socially recognized as rational is the product of certain economic and social conditions. It is only by relating it to its individual and collective genesis that one can understand its economic and social conditions of possibility and, consequently, both the necessity and the sociological limits of economic reason and of apparently unconditioned notions such as needs, calculation or preferences.

It is only by grasping how economic structures (past and present) become part of individuals' dispositions, which then impact the decisions that people make, can we have a complete understanding of neoliberal capitalism. Thus, for Bourdieu, this became the economic habitus. We use this as the starting point for our concept of the "neoliberal habitus," which shares similarities with Bourdieu's economic habitus. There are, however, differences between the two concepts. Specifically, we argue that a large part of the neoliberal habitus is shaped by insecurity.

There is some evidence that Bourdieu himself thought that insecurity was a fundamental part of a neoliberal habitus. In his most direct examination and argument against neoliberalism in *Acts of Resistance: Against the Tyranny of the Market* (1998), Bourdieu provides us with a basis for an examination of a neoliberal habitus. Writing specifically about job insecurity, Bourdieu (1998:98) spoke of "the destabilized habitus produced by insecurity." In other words, individuals in the global neoliberal capitalist field have internalized past neoliberal social structures that have been influenced by insecurity, which then shape their dispositions.

A Note on Neoliberalism, Incarceration, and Insecurity

Perhaps the most important yet unrecognized way power operates within the neoliberal capitalist field is through the systematic removal of the most vulnerable members of the population from the space. The spread of neoliberalism coincided with dramatically rising incarceration rates (World Prison Brief 2024; see Appendix A for cross-national incarceration rates) in many advanced capitalist countries[5] since the 1970s, with the US leading the way in this punitive turn (Wacquant 2009). The regulation of those in poverty by the "left hand" of the State (i.e., social welfare programs [Piven and Cloward 1993]) has been replaced by a paternalistic "right hand" (Bourdieu 1998) that regulates through a dual system of paternalistic workfare programs and a massively expanded penal system (Wacquant 2009:290–291). The prison system is now used as a means of regulating the low-wage labor market and a way for the State to deal with the consequences of increased insecurity associated with labor market deregulation and welfare state retrenchment. Western (2006) convincingly shows how the rise of mass incarceration in the US has fundamentally limited the ability of social scientists and policymakers to measure racial inequality in labor market outcomes, such as joblessness and wages, given the vast racial disparities in incarceration rates.

The incarcerated population is not a representative cross-section of adults. It draws disproportionately from individuals that prior to incarceration were most likely to experience one or more types of insecurity due to their economically vulnerable social positions. As a result, the (potentially) most insecure individuals are rendered invisible by the punitive right hand of the State. This biases estimates of the size of the insecure population. In the era of mass incarceration, the most insecure individuals simply do not count toward official statistics. Their entanglement with the criminal justice system renders them "illegible" (Butler 2004) in the eyes of the State, which is a reminder that the State has a monopoly over symbolic as well as physical violence (Bourdieu 2014:4). The power of the State to classify individuals as criminals (vs. non-criminals), confine them in prisons for extended periods, and exclude them from official calculations of key labor market indicators (e.g., unemployment and median hourly wages) also indicates how the classificatory or symbolic power of the State is interwoven with its physical power of confinement. It hardly seems like a coincidence that the same neoliberal policies creating increased levels of insecurity have also found a way to conceal the true extent of the consequences for the most powerless segments of society.

Plan for this Book

In this chapter, we have briefly defined neoliberalism and presented our definition of the general concept of "insecurity." We then proceeded to overview Bourdieu's theory of practice, as that is the perspective and methodology that we employ in our analysis of what we refer to as the "neoliberal global capitalist field." Chapter 2 provides a history of neoliberalism first in the Global North (especially in the US and UK) and then as neoliberalism was exported to the Global South, and we end with a discussion of how neoliberalism and insecurity are linked.[6] Chapters 3–5 provide overviews of the concepts of food, energy, and job insecurity, respectively. These chapters focus on how structural political economy, especially neoliberalism, has created substantial food, energy, and job insecurity throughout the world. Chapter 6 shifts focus to the individual, micro-level impacts of neoliberalism on people; building on the scholarship of Michel Foucault and others working in that tradition, we describe how the philosophy of neoliberalism affects how individuals approach their lives with a strong focus on individuality, competition, self-regulation, and self-reliance dominating the lives of people living in the neoliberal era. In Chapter 7, we provide the results of multiple correspondence analyses, based on survey data that we collected, in which we attempt to map locations in the US neoliberal capitalist space (which is nested within the larger global neoliberal capitalist field). Chapter 8 is the conclusion. In Chapter 8, we summarize the previous chapters, present theoretical advancements and lessons learned from our investigation of the global neoliberal capitalist field through the theory of practice, and draw conclusions regarding the relationship between neoliberalism and insecurity in advanced capitalism.

Notes

1 Scholars also refer to a third type, labor market insecurity, which refers to one's perceived chances of finding a comparable job in the labor market if one was to begin a job search (see Anderson and Pontusson 2007).

2 However, as Gros (2014:17) notes, the etiology of the word "security" has a much longer history. "The word 'security' derives from the Latin *securitas*, which can be deconstructed into *sine curae*: without troubles, without cares. Ther Greek equivalent, *a-taraxia*, also means without worries, without unrest."

3 We provide an in-depth discussion of the difference between a field and a social space in our presentation of the space of US neoliberal capitalism in Chapter 7. We appreciate Wacquant's (2019, 2024) efforts to highlight important differences between the more general concept of a social space and the field as a special type of social space with firm boundaries that are sufficiently differentiated and autonomous. We acknowledge that one could argue that global neoliberal capitalism is a field or a social space, depending on the strictness of the definition. We conceptualize national variations in neoliberal capitalism as national spaces nested within a global meta-field, which suggests they are shaped by a common set of forces but also exhibit differences based on national differences in institutions and historical trajectory.

4 The field of power is a meta-field comprising dominant positions in several key fields (Bourdieu 1996:264).
5 Some researchers (see, for example, Clark and Herbolsheimer 2021) observe a "criminological Kuznets curve," where economic growth is associated with increases in incarceration in less developed countries, while economic development in affluent countries decreases incarceration. However, it should be noted that these analyses were based on data from 2000 to 2015, decades after the beginning of the neoliberal capitalist era. In the neoliberal years before 2000, affluent countries experienced growing incarceration.
6 We note that no single definition of the "Global South" is unproblematic. Following McCall's (2005) "intercategorical complexity" approach and a number of recent studies on postcolonialism (e.g., Connell 2007; Go 2016; Steinmetz 2023), we provisionally adopt the categories of "Global South" and "Global North" in an effort to highlight unequal global relations and the implications for the historical development of neoliberalism and its impact on insecurity throughout the world. The irony of using a binary (Global North/South) is, however, not lost on us.

References

Anderson, Christopher J. and Jonas Pontusson. 2007. "Workers, Worries and Welfare States: Social Protection and Job Insecurity in 15 OECD Countries." *European Journal of Political Research* 46(2): 211–235. https://doi.org/10.1111/j.1475-6765.2007.00692.x.

Barnett, Clive. 2005. "The Consolations of 'Neoliberalism.'" *Geoforum* 36(1): 7–12. https://doi.org/10.1016/j.geoforum.2004.08.006.

Bourdieu, Pierre. 2024. *The Interest in Disinterestedness. Lectures at the Collège de France, 1987–1989*. Cambridge: Polity Press.

Bourdieu, Pierre. 2023. *Politics and Sociology: General Sociology, Volume 5. Lectures at the Collège de France, 1985–1986*. Cambridge: Polity Press.

Bourdieu, Pierre. 2022. *Principles of Vision: General Sociology, Volume 4. Lectures at the Collège de France, 1984–1985*. Cambridge: Polity Press.

Bourdieu. Pierre. 2021. *Forms of Capital: General Sociology, Volume 3. Lectures at the Collège de France, 1983–1984*. Cambridge: Polity. Press

Bourdieu, Pierre. 2020. *Habitus and Field: General Sociology, Volume 2. Lectures at the Collège de France, 1982–1983*. Cambridge: Polity. Press

Bourdieu, Pierre. 2014. *On the State*. Cambridge: Polity. Press

Bourdieu, Pierre. 2013. *Algerian Sketches*. Cambridge: Polity. Press

Bourdieu, Pierre. 2005. *The Social Structure of the Economy*. Cambridge: Polity Press.

Bourdieu, Pierre. 2000. *Pascalian Meditations*. Cambridge: Polity Press.

Bourdieu, Pierre. 1998. *Acts of Resistance: Against the Tyranny of the Market*. New York: The New Press.

Bourdieu, Pierre. 1996. *The State Nobility*. Stanford, CA: Stanford University Press.

Bourdieu, Pierre. 1991. *Language & Symbolic Power*. Cambridge, MA: Harvard University Press.

Bourdieu, Pierre. 1990. *The Logic of Practice*. Stanford, CA: Stanford University Press.

Bourdieu, Pierre. 1984. *Distinction: A Social Critique of the Judgement of Taste*. Cambridge, MA: Harvard University Press.

Bourdieu, Pierre. 1983. "The Field of Cultural Production, Or: The Economic World Reversed." *Poetics* 12: 311–356.
Bourdieu, Pierre. 1977. *Outline of a Theory of Practice*. Cambridge: Cambridge University Press.
Bourdieu, Pierre. 1962. *The Algerians*. Boston, MA: Beacon Press.
Bourdieu, Pierre and Jean-Claude Passeron. 1977. *Reproduction in Education, Society and Culture*. Thousand Oaks, CA: Sage.
Bourdieu, Pierre and Abdelmalek Sayad. 2020. *Uprooting: The Crisis of Traditional Agriculture in Algeria*. Cambridge: Polity Press.
Bourdieu, Pierre and Loïc J. D. Wacquant. 1992. *An Invitation to Reflexive Sociology*. Chicago, IL: University of Chicago Press.
Buchholz, Larissa. 2016. "What is a Global Field? Theorizing Fields Beyond the Nation-State." *The Sociological Review* 64(2): 31–60.
Butler, Judith. 2004. *Undoing Gender*. New York: Routledge.
Cassirer, Ernst. 1953 [1923]. *Substance and Function & Einstein's Theory of Relativity*. Chicago, IL: Dover Publications.
Castree, Noel. 2010. "Neoliberalism and the Biophysical Environment 1: What 'Neoliberalism' Is, and What Difference Nature Makes to It." *Geography Compass* 4(12): 1725–1733. https://doi.org/10.1111/j.1749-8198.2010.00405.x.
Clark, Rob and Chancey Herbolsheimer. 2021. "The Iron Cage of Development: A Cross-National Analysis of Incarceration. 2000–2015." *Sociological Forum* 36(2): 381–404. https://doi.org/10.1111/socf.12683.
Connell, Raewyn. 2007. *Southern Theory*. New York: Routledge.
Dardot, Pierre and Christian Laval. 2014. *The New Way of the World*. London and New York: Verso.
Emirbayer, Mustafa and Matthew Desmond. 2015. The Racial Order. Chicago, IL: University of Chicago Press.
Fligstein, Neil and Doug McAdam. 2012. *A Theory of Fields*. Oxford: Oxford University Press.
Food and Agriculture Organisation of the United Nations (FAO). 2000. *The State of Food Security and Nutrition in the World*. Rome, Italy: FAO. Retrieved January 26, 2024, from https://www.fao.org/publications/home/fao-flagship-publications/the-state-of-food-security-and-nutrition-in-the-world/en.
Foucault, Michel. 2008. *The Birth of Biopolitics: Lectures at the Collège de France, 1978–1979*. New York: Palgrave Macmillan.
Go, Julian. 2016. *Postcolonial Thought and Social Theory*. Oxford: Oxford University Press.
Go, Julian and Monika Krause. 2016. "Fielding Transnationalism: An Introduction." *The Sociological Review* 64(2): 6–30. https://doi.org/10.1111/2059-7932.12000.
Gros, Frédéric. 2014. "The Fourth Age of Security." Pp. 7–28 in *The Government of Life: Foucault, Biopolitics, and Neoliberalism*, edited by Vanessa Lemm and Miguel Vatter. New York: Fordham University Press.
Habermas, Jürgen. 1988. *Theory and Practice*. Boston, MA: Beacon Press.
Harvey, David. 2005. *A Brief History of Neoliberalism*. Oxford: Oxford University Press.
Hernández, Diana. 2016. "Understanding 'Energy Insecurity' and Why It Matters to Health." *Social Science & Medicine* 167: 1–10. https://doi.org/10.1016/j.socscimed.2016.08.029.

Husserl, Edmund. 1973 [1948]. *Experience and Judgment*. Evanston, IL: Northwestern University Press.

Kopnina, Helen. 2015. "Neoliberalism, Pluralism and Environmental Education: The Call for Radical Re-Orientation." *Environmental Development* 15: 120–30. https://doi.org/10.1016/j.envdev.2015.03.005.

Larner, Wendy. 2000. "Neoliberalism: Policy, Ideology, Governmentality." *Studies in Political Economy* 63: 5–25. https://doi.org/10.1080/19187033.2000.11675231.

Lemke, Thomas. 2002. "Foucault, Governmentality, and Critique." *Rethinking Marxism: A Journal of Economics, Culture & Society* 14: 49–64. https://doi.org/10.1080/089356902101242288.

Liverman, Diana. M. and Vilas, Silvina. (2006). "Neoliberalism and the environment in Latin America." *Annual Review of Environment and Resources*, 31: 327–363. https://doi.org/10.1146/annurev.energy.29.102403.140729.

Lorey, Isabell. 2015. *State of Insecurity: Government of the Precarious*. New York: Verso.

Mansfield, Becky. 2004. "Rules of Privatization: Contradictions in Neoliberal Regulation of North Pacific Fisheries." *Annals of the Association of American Geographers* 94(3): 565–584. https://doi.org/10.1111/j.1467-8306.2004.00414.x.

Martin, John Levi. 2003. "What is Field Theory?" *American Journal of Sociology* 109: 1–49. https://doi.org/10.1086/375201.

McCall, Leslie. 2005. "The Complexity of Intersectionality." *Signs: Journal of Women in Culture and Society* 30: 1771–1800.

Mead, George. H. 1967 [1934]. *Mind, Self, & Society: From the Standpoint of a Social Behaviorist*. Chicago, IL: University of Chicago Press.

Mudge, Stephanie L. 2016. "Neoliberalism, Accomplished and Ongoing." Pp. 93–104 in *The Handbook of Neoliberalism*, edited by Simon Springer, Kean Birch and Julie MacLeavy. New York and London: Routledge.

Mudge, Stephanie L. 2008. "What is Neoliberalism?." *Socio-Economic Review*, 6(4): 703–731. https://doi.org/10.1093/ser/mwn016.

Parr, Adrian. 2013. *The Wrath of Capital: Neoliberalism and Climate Change Politics*. New York: Columbia University Press.

Peck, Jamie and Adam Tickell. 2007. "Conceptualizing Neoliberalism, Thinking Thatcherism." Pp. 26–50 in *Contesting Neoliberalism: Urban Frontiers*, edited by Helga Leitner, Jamie Peck, and Eric S. Sheppard. New York: Guilford Press.

Piven, Frances Fox and Richard Cloward. 1993. *Regulating the Poor, 2nd Edition: The Functions of Public Welfare*. New York. Vintage.

Sparke, Matt. 2016. "Health and the Embodiment of Neoliberalism: Pathologies of Political Economy from Climate Change and Austerity to Personal Responsibility." Pp. 237–251 in *The Handbook of Neoliberalism*, edited by Simon Springer, Kean Birch, and Julie MacLeavy. New York: Routledge.

Steinmetz, George. 2023. *The Colonial Origins of Modern Social Thought: French Sociology and the Overseas Empire*. Princeton, NJ: Princeton University Press.

Swartz, David. 1997. *Culture & Power: The Sociology of Pierre Bourdieu*. Chicago, IL: University of Chicago Press.

Taylor, Astra. 2023. *The Age of Insecurity: Coming Together as Things Fall Apart*. Toronto, : House of Anansi Press.

Wacquant, Loïc. 2019. "Bourdieu's dyad: On the Primacy of Social Space and Symbolic Power." Pp. 15–21 in *Empirical Investigations of Social Space*, edited by

Jorg Blasius, Frederic Lebaron, Brigitte Le Roux, and Andreas Schmitz. Cham: Springer.

Wacquant, Loïc. 2016. "A Concise Genealogy and Anatomy of Habitus." *The Sociological Review* 64: 64–72. https://doi.org/10.1111/1467-954X.12356.

Wacquant, Loïc. 2014. "*Homines in Extremis*: What Fighting Scholars Teach Us about Habitus." *Body & Society* 20: 3–17.

Wacquant, Loïc. 2009. *Punishing the Poor: The Neoliberal Government of Social Insecurity*. Durham, NC: Duke University Press.

Western, Bruce. 2006. *Punishment and Inequality in America*. New York: Russell Sage Foundation.

World Health Organization. 2006. *Fuel for Life: Household Energy and Health*. Retrieved from https://iris.who.int/bitstream/handle/10665/43421/9241563168_eng.pdf.

World Prison Brief. 2024. "World Prison Brief Data." Institute for Crime & Justice Policy Research: Birkbeck University of London (accessed February 16, 2024). Available at: https://www.prisonstudies.org/world-prison-brief-data.

2

NEOLIBERALISM IN THE GLOBAL NORTH AND SOUTH

A Little History

The history of neoliberalism has been written many times by scholars in a variety of disciplines (see, for example, Cahill et al. 2018; Davies 2017; Harvey 2005; Kotsko 2018; Springer et al. 2016; Wilson 2018). As a result of these scholarly differences, and depending on the context, neoliberalism has been treated as an economic, political, and/or ideological concept (Rossi and Vanolo 2012). Recall from Chapter 1 that "neoliberalism," whether employed economically, politically, or ideologically, can be described as a philosophy that suggests human beings prosper most when economic markets are prioritized by States that do their best to reorient government and life around a free market approach, which translates to the most efficient distribution of resources, thereby generating the maximum possible economic growth. What is not up for debate is that many of the ideas that underpin "neo"-liberalism first appeared in eighteenth-century political economy, usually referred to as "liberalism." Economists Adam Smith, David Ricardo, and other liberal economists placed high value on private property and free markets. These economic values coincided with the rise of capitalism as an economic system.

Once the US, the UK, Western Europe, and, soon after, most of the rest of the world turned to capitalism as its economic system of choice, debates raged for the next several hundred years about how to produce economic growth – capitalism's only goal. While some favored the liberal ideas of protection of property and the efficiency of free markets to allocate resources (which translated into a smaller State), others argued that a more involved State was necessary to regulate capitalism to both foster economic growth

DOI: 10.4324/9781003326892-2

and provide basic social services to those who need them. Bourdieu alludes to the importance of the role of the State, or the "bureaucratic field" (Bourdieu 2014:123, 2024:126), with respect to interfacing with the economy, "of all the characteristics of societies in which the economic order is 'immersed', the most important for contemporary societies is the form and force of its state tradition" (Bourdieu 2005:12). In other words, one of the biggest decisions for societies to make was whether to endorse the limited State intervention of liberalism or the approach where the State takes a more active role in regulating capitalism and the economy. The value of the second approach was highlighted by the economic historian Karl Polanyi in his classic, *The Great Transformation: The Political and Economic Origins of Our Time*, first published in 1944. Polanyi (1944) documented the problems with a self-regulating economic marketplace, from an economic standpoint, but arguably more important was his emphasis on the horrible social consequences of liberal capitalism and a focus on free markets. This debate about what type of capitalism is best continues today across the globe (however, there is less debate about whether capitalism is the best form of economic organization). A brief review of the economic history of the US and UK is illustrative of this debate. Such a review demonstrates how forms of capitalism have come and gone, while the existence of capitalism itself (in some form) has not been questioned. In the following section, we focus on countries in the Global North, and how the Global North exported neoliberal economic reforms (by force if necessary) to the Global South.

Let's fast-forward from the eighteenth century to the late 1940s, focusing on the reconstruction of Europe after the conclusion of World War II (WWII). Much of Europe was decimated from war. The US stepped in with a massive aid package, officially named the European Recovery Program but colloquially referred to as the "Marshall Plan," after its primary architect, then US Secretary of State George C. Marshall. In 1948, the US government provided $13.3 billion to Western European nations (De Long and Eichengreen 1991). This translates to roughly $173 billion in adjusted 2023 US dollars. While the Marshall Plan encouraged economic policies that can be characterized as neoliberal in nature, particularly those that focused on removing barriers to economic cooperation between nations, this approach to reconstruction (economic and otherwise) was based on strong State intervention.

Back "across the pond" in the US, unease about the economy lingered from the Great Depression (1929–1939) and was exacerbated by the strain of two world wars that bookended the Depression. Beginning in 1933 and lasting for roughly five years, US President Franklin D. Roosevelt enacted a series of reforms and programs, which collectively became known as the "New Deal." The New Deal was designed to prevent another Great Depression and the human suffering that accompanied it (Hiltzik 2011). In many ways, the New Deal embodied much of the spirit of what Polanyi was observing and writing about during roughly the same period. In short, State intervention in the economy became necessary, as unregulated markets were one of the causes of the Great Depression.

While the US economy was forced to transform into a wartime economy to meet the needs of the military during WWII, after the war was over, the US continued to employ a substantial amount of State intervention in the economy. In the post-WWII era, US economic policy was heavily influenced by the work of economist John Maynard Keynes.[1] Keynesian economic theory is characterized by the importance of State regulation of markets and the creation of economic and social welfare programs (funded and run by the government). The US experienced unprecedented growth and prosperity for the next several decades following the Keynesian model. Consequently, liberal ideas of free market efficiency and related economic ideology were marginalized during this period. Alas, as the saying goes, "nothing lasts forever," and that was the case with the Keynesian-influenced economic policies in the US. A combination of factors in the 1970s, highlighted by the oil embargo, manifested in a long period of "stagflation" in the US – the combination of stagnant economic growth and inflation (Barsky and Kilian 2000; Blinder 1979; Harvey 2005). Stagflation proved to be a difficult problem for economists to solve, opening the door for neoliberal economic philosophy and its proponents to advocate for a seismic shift in economic policy in the US. Similarly, in the UK, a prolonged economic downturn gave the neoliberals a foothold in UK policy and government circles, and soon Prime Minister Margaret Thatcher would elevate neoliberal economic policy to the dominant economic (and political) approach in the UK.

Before we turn our attention to the beginning of the neoliberal era, we should briefly return to the post-WWII period. While economic policies that favored unfettered free markets (whether these policies were actually referred to as "neoliberal" at that point is not important) were not in vogue during this time, beginning in earnest in 1947,[2] there was a small, dedicated group of economists who regularly gathered and discussed the virtues of neoliberal economic theory and policy. This group referred to itself as the Mont Pelerin Society (MPS), after the location of the group's founding – Mont Pelerin, Switzerland (Nik-Khan and Van Horn 2016). One of the co-founders of the MPS and arguably the most influential was the Austrian economist, Friedrich August von Hayek. His most famous work, *The Road to Serfdom* (1944), was central to the views of the MPS at that time. Hayek argued that certain forms of State intervention into the economy came with a loss of freedom for individuals. The main thesis of the book is that "centralized planning" – essentially Hayek's phrase for "State intervention" – would lead to fascism, due to the small number of people (i.e., the State or government) making decisions regarding resource allocation, among other things, that would not be in the best interests of the masses.

The solution to this problem, and to keep the US, UK, and Western Europe off the path toward fascism, was to adopt neoliberal, free market policies, while recognizing that the State had a role to play facilitating national integration into the global capitalist free market economy (Dardot and Laval 2014).

Hayek's free market advocate counterpart in the US was University of Chicago economist Milton Friedman (Rodrigues 2018). Friedman used the University of Chicago Department of Economics to train a generation of what we would now refer to as neoclassical economists. Friedman, his former students (who informally became known as the "Chicago boys"; Nik-Khan and Van Horn 2016; Van Horn and Nik-Khan 2018), and free market think tanks (Peck and Tickell 2007) continued to advocate for market-based, neoliberal economic policies. At that point, however, they were a group of academics, with a mostly untested theoretical idea (or set of ideas). The Chicago boys would get their wish for a kind of natural neoliberal laboratory, though, with some help from the US Central Intelligence Agency, a Chilean General (Augusto Pinochet), and his military junta that took control of the government of Chile in a military coup d'état, which toppled the democratically elected president of Chile, Salvador Allende – a socialist.[3] Pinochet and his military junta almost immediately began receiving economic advice from the Chicago boys (Rodrigues 2018). The days of social democratic policies in Chile were over. Pinochet moved swiftly to cut social spending, privatize social security, and also privatize sectors of the economy such as education and banking. From an economic perspective, the reforms received mixed reviews; the social impacts, however, were far worse.[4]

After that brief digression, let's return to 1979 and the election of Margaret Thatcher as prime minister of the UK. Thatcher was a true believer in the power of neoliberal economics and had, throughout her time as prime minister, delivered what have become famous quotes associated with the virtues of individual responsibility, free markets, and neoliberalism. Perhaps the most well known of which summed up her views on government, society, and individuals is the following.

> I think we have gone through a period when too many children and people have been given to understand 'I have a problem, it is the Government's job to cope with it!' or 'I have a problem, I will go and get a grant to cope with it!' 'I am homeless, the Government must house me!' and so they are casting their problems on society and who is society? There is no such thing! There are individual men and women and there are families and no government can do anything except through people and people look to themselves first.
>
> *(Thatcher 1987)*

For Thatcher, small government was a bedrock of economic and other policies. Throughout her time as prime minister, she privatized industries, fought labor unions, tightly controlled the government's budget and implemented other policies out of the neoliberal playbook (Harvey 2005).

Thatcher found her companion in neoliberalism when Ronald Reagan became the president of the US in 1980. Reagan demonstrated his neoliberal credentials early into his eight years as president, when he broke the striking air traffic controllers' union in 1981 by firing over 10,000 air traffic controllers. Reagan favored supply-side economic policies[5] that became known as "Reaganomics." Reaganomics featured tax cuts, privatization of State-controlled industries, a reduction in the monetary supply, cuts to social spending (including famously closing many State-funded mental health facilities, whose former patients subsequently contributed to the growing homeless population throughout the US), and essentially reducing as much government regulation as possible. Under Reagan (and continued under his successor, President George H.W. Bush), neoliberalism entrenched itself within the US, at the same time it had in the UK during the Thatcher administration. Other Western European nations followed the US and UK on the path to neoliberalization (Schmidt 2016, 2018).

Sometimes overlooked when discussing the history of neoliberalism is the German variety – "ordoliberalism" (Bonefeld 2012; Cerny 2016; Jessop 2019) – which first appeared after WWII. The word ordoliberalism highlights the perspective's focus on order as necessary to make market-based societies function efficiently. This includes structuring neoliberal's core value – competition. The structuring mechanism of competition is the State. Therefore, ordoliberals saw an active role for the State in creating and "ordering" the competition necessary for neoliberalism to be successful. German ordoliberalism provided much of the backbone for the creation of, and policies implemented by, the European Union. Dardot and Laval (2014:205) note that ordoliberalism, "was to become standard doctrine for the governmental elite of the [European] Union from the 1980s." Since its creation on November 1, 1993, in Maastricht in the Netherlands, the European Union has consistently advocated for neoliberal approaches to the economy and life.

Conservative politicians and political parties did/do not have a monopoly on devotion to neoliberal economic policies. Beginning with President Bill Clinton (a Democrat) in the US in 1992, and a few years later, Tony Blair (of the Labour Party), both left-center politicians from their country's major progressive political party, neoliberal capitalism was still the primary economic philosophy used by government policymakers. This was true even though these administrations claimed that their approach (sometimes referred to as "the third way"; Giddens 1998; Jones 2018) was akin to a "kinder, gentler capitalism," primarily because they provided more funding for social programs than their predecessors. Make no mistake, though, neoliberal economic policy was still the order of the day. Arguably the most famous example of neoliberalism in the US during the Clinton administration was what became known as "welfare reform." This program, officially named the Personal Responsibility and Work Opportunity Reconciliation Act, left many low-income individuals and families without any government aid. Welfare reform reduced the amount of time individuals could receive aid, while adding the requirement that benefit seekers needed to be actively looking for work. This change has been noted by scholars as the move from a welfare model to a "workfare" approach to government aid (Greer 2016; Wacquant 2010). This is directly in line with the neoliberal values of individual responsibility and small government.

At the turn of the twenty-first century, the George W. Bush administration in the US, in addition to nation-building through the Doctrine of Preemption (Anghie 2004) under the guise of spreading democracy, continued to advocate for free markets, both at home and especially abroad. While much of the world's attention was focused on the wars in Afghanistan and Iraq, neoliberalism was running wild. In the Global North, this eventually came to a head in the US, with the housing bubble and the subsequent sub-prime mortgage crisis. In September 2008, the proverbial cat was out of the bag as the collapse of the investment bank Lehman Brothers became public. The collapse of other US banks followed, and these economic problems rapidly spread to other sectors of the US economy, other national economies, and consequently the global capitalist economy, leading to what became known as the "Great Recession" (Grusky, Western and Wimer 2011).

This is the point where the phrase "too big to fail" entered the global lexicon. Pointing to the catastrophic repercussions of letting many large banks and corporations go bankrupt, the George W. Bush administration passed the first of several government "bailout" acts (beginning with the Emergency Economic Stabilization Act of 2008), providing hundreds of billions of US dollars of aid to large banks and corporations. This tremendous level of government intervention in the economy was clearly not a neoliberal solution; rather, it seemed that neoliberal policies were primary causes of the recession. The government bailouts continued under President Barak Obama when he was elected in 2008. On the back of these bailouts, in the US and in other affluent countries, national and the global economies recovered. The general success of the bailouts, especially in the US, did little to persuade government policy makers to jettison neoliberal economic policies. Obama simultaneously touted bailout victories and supported neoliberal economics. For example, he supported the proposed Transatlantic Trade and Investment Partnership (T-TIP), a free trade and investment agreement between the US and the European Union (the T-TIP was scuttled by Donald Trump when he became president of the US for the first time in 2017). Similarly, the UK moved on from the Great Recession by implementing a program of austerity measures under the Tory government of Prime Minister David Cameron, which reduced the standard of living for the average UK citizen across the country. Despite the bump in the road (i.e., the Great Recession), neoliberalism continued its movement throughout the world.

Before we turn to a discussion of some of the recent reactions against neoliberalism over the last decade, we need to take some time to review what was going on in the Global South during the same period we just covered for the Global North.

Exporting Neoliberalism

Neocolonialism occurs when one country employs political, economic, and other avenues to exert influence and control over another country (Langan 2018). In its most serious cases, the countries who are on the receiving end of neocolonial relationships become and remain dependent on the countries who are exerting influence on them. Part of our argument, which has been made elsewhere (Long, McElroy and Lynch 2024), is that the process of neoliberalization (i.e., becoming more neoliberal) and the resultant neoliberal policies increase the probability that nations in the Global South will enter neocolonial relationships with countries in the Global North – sometimes voluntarily, other times coerced.

Returning to the period toward the end of WWII and immediately after, the seeds for the modern global capitalist economy were sown. In 1944, at a conference at the Mount Washington Hotel in Bretton Woods, New Hampshire, representatives from all Allied nations in WWII signed what was to become known as the Bretton Woods Agreement (Bordo 1993). The impetus for the conference and the subsequent Agreement came from a desire for the Allied countries to rebuild after WWII without the (primarily economic based) tensions that characterized post-World War I (WWI) reconstruction. The delegates at the conference agreed that floating exchange rates between countries partly sabotaged the plans to rebuild after WWI. Therefore, an integral part of the Bretton Woods Agreement was to create fixed currency exchange rates that were based on the US dollar and the gold standard. To help with the economic restructuring, the Agreement created the International Monetary Fund (IMF) and the International Bank for Reconstruction and Development (which has subsequently become part of the World Bank). A few years later, the General Agreement on Tariffs and Trade (GATT) was created by some of the Allied countries from WWII. The remit of GATT was to help encourage economic cooperation between nations. In 1995, GATT gave way to a more comprehensive institution, the World Trade Organization (WTO), whose primary purpose was to facilitate free trade between countries and, if necessary, mediate trade disputes between countries or regions (Narlikar, Daunton and Stern 2012,).

With these international financial institutions in place, we can now move forward to the ascension of Thatcher in the UK and Reagan in the US, and their embrace of neoliberalism. While Reagan and Thatcher were busy restructuring their economies along neoliberal lines, the international financial institutions (who were/are controlled by the US, UK, and Western Europe) were looking to take neoliberalism global. Long et al. (2024:94–95) describe how this process has played out since 1980:

> Any discussion of neoliberalism and neo-colonial relationships between countries would be remiss without highlighting the role of the World Bank and the International Monetary Fund (IMF) structural adjustment programs (SAPs) from 1980–2000. While framed as mechanisms to promote economic growth and development, and the alleviation of poverty, SAPs were employed to maintain nations in dependency positions. Post-2000 and continuing today, similar policy measures continue to place many countries in dependent positions; however these policies, while still highly neoliberal in nature, have been rebranded as poverty reduction strategies by international monetary institutions. These programs are the international embodiment of the neoliberal agenda and policy packages being forced on poor countries in the Global South that help maintain them in states of dependency.

So, how exactly does the dependency – and potentially neocolonial – relationships that countries in the Global South have often found themselves in develop? As the quote highlights, structural adjustment programs (SAPs), and subsequently the poverty reduction strategies of the IMF and the World Bank, have been central to this process. SAPs are loans (containing sizable interest rates) that are provided from the IMF and/or the World Bank primarily to countries in the Global South to aid in economic development, which is viewed by the neoliberal Bretton Woods institutions as occurring through an emphasis on small government and export-oriented economies that imposed little to no tariffs to encourage trade. This view of economic development and growth is institutionalized in the loan agreements between the international financial institutions and the recipient countries through a range of "conditionalities" – the receiving country must agree to a suite of neoliberal economic reforms to receive the loan. As Brohman (1996) notes, these reforms often include some combination of the following: reduced government spending in all sectors, privatization of previously State-run industries, market deregulation, elimination of minimum wage laws, and other mechanisms to reorient the domestic economy of the recipient country to one based on exports.

As noted earlier, SAPs not only required economic restructuring by the recipient country as a condition of the loan, but these loans were also not provided interest-free. The accumulation and payment of even the interest on these loans became difficult, if not impossible, for many SAP recipients (George 1988, 1992), leading to neocolonial relationships between the international monetary institutions and the countries who could not pay back their structural adjustment loans. The development projects funded by the IMF and the World Bank have been used to further entrench the dependency of Global South countries on the Global North. For example, as Long et al. (2024:95) note, SAPs "facilitate building economic infrastructure useful to consumption patterns in developed nations and constrain and direct raw material and goods export flows in a manner beneficial to developed nations." The development projects required by SAPs help to open Global South nations for resource extraction, which are then traded, in unequal terms (Emmanuel 1972), to companies in the Global North in the global neoliberal capitalist economy. It is not only international financial institutions that place Global South countries in neocolonial relationships based on neoliberal policies, corporations based in Global Northern countries, primarily through foreign direct investment (FDI), can also force Global Southern countries into dependency relationships.

FDI is another tool in the neoliberal toolbox that, while attempting to generate economic growth, has the potential to place countries in dependency relationships with large corporations that are usually based in Global North countries.[6] A simple definition of FDI is money from a corporation (or other type of firm) located in one country that is then invested into another country. The World Bank, in their World Bank Databank, measures FDI as ownership of a controlling number of shares in a business in one country by a business or other entity located in a second country (World Bank 2024). Investment in foreign entities and capital, flowing easily between nations, is what neoliberal economic policies are designed to encourage, arguing that both the investing country and the receiving country will benefit economically. This harkens back all the way to the concept of what later became known as "comparative advantage,"[7] postulated by eighteenth-century liberal economist, David Ricardo. The theory suggests that all countries have a "comparative advantage" in producing certain products due to factors unique to their country. Countries, then, should focus on producing only what they have a comparative advantage in – that is, they can produce a particular good more efficiently than other countries of the world. Countries then trade for all other goods that are needed in that nation. Therefore, if all countries produced only what they have a comparative advantage for and trade for everything else, economic growth would be created the world over, and the needs for all types of goods would be met.

Alas, what often appears reasonable in theory does not always work out in practice. Comparative advantage may have succeeded in generating economic growth for all countries if all goods were of equal value. This, of course, is not the case. Generally, countries in the Global South are exporting raw materials, while importing more expensive finished products. This situation has been referred to as the "unequal terms of trade" that occurs on the global capitalist market. Arghiri Emmanuel (1972) was one of the first to extensively highlight this problem in his now classic work, *Unequal Exchange: A Study of the Imperialism of Trade*.

There are several problems with international trade (whether between firms or countries) based on comparative advantage approaches. First, as noted above, is the unequal terms of trade based on what is imported and exported. Global North countries (or firms headquartered in those countries) typically come out on top financially in trade relationships with Global South countries based on the value of what is being traded between the two nations (or firms). Second, relatedly, given that natural resources are a main export of many nations in the Global South and that many heavily polluting industries have relocated production to these regions, environmental sociologists have introduced an "ecostructural theory of foreign investment dependence," which highlights how

> the transnational organization of extraction and production in the context of foreign investment dependence partially allows for more developed countries and the transnational firms headquartered within them to treat less developed countries as *supply depots* as well as *sinks for waste*.
> (*Jorgenson 2010:459–460, emphasis added*)

Countries from the Global North can pillage poor countries of their natural resources to subsidize their citizens' high consumption lifestyles, while also outsourcing the pollution of those same Global North consumers back to the Global South. Third, in some cases, the only real comparative advantage that very poor countries have in the global neoliberal capitalist economy is the relatively cheap cost of labor. These countries, therefore, invite transnational firms to produce products in their country by luring them with cheap labor (usually under unsafe conditions) and lax environmental regulations. This does not seem like all countries are benefiting from neoliberal comparative advantage approaches to the global marketplace.

In sum, then, not only did neoliberalism take over the economic, political, and policy arenas of affluent countries such as the US, UK, and those in Western Europe, but once entrenched in those countries, the export of neoliberalism to the developing world began and escalated quickly. Eventually, neoliberal policies became the norm, the world over. As a result, the global spread of neoliberalism has also meant increasing levels of insecurity (e.g., see Dixon 2020).

Neoliberalism's roots are in countries, such as the US and the UK, with a history of colonialism (Go 2011), which further highlights the connection between the two forces. Colonialism and neocolonialism are also relevant for our study of insecurity for two main reasons. First, the discipline of sociology emerged within the dominant imperial powers of the late 1800s and early 1900s (Connell 2007; Go 2013; Steinmetz 2013, 2023). Second, Bourdieu's transition from philosophy to sociology and the early work that eventually led to the development of his theory of practice took place in Algeria during the war for independence in the late 1950s (Go 2013; Pérez 2024; Steinmetz 2023). Bourdieu's concept of habitus (Bourdieu 1984, 1990) is typically described as a stable set of dispositions, but his early research on war-torn Algeria and the forced resettlement of Algerian peasants (Bourdieu and Sayad 2020), as well as the rapid transition to a capitalist economy, revealed dispositions characterized by internal conflict and division rather than by stability and internal cohesion. Bourdieu (2000, p.64) would refer to the situation in Algeria in his later work when he introduced the concept of a divided or "cleft" habitus. Countries from the Global South may be more likely to experience unstable economic conditions due to the spread of neoliberalism through neocolonial relationships, which makes it important to include countries from both sides of the North/South global divide to understand insecurity. Additionally, these twin forces of neoliberalism and neocolonialism highlight the need for reflexivity, given that many of the concepts employed in academic fields are shaped by State power (Bourdieu 2014, 2024).

Reactions against Neoliberalism and Where We Are Now

While neoliberal policies became the norm throughout the world during the last decades of the twentieth century and the first two decades of the twenty-first century, we do not want to give the impression that neoliberalism has been universally embraced by all countries, across administrations, and consistently over the last 45 years. Of course, there have been countless grassroots protests against neoliberalism and neoliberal policies across the globe as long as neoliberalism has been around (e.g., Andretta 2017; Ayres 2004; Saad-Filho 2013; Wood 2004). However, our focus in this review is the degree that countries (and specific administrations within countries) have turned away from neoliberalism and have taken more nationalist approaches to government (Worth 2018).

In 2016, two events, the election of Donald Trump as president of the US and the successful Brexit referendum in the UK where UK citizens voted by a narrow margin (Leave = 52%, Remain = 48%) to leave the European Union, appeared to signify the beginning of a post-neoliberal era (at least in the Global North). Long, Defeyter, and Stretesky (2021:23) summarize neoliberalism in the US during the first Trump administration, when they note that,

> others may point to the election of Donald Trump in 2016 as a reaction by US citizens to neoliberal policies as he argued that in order to 'Make

> America Great Again,' the country needed to take a protectionist turn and reinstate tariffs and quotas on imports and remove themselves from free trade agreements. While the Trump Administration followed through on some of that, little, if anything, has changed for neoliberal capital on a global level. Furthermore, the Trump Administration did not increase social spending, so neoliberalism's effects on inequality and poverty in the US still remain very strong.

The nationalist rhetoric that became synonymous with the first Trump administration predominately focused on anti-immigration issues, from his repeated attempts to pass a "travel ban" on citizens originally from Iran, Iraq, Libya, Somalia, Sudan, Syria, and Yemen. The countries on the travel ban list vacillated over the different attempts by Trump to pass the ban, but the list was always dominated with Muslim-majority countries. Under the second Trump administration, set to begin in January 2025, we may see a revival of nativist rhetoric and attempts to revisit the travel ban. Time will tell.

Around the same time, a related situation was unfolding in the UK. UK citizens voted to leave the European Union in June 2016. Proponents of Brexit argued that the UK would generate more economic growth without having to pay its EU fees and abide by its regulations. Central among the concerns of supporters of Brexit was the free movement of people between EU countries, arguing that this was causing UK citizens to lose jobs to citizens of other EU countries. In many ways, it became a referendum on immigration, with many UK citizens adopting the xenophobic rhetoric of the leaders of Brexit. The anti-immigrant sentiment in both countries was high. This right-wing ideology spread to Western Europe. For example, far-right politicians started to fare better in European elections than they had in the recent past, starting with several unsuccessful attempts at the French presidency by far-right candidate Marine Le Pen in France. More recent, successful attempts of far-right politicians in Western Europe include Giorgia Meloni who became the first woman prime minister of Italy, and Geert Wilders of the Dutch Party for Freedom, who recently won the most seats of any party in the Dutch House of Representatives. Again, much of their electoral platforms consisted of anti-immigration and Euroscepticism viewpoints. In the case of the UK, a recent report by economists Du et al. (2024) in the Centre for Business Prosperity at Aston University in the UK shows a precipitous decline in imports and exports between the UK and the EU after the implementation of Brexit.

With several of the leading national economies (e.g., US, UK, France, Italy, and the Netherlands) grappling with more nationalist policies, which, at least in theory, included rebuffs against the global neoliberal capitalist economy, it may appear to some that the power and influence of neoliberalism is starting to wane. Some scholars have suggested that we are moving past the neoliberal era (e.g., Antonio 2024; Brand 2016; Springer 2015). Nevertheless, nationalist governments focused on their popular anti-immigrant policies have continued to participate in the global neoliberal capitalist economy. Trump lost the 2020 presidential election to Joe Biden, who, like Barak Obama, Bill Clinton, and other recent US presidents from the Democratic Party, was an ardent neoliberalist (Berman 2022) – even if they nominally increased social spending and programs for the less fortunate. After Brexit, the UK has regularly (with mixed success) attempted to negotiate bilateral free trade agreements with many countries to replace the EU agreements they had before Brexit. For instance, the post-Brexit trade agreement called the Trade and Cooperation Agreement, which was established to maintain trade between the UK and the EU, has resulted in the disruptions to the production and distribution of consumer goods (Du et al. 2024). Although it is unclear what will happen with these new right-wing governments in Western Europe, our position in this book is that neoliberal economic philosophy and related policies still dominate in most countries, and certainly at the level of the global economy. This was especially apparent during the COVID-19 pandemic, when many industries were brought to a standstill because most products are manufactured with parts from numerous countries. When the world shut down to slow the spread of the pandemic, it highlighted how interlinked global supply chains are (Meier and Pinto 2024) and how a slowdown in production of one component, in one country, can lead to slowdowns in other countries and, ultimately, unsatisfied consumers. Relatedly, insecurity of all types increased during the COVID-19 pandemic.

During the writing of this book, Donald Trump was reelected president of the US, partially due to his support of more isolationist economic and social policies. While this is somewhat a reaction against neoliberalism, it will be interesting to see how effective the second Trump administration can be at partially extricating the country from global capitalism.

Neoliberalism and Insecurity

We have now outlined the concepts of "insecurity" (in Chapter 1) and "neoliberalism" (primarily in Chapter 2). We have also detailed our approach to the study of how these concepts are interrelated. Specifically, to bridge the dualism of theoretical approaches to neoliberalism, our approach employs Bourdieu's theory of practice to understand and map what we refer to as the global neoliberal capitalist field. Central to our argument is that insecurity, in both its general and specific forms, is an integral part of neoliberalism and, therefore, the global neoliberal capitalist field.

In the following chapters, we expand on the relationship between neoliberalism and insecurity in advanced capitalism. Chapters 3–5 detail the structural political economic implications of neoliberalism on food, energy, and job insecurity, respectively. In Chapter 6, we turn to the impacts of the association between neoliberalism and insecurity on individuals (and households), traditionally conceived as the micro-level impacts of the neoliberalism-insecurity nexus. In Chapter 7, we examine the interdependence of purported micro- and macro-level factors through our application of Bourdieu's theory of practice, both as a theoretical framework for understanding the global neoliberal capitalist field and also empirically using a field-theoretic approach to investigate the US neoliberal capitalist space through geometric data analysis (Le Roux and Rouanet (2010a), specifically, multiple correspondence analysis approaches (Beh and Lombardo 2021; Hjellbrekke 2019; Le Roux and Rouanet 2010b). This empirical approach was favored by Bourdieu himself as it enabled him to map individuals' locations in fields based on the composition of the capitals that organized that specific social space or field (e.g., in our case, economic capital and security capital) (e.g., see Bourdieu 1984, 1988, 1996, 2005).

Bourdieu observed how widespread the impact was on individuals living under neoliberalism in the late twentieth century, and these observations remain relevant today. Bourdieu noted that,

> insecurity acts directly on those it touches (and who it renders incapable of mobilizing themselves) and indirectly on all the others, through the fear it arouses, which is methodically exploited by all the *insecurity-inducing strategies*, such as the introduction of the notorious 'flexibility', which, it will have become clear, is inspired as much by political as economic reasons.
>
> *(Bourdieu 1998:84)*

In other words, Bourdieu recognized that insecurity was synonymous with neoliberalism. Insecurity affects, either directly or indirectly, every person in a neoliberal world, and therefore we argue that it is one of the organizing principles (or capitals) of the global neoliberal capitalist field.

Conclusion

This chapter provided a history of neoliberalism, beginning with eighteenth-century liberal political economy, primarily of Western Europe. We traced the development of neoliberalism in the Global North from post-WWII to the present day, and looked at how countries and corporations in the Global North exported neoliberalism to countries in the Global South. We have suggested that the rise of reactions against neoliberalism (and globalization) have included the election (and reelection) of Donald Trump as president of the US, the Brexit vote in the UK to leave the European Union, and the rise of far-right governments in several European countries. While some literature suggests there is a rising neoliberal backlash, and that we may be in a post-neoliberal era, we have argued that this is not the case. As we have asserted, neoliberalism and insecurity should be studied together. We continue our examination of insecurity and neoliberalism in Chapter 3 by focusing on the topic of food insecurity. We discuss how food insecurity is conceptualized, measured, and distributed in both the Global North and Global South.

Notes

1 For a detailed description and analysis of Keynes' economic approach, see (Minsky 1975).
2 Dardot and Laval (2014:49) remind us that "[t]he creation of the Mont Pelerin Society in 1947 is often incorrectly cited as marking the birth of neoliberalism. In fact, the founding moment of neoliberalism came earlier: it was the Walter Lippmann Colloquium held over five days from 26 August 1938." The discussion by economists at the Colloquium, while foundational to neoliberalism, were interrupted by WWII. The MPS took up the mantle of the work started by those in attendance at the Colloquium after the conclusion of the war.
3 The US CIA was at least aware of the coup beforehand and may have been involved in planning/facilitating it (Shiraz 2011).
4 Kingstone (2018) notes that [e]ven the Chilean military has conceded that it systematically violated human rights.
5 See Lucas Jr. (1990) for a review of supply-side economics.
6 A substantial debate has developed over the last 50 years in the cross-national FDI literature regarding whether, to what extent, and through what mechanism FDI harms countries in the Global South. That debate continues today (see Bornschier and Chase-Dunn 1985; Dixon and Boswell 1996; Firebaugh 1996 for some of the genesis of the debate).
7 The term "comparative advantage" was actually introduced later by John Stewart Mill (1844) to describe Ricardo's theory.

References

Andretta, Massimiliano. 2017. "Neoliberalism and Its Discontents in Italy: Protests without Movement?" Pp. 201–241 in *Late Neoliberalism and Its Discontents in the Economic Crisis*, edited by D. Della Porta, Massimiliano. Andretta, and others. Cham: Palgrave Macmillan.

Anghie, Antony. 2004. "The Bush Administration Preemption Doctrine and the United Nations." *Proceedings of the ASIL Annual Meeting* 98:326–329. https://doi.org/10.1017/S0272503700061565.

Antonio, Robert J. 2024. "After Neoliberalism: Social Theory and Sociology in the Interregnum." *The American Sociologist.* 55:11–23. https://doi.org/10.1007/s12108-022-09562-z.

Ayres, Jeffrey M. 2004. "Framing Collective Action against Neoliberalism: The Cases of the 'Anti-Globalization' Movement." *Journal of World Systems Research* 10(1):11–34. https://doi.org/10.5195/jwsr.2004.311.

Barsky, Robert and Lutz Kilian. 2000. "A Monetary Explanation of the Great Stagflation of the 1970s." Working Paper 7547. National Bureau of Economic Research. https://www.nber.org/papers/w7547.

Beh, Eric J. and Rosaria Lombardo. 2021. *An Introduction to Correspondence Analysis*. Oxford: Wiley.

Berman, Elizabeth Popp. 2022. *Thinking Like an Economist: How Efficiency Replaced Equality in U.S. Public Policy*. Princeton, NJ: Princeton University Press.

Blinder, Alan S. 1979. *Economic Policy and the Great Stagflation*. New York: Academic Press.

Bonefeld, Werner. 2012. "Freedom and the Strong State: On German Ordoliberalism." *New Political Economy* 17(5): 633–656. https://doi.org/10.1080/13563467.2012.656082.

Bordo, Michael D. 1993. "The Bretton Woods International Monetary System: A Historical Overview." Pp. 3–108 in *A Retrospective on the Bretton Woods System: Lessons for International Monetary Reform*, edited by Michael D. Bordo and Barry Eichengreen. Chicago, IL: University of Chicago.

Bornschier, Volker and Christophe Chase-Dunn. 1985. *Transnational corporations and underdevelopment*. New York: Praeger.

Bourdieu, Pierre. 2024. *The Interest in Disinterestedness*. Cambridge: Polity Press.

Bourdieu, Pierre. 2014. *On the State*. Cambridge: Polity Press.

Bourdieu, Pierre. 2005. *The Social Structure of the Economy*. Cambridge: Polity Press.

Bourdieu, Pierre. 2000. *Pascalian Meditations*. Cambridge: Polity Press.

Bourdieu, Pierre. 1998. *Acts of Resistance: Against the Tyranny of the Market*. New York: The New Press.

Bourdieu, Pierre. 1996. *The State Nobility*. Stanford, CA: Stanford University Press.

Bourdieu, Pierre. 1990. *The Logic of Practice*. Stanford, CA: Stanford University Press.

Bourdieu, Pierre. 1988. *Homo Academicus*. Stanford, CA: Stanford University Press.

Bourdieu, Pierre. 1984. *Distinction: A Social Critique of the Judgement of Taste*. Cambridge, MA: Harvard University Press.

Bourdieu, Pierre and Abdelmalek Sayad. 2020. *Uprooting: The Crisis of Traditional Agriculture in Algeria*. Cambridge: Polity Press.

Brand, Ulrich. 2016. "Postneoliberalism." Pp. 583–591 in *The Handbook of Neoliberalism*, edited by Simon Springer, Kean Birch, and Julie MacLeavy. New York: Routledge.

Brohman, John. 1996. *Popular Development: Rethinking the Theory and Practice of Development*. Hoboken, NJ: Wiley-Blackwell.

Cahill, Damien, Melinda Cooper, Martijn Konings, and David Primrose (eds.). 2018. *The Sage Handbook of Neoliberalism*. Thousand Oaks, CA: Sage.

Cerny, Philip G. 2016. "In the Shadow of Ordoliberalism: The Paradox of Neoliberalism in the 21st century." *European Review of International Studies* 3(1): 78–91. https://www.jstor.org/stable/26593549.

Connell, Raewyn. 2007. *Southern Theory*. Cambridge: Polity Press.

Dardot, Pierre and Christian Laval. 2014. *The New Way of the World*. London and New York. Verso.

Davies, William. 2017. *The Limits of Neoliberalism: Authority, Sovereignty and the Logic of Competition*. Thousand Oaks, CA: Sage.

De Long, J. Bradford and Barry Eichengreen. 1991. "The Marshall Plan: History's Most Successful Structural Adjustment Program." Working Paper 3899. National Bureau of Economic Research. Available at: https://www.nber.org/papers/w3899.

Dixon, Jeffrey C. 2020. "Understanding Perceived Worker Insecurity in Europe, 2002–2016: Economic Freedom and Neoliberalism as Alternative Theories?" *Sociological Perspectives* 63(1): 5–28. https://doi.org/10.1177/0731121419862233.

Dixon, William J. and Terry Boswell. 1996. "Dependency, Disarticulation, and Denominator Effects: Another Look at Foreign Capital Penetration." *American Journal of Sociology* 102(2): 543–562. https://www.jstor.org/stable/2782635.

Du, Jun, Liu, Xingyi, Shepotylo Oleksandr and Yujie Shi. 2024. *Unbound: UK Trade Post-Brexit.* Centre for Business Prosperity at Aston University. 16 September 2024. Available at https://www.aston.ac.uk/sites/default/files/2024-09/Full%20Report.pdf.

Emmanuel, Arghiri. 1972. *Unequal Exchange: A Study of the Imperialism of Trade.* London: Monthly Review Press.

Firebaugh, Glenn. 1996. "Does Foreign Capital Harm Poor Nations? New Estimates Based on Dixon and Boswell's Measure of Capital Penetration." *American Journal of Sociology* 102(2): 563–575. https://doi.org/10.1086/230957.

George, Susan. 1992. *The Debt Boomerang: How Third World Debt Harms Us All.* New York: Routledge.

George, Susan. 1988. *A Fate Worse Than Debt: The World Financial Crisis and the Poor.* New York: Grove Press.

Giddens, Anthony. 1998. *The Third Way.* Cambridge: Polity Press.

Go, Julian. 2013. "Decolonizing Bourdieu: Colonial and Postcolonial Theory in Pierre Bourdieu's Early Work." *Sociological Theory* 31(1): 49–74. https://doi.org/10.1177/073527511347708.

Go, Julian. 2011. *Patterns of Empire: The British and American Empires, 1688 to the Present.* Cambridge: Cambridge University Press. https://doi.org/10.1017/CBO9780511996559.

Greer, Ian. 2016. "Welfare Reform, Precarity, and the Re-Commodification of Labour." *Work, Employment, and Society* 30(1): 162–173. https://www.jstor.org/stable/26655454.

Grusky, David B., Bruce Western, and Christopher Wimer (eds.). 2011. *The Great Recession.* New York: Russell Sage Foundation.

Harvey, David. 2005. *A Brief History of Neoliberalism.* Oxford: Oxford University Press.

Hayek, Friedrich A. von. 1944. *The Road to Serfdom.* London: Routledge Press.

Hiltzik, Michael. 2011. *The New Deal: A Modern History.* New York: Free Press.

Hjellbrekke, Johs. 2019. *Multiple Correspondence Analysis for the Social Sciences.* Abingdon: Routledge.

Jessop, Bob. 2019. "Ordoliberalism and Neoliberalization: Governing through Order or Disorder." *Critical Sociology* 45(7–8): 967–981. https://doi.org/10.1177/0896920519834068.

Jones, Daniel Stedman. 2018. "The Neoliberal Origins of the Third Way: How Chicago, Virginia and Bloomington Shaped Clinton and Blair." Pp. 167–178 in *The Sage Handbook of Neoliberalism*, edited by Damien Cahill, Melinda Cooper, Martijn Konings, and David Primrose. New York: Sage. https://doi.org/10.4135/9781526416001.

Jorgenson, Andrew K. 2010. "World-Economic Integration, Supply Depots, and Environmental Degradation: A Study of Ecologically Unequal Exchange, Foreign

Direct Investment Dependence, and Deforestation in Developing Countries." *Critical Sociology* 36(3): 453–477. https://doi.org/10.1177/0896920510365204.

Kingstone, Peter. 2018. "The Rise and Fall (and Rise Again?) of Neoliberalism in Latin America." Pp. 201–218 in *The Sage Handbook of Neoliberalism*, edited by Damien Cahill, Melinda Cooper, Martijn Konings, and David Primrose. London: Sage.

Kotsko, Adam. 2018. *Neoliberalism's Demons: On the Political Theology of Late Capital*. Stanford, CA: Stanford University Press.

Langan, Mark. 2018. *Neo-colonialism and the poverty of 'development' in Africa*. Basingstoke: Palgrave Macmillan.

Le Roux, Brigitte and Henry Rouanet. 2010a. *Geometric Data Analysis: From Correspondence Analysis to Structured Data Analysis*. Dordrecht: Kluwer Academic Press.

Le Roux, Brigitte and Henry Rouanet. 2010b. *Multiple Correspondence Analysis*. Thousand Oaks, CA: Sage.

Long, Michael A., Margaret Anne Defeyter, and Paul B. Stretesky. 2021. *Holiday Hunger in the UK: Local Responses to Childhood Food Insecurity*. Abingdon: Routledge.

Long, Michael A., Jericho R. McElroy, and Michael J. Lynch. 2024. "Environmental Crimes and the Treadmill of Production: Neoliberal Policy and Neo-Colonialism." Pp. 88–105. in *Handbook of Environmental Crime and Criminal Enforcement*, edited by Susan L. Smith and Iina Sahramäki. Cheltenham: Edward Elgar Publishing.

Lucas Jr, Robert E. 1990. "Supply-Side Economics: An Analytical Review." *Oxford Economic Papers* 42(2): 293–316. https://doi.org/10.4337/9781035309511.00013.

Meier, Mattias and Eugenio Pinto. 2024. "COVID-19 Supply Chain Disruptions." *European Economic Review* 162: 104–674. https://doi.org/10.1016/j.euroecorev.2024.104674.

Mill, John Stewart. 1844. *Essays on Some Unsettled Questions of Political Economy*. London: John W. Parker.

Minsky, Hyman P. 1975. *John Maynard Keynes*. New York: Columbia University Press.

Narlikar, Amrita, Martin Daunton, and Robert M. Stern. 2012. *The Oxford Handbook on the World Trade Organization*. Oxford: Oxford University Press.

Nik-Khan, Edward and Robert Van Horn. 2016. "The Ascendancy of Chicago Neoliberalism." Pp. 27–38 in *The Handbook of Neoliberalism*, edited by Simon Springer, Kean Birch, and Julie MacLeavy. New York: Routledge.

Peck, Jamie and Adam Tickell. 2007. "Conceptualizing Neoliberalism, Thinking Thatcherism." Pp. 26–50 in *Contesting Neoliberalism: Urban Frontiers*, edited by Helga Leitner, Jamie Peck, and Eric Sheppard. New York: Guilford Press.

Pérez, Amín. 2024. *Bourdieu & Sayad against Empire*. Cambridge: Polity Press.

Polanyi, Karl. 1944. *The Great Transformation: The Political and Economic Origins of Our Time*. Boston, MA: Beacon Press.

Rodrigues, João. 2018. "Embedding Neoliberalism: The Theoretical Practices of Hayek and Friedman." Pp. 129–142 in *The Sage Handbook of Neoliberalism*, edited by Damien Cahill, Melinda Cooper, Martijn Konings, and David Primrose. Thousand Oaks, CA: Sage.

Rossi, Ugo, and Alberto Vanolo. 2012. *Urban Political Geographies*. Thousand Oaks, CA: Sage.

Saad-Filho, Alfredo. 2013. "Mass Protests under 'Left Neoliberalism': Brazil, June-July 2013." *Critical Sociology* 39(5): 657–669. https://doi.org/10.1177/0896920513501906.

Schmidt, Vivien A. 2016. "The Roots of Neo-Liberal Resistance: Explaining Continuity and Change in Background Ideas in Europe's Political Economy." *British Journal of Politics and International Relations* 18(2): 318–334. https://doi.org/10.1177/136914811561279.

Schmidt, Vivien A. 2018. "Ideas and the Rise of Neoliberalism in Europe." Pp. 66–82 in *The Sage Handbook of Neoliberalism*, edited by Damien Cahill, Melinda Cooper, Martijn Konings, and David Primrose. Thousand Oaks, CA: Sage.

Shiraz, Zakia. 2011. "CIA Intervention in Chile and the Fall of the Allende Government in 1973." *Journal of American Studies* 45(3): 603–613. https://www.jstor.org/stable/23016792.

Springer, Simon. 2015. "Postneoliberalism?" *Review of Radical Political Economics* 47(1): 5–17. https://doi.org/10.1177/0486613413518724.

Springer, Simon, Birch, Kean, and MacLeavy, Julie. (eds.). 2016. *The Handbook of Neoliberalism*. New York: Routledge.

Steinmetz, George. 2023. *The Colonial Origins of Modern Social Thought: French Sociology and the Overseas Empire*. Princeton, NJ: Princeton University Press.

Steinmetz, George, ed. 2013. *Sociology & Empire: The Imperial Entanglements of a Discipline*. Durham, NC: Duke University Press.

Thatcher, Margaret. 1987. "Interview for 'Woman's Own' ('No Such Thing as Society')." In *Margaret Thatcher Foundation: Speeches, Interviews and Other Statements*. London. Available at: https://newlearningonline.com/new-learning/chapter-4/neoliberalism-more-recent-times/margaret-thatcher-theres-no-such-thing-as-society.

Van Horn, Robert and Edward Nik-Khan. 2018. "Planning the 'Free' Market: The Genesis and Rise of Chicago Neoliberalism. Pp. 98–112 in *The Sage Handbook of Neoliberalism*, edited by Cahill, Damien, Cooper, Melinda, Konings, Martijn, and Primrose, David. New York: Sage.

Wacquant, Loïc. 2010. "Crafting the Neoliberal State: Workfare, Prisonfare, and Social Insecurity." *Sociological Forum* 25(2): 197–220. https://doi.org/10.1111/j.1573-7861.2010.01173.x.

Wilson, Julie A. 2018. *Neoliberalism*. New York: Routledge.

Wood, Lesley J. 2004. "Breaking the Bank & Taking to the Streets: How Protesters Target Neoliberalism." *Journal of World-Systems Research* 10(1): 69–89. https://doi.org/10.5195/jwsr.2004.313.

World Bank. 2024. World Bank Databank (accessed January 28, 2024). Available at: https://databank.worldbank.org/.

Worth, Owen. 2018. "Resistance to Neoliberalism Before and Since the Global Financial Crisis." Pp. 609–619 in *The Sage Handbook of Neoliberalism*, edited by Damien Cahill, Melinda Cooper, Martijn Konings, and David Primrose. New York: Sage.

3

THE POLITICAL ECONOMY OF FOOD AND FOOD INSECURITY

On October 16, 2023, the UN Secretary-General António Guterres (United Nations 2023:4) declared, "in our world of plenty, it is outrageous that a person dies of hunger every few seconds." Indeed, approximately 9 million people die from hunger each year (World Food Programme 2021:3). Moreover, millions of additional people die each year from hunger-related complications (United Nations 2002:15). In this chapter, we return to the issue of food insecurity as discussed in Chapter 1. We emphasize that while food insecurity persists, there is more than enough food to feed the world. That is, if we evenly distribute available food to people across the globe, there would be enough food for every person to consume approximately 2,700 calories per day. Therefore, no global citizen must be food insecure or die from hunger (Mercy Corps 2020:36). The present chapter takes up the structural reasons for food insecurity by highlighting the global nature of the food system itself. Here, when we refer to the food system, we refer to all those global, regional, national, and/or local actors that are involved in the production, distribution, consumption, and disposal of food (von Braun et al. 2023). Importantly, neoliberal policies, discussed in Chapters 1 and 2, have dramatically increased the power of some actors in the food system, such as agribusinesses, through their networks of international trade and production styles where monoculture farming is increasingly common.

The current chapter begins with a brief examination of factors that shape the food system and have contributed to global patterns of food insecurity across the globe after World War II. Within that discussion, we especially emphasize the significant role of food production and trade networks that distribute food that is produced, often in the form of food aid. This discussion

DOI: 10.4324/9781003326892-3

leads us to the global food crisis in the 1970s and contemporary definitions of food insecurity. We then describe how food insecurity is measured and how food insecurity plays out in both the Global South and in the Global North. Next we discuss the increasing power of large agribusinesses that currently dominate the global food system and shape people's economic capital across the globe in the pursuit of profit. Finally, we conclude with an empirical investigation of the relationship between neoliberalism and food insecurity at the structural (i.e., national) level and consider the ways we might apply Bourdieu's field-theoretic approach to understand food insecurity.

The Rise of Global Food Insecurity after WWII

Frank Lidgett McDougall is best known for his role in helping to establish the Food and Agriculture Organization (FAO), a branch of the United Nations that was tasked with raising levels of nutrition (Way 2013). McDougall was born in 1884 as the son of a farmer in Blackheath, England, and moved to Australia when he was 25 years old (Stirling, 1986). Early in life, McDougall became a strong proponent of "empire trade" – a set of policies that would bolster British trade by removing tariffs within the British Empire. McDougall argued that this empire trade policy would not only improve the purchasing power of the British public but also "raise the standards of living among the backward peoples of the Empire to enlarge their purchasing power for British exports" (Taylor 1926:79). The policy of empire trade is best summarized in a 1934 propaganda film, under the same name (Conservative and Unionist Film Association 1934, see the film on http://www.colonialfilm.org.uk). While McDougall's early views on trade are not often mentioned, it is nevertheless appropriate that he went on to become an advocate for the FAO, one of the largest global food organizations that would come to be associated with liberal trade policies on a global level (McDougall 1951; O'Brien 2000; Thackeray and Toye 2018). Importantly, there are parallels in McDougall's views of empire trade (see McDougall 1925) that privileged Britain's well-being over its colonies and modern trade policies under the World Trade Organization (WTO) that favor the Global North over the Global South. We will return to this issue shortly, explaining its link to food insecurity, but in a privately circulated memorandum advocating for the establishment of an international food organization, McDougall (n.d., 26, 28) explained,

> We have promised to our own citizens, and to the peoples of the world, freedom from want through an expansive economy with full employment, better labour conditions and social security...Freedom from want of food must be given high priority...it is not only the most essential

> of human needs but the production of food is the principle economic activity of men [sic].

The McDougall memorandum drafted in consultation with the US Department of Agriculture (USDA) was also written at a time when emerging neoliberal ideals were favored by the US. These neoliberal ideas were being developed by the Bretton Woods System and its newly formed institutions, the World Bank and International Monetary Fund, described in Chapter 2. Together, these institutions have helped shape global food insecurity to the present day. And while McDougall's vision of empire trade was never realized for Britain, what developed over the past 70 years is a global neoliberal capitalist field that has significant consequences for food insecurity and forms of security capital that people come to possess to combat that insecurity.

The story begins with the development of the FAO that was created in 1945 as a dedicated agency of the United Nations, which itself had only just been established (Phillips 1983). At the end of WWII, many countries were facing food shortages (Hamblin 2012), and the FAO (1948) estimated that food production in countries directly impacted by conflict was significantly lower than during pre-war times. The mission of the FAO was to increase nutrition and reduce hunger for all countries in the world. The establishment of the FAO was followed closely by the UN's 1948 fundamental right to food, which appeared in Article 25, Section 1, in the Universal Declaration of Human Rights, stating:

> Everyone has the right to a standard of living adequate for the health and well-being of himself [sic] and of his [sic] family, including food, clothing, housing and medical care and necessary social services, and the right to security in the event of unemployment, sickness, disability, widowhood, old age or other lack of livelihood in circumstances beyond his control (United Nations General Assembly 1948: Article 24).

The 1948 FAO report recommended that the global distribution of food to improve nutrition for all could better meet the rights of global citizens through (1) increasing food production, (2) promoting global food trade, and (3) providing more food aid. Early FAO reports note that these three tactics were successful in addressing global hunger, and FAO policies were pushed across the globe with significant support from the US who helped shape these policies. As FAO data in Table 3.1 suggest, food production, aid, and trade increased significantly after WWII, and they are all important components for understanding food systems and food insecurity at a global level. We address each of these components.

TABLE 3.1 Agriculture Production, Volume of Agricultural Exports, and Food Aid, 1948–1969

	1948–1952 average	*1956*	*1957*	*1958*	*1959*	*1960*	*1961*	*1962*	*1963*	*1964*	*1965*	*1966*	*1967*	*1968*	*1969*
Agriculture Production	87			114	116	120	121	126	128	131	133	138	143	147	148
Per Capita Agriculture Production	93			105	106	107	106	108	108	108	107	109	111	112	110
Volume of Agricultural Exports		95	98	97	105	111	119	121	126	131	134	137	138	142	142
[a]Food Aid in Total Agriculture (in millions of US dollars)												87.0	172.5	367.3	412.9

Source: FAO, 1970. The State of Food and Agriculture, 1945–1970. https://www.fao.org/3/a4700e/a4700e.pdf.

[a] For "Aid in Total Agriculture," 1966 represents the 1966/1967 fiscal year, and so forth.

Food Production

As the war ended, potential food shortages in many parts of the world were inextricably tied to the view that more agricultural production was needed (Brannan 1951). These increases were realized, in part, through a new food epoch, which was only just beginning to take shape in the mid-1940s (Friedmann 1982). Above all, the era was primarily driven by fossil fuel-produced energy, which enabled the development of genetically modified high-yield crops through advances in industrial technology (e.g., tractor power), as well as the use of chemical fertilizers and pesticides (Johnson 1945:262). This historical era in crop technology was retrospectively named the "Green Revolution" by William Gaud, the head of the US Agency for International Development (USAID), in 1968. The Green Revolution is often credited with decoupling land area from crop yields (Stevenson et al. 2013). Agrotechnology developments that occurred during the Green Revolution were believed to be so important in the production of grain that the area of land devoted to growing grain was no longer the primary predictor of levels of grain production. Gaud attributed the beginning of the revolution to Norman Borlaug, who was working to increase wheat production in Mexico, with support from a grant obtained from the Rockefeller Foundation, a philanthropic organization started by John Rockefeller, a billionaire oil and gas tycoon (Robin 2010). Borlaug was eventually awarded a Nobel Peace Prize in 1970, and crowned the "father of the green revolution" (Quinn 2008). Gaud, for his part, summarized the early successes of Borlaug's work and the Green Revolution, noting that new innovations had led to historical levels of wheat production across the world, especially in Pakistan and Turkey, as well as rice production in the Philippines (Gauld 1968). Importantly, and as Bauerly (2016) suggests, the Green Revolution benefited US corporations, and US food surpluses, created by the modernization, expansion, and intensification of US farming, resulted in a US-dominated global agro-industrial complex that lasted from 1947 until 1973 (Friedmann 1987). During this time, nutritional energy per capita increased across the globe (Krausmann and Langthaler 2019; see Table 3.4).

Food Aid

After WWII, the FAO worked with the US government to increase food aid to needy European countries. This aid was coordinated through the United Nations Relief and Rehabilitation Administration and the Marshall Plan (Wood 1986). The Marshall Plan allowed for aid in the form of food, feed, and fertilizer. According to Friedmann (1982), aid under the Marshal Plan accounted for approximately $13.5 million annual aid to Europe. However, food aid was (1) largely driven by US surplus agriculture and (2) changed over a short period of time. This was accomplished through the Agricultural Trade Development and Assistance Act of 1954, or Public Law 480 (PL480; Barrett and Maxwell 2004; Friedmann 1982). The stated purpose of the act, also known as 'Food for Peace,' was to help address global hunger by increasing food security in other countries, while a more hidden purpose of the act was to "increase the consumption of United States agricultural commodities in foreign countries [and] improve the foreign relations of the United States" (Davis 1960:145). Importantly, this was accomplished by expanding food aid beyond Europe, so that the US could sell surplus food to nations identified as being susceptible to communism. Title 1 of PL480 aided in this task by establishing *loans* to countries that could be used to purchase low-priced American surplus food. As a result, US food "aid" increased annually in the form of loans for food, and it quickly became the main method of provision around the globe, especially to countries in the Global South. As Table 3.2 suggests, loans (in equivalent foreign currency) under Title 1 increased from $73 million, or 2% of all foreign aid, in 1955, to $1,090 million, or 21%, of all foreign aid in 1963 (DeBlois 1967).

PL480 loans for US agricultural surplus aimed to stimulate economic development and multilateral trade. Loans for food were to be given and repaid in the borrowing country's currency, with pre-loan agreements that included "relending policies." These policies allowed a portion of PL480 loan proceeds to be re-lent to private investors in borrowing countries, enabling them to implement development projects that would ultimately benefit US industry (Cheek 1958). Table 3.3 lists the agreed and planned loans for the first 38 countries given aid under PL480, Title 1. Thus, what began as a means of selling surplus food produced under the US Green Revolution eventually became a vehicle for profitmaking, mandating funding for additional projects that could be used to stimulate economic growth and boost US markets for traded goods, mainly though the creation of food aid and new markets by using low-income countries outside of Europe. As Rietkerk (2015:719) succinctly summarizes, "food aid transformed into investment capital." Indeed, global food aid structured the way economic capital was distributed across the globe.

However, American food aid soon had negative effects on borrowing countries (Freidmann 1982). Food aid loans not only imposed debt on borrowing countries but also appeared to increase inflation as well as displace national agriculture production, making borrowing countries more dependent on US financial aid and more susceptible to fluctuations in global food prices (Freidmann 1982; Laaksonen 2023). As a result, food policies post-WWII did not create sustainable ways for countries to establish food security, as is documented by several studies on the topic in the Global South (see, for example, McHenry and Bird 1977; Sethi 2018; Vansteenkiste 2017). As we will discuss later, large corporations were often rewarded for helping provide food aid, with greater shares of the food systems markets. Cargill, for

TABLE 3.2 Title 1 Food Aid Under Public Law 480, 1955, and 1966

	1955	*1956*	*1957*	*1958*	*1959*	*1960*	*1961*	*1962*	*1963*	*1964*	*1965*	*1966*	*1955 through 1966*
Food Aid, Title 1 (in million $)	73	439	908	658	724	824	951	1030	1090	1064	1,144	906	9,811
% All Foreign Aid	2	13	19	16	19	18	19	20	21	18	19	14	17

Source: DeBlois, Eleanor N. 1967. 12 Years of Achievement under Public Law 480. Washington, DC: Economic Research Service. Table 1.

TABLE 3.3 First Round of US Food Aid by under Title 1 (PL480) by Country Receiving Loan

Country	*Title 1 Sales Agreements*
Argentina	31.1
Austria	43.2
Bolivia	6.8
Brazil	179.9
Burma	22.7
Chile	40.2
China	9.8
Colombia	29.2
Ecuador	8.1
Egypt	19.5
Finland	27.2
France	4.6
Germany	1.2
Greece	66.3
Iceland	2.8
India	360.1
Indonesia	98.7
Iran	12.9
Israel	87.3
Italy	128.1
Japan	151.4
Korea	82.3
Mexico	28.2
Netherlands	0.3
Pakistan	186.1
Paraguay	3.0
Peru	14.4
Philippines	10.3
Poland	65.4
Portugal	7.2
Spain	184.3
Thailand	4.6
Turkey	111.6
UK	35.6
Yugoslavia	230.4

Source: World Bank. 1958. United Sates Loans Repayable in Local Currencies. https://documents1.worldbank.org/curated/en/714551468142477048/pdf/multi-page.pdf

instance, benefited significantly from money generated from PL480. Alexander (2024:443) points out that, between 1955 and 1965, Cargill's agricultural sales increased from "$800 [million] to $2 billion." Thus, the promise of future commercial markets, which would be leveraged by companies such as Cargill, not only dictated the conditions of agricultural production that could increase sales but was often a condition of food aid loans (Kneen 2006).

Food Trade

When it comes to trade, Friedmann (1993:30) suggests that "the rules [of trade] implicitly governing agrifood relations were established in the years immediately after World War II and worked stably enough for nearly twenty-five years." An important part of that postwar stability is GATT, established in 1947 in a multilateral agreement to reduce tariffs and barriers to trade. GATT was essentially a global blueprint for international commerce (Schwenger 1958). Watkins (1991) pointed out that when it came to agricultural trade, GATT was also used by the US to rid itself of surplus food by getting it into the world market. Importantly, however, the US did not campaign for GATT until the war had ended. This support represented a sharp contradiction to pre-war food trade policies, where US food production was heavily protected by the government subsidies that kept US markets insulated from global economic forces associated with free trade (Watkins 1991). GATT was certainly beneficial to the US economy and the agriculture industry. After years of protectionist policies and newly developed agriculture technology (i.e., the Green Revolution), GATT allowed the US and its corporations to dominate the trade market, flooding the world markets with food surpluses. Thus, the global trade system envisioned under GATT was now viewed by the US as "freer, predictable, more competitive and more beneficial" (Singh 2017:565). Moreover, GATT, along with Title 1 of PL480, helped leverage the expansion of US agricultural production following World War II while still maintaining the protectionist policies that favored US agriculture (Friedmann 1993). Indeed, when countries in the Global South challenged economic policies eventually adopted in GATT (e.g., the challenges in the pre-GATT Havana negotiations [see Margulis 2017), countries such as the US simply refused to participate in trade negotiations. Nevertheless, the eventual GATT policy on agriculture that emerged was created in the interests of the US and is still described as an "agro-export program of global significance" (McMichael 2000:21). Neoliberal trade policies were enforced in the Global South, while subsidies and tariff protections were used as an advantage in the Global North. GATT set the stage for the WTO (created in 1995) and the new global order governed by Bretton Woods, as discussed in Chapters 1 and 2. While GATT increased the global trade of food, it also had some disastrous health consequences for countries that could not compete in this new and unequal economic order (Lang 1999). Countries in the Global North were able to benefit from their distortion of trade liberalization policies under GATT, while counties in the Global South were forced to engage in neoliberal development practices that threatened future national food sustainability and harmed the environment (Singh 2017). As Friedmann (1993:37) observes,

> As third world states sought to develop national economies, their agrarian strategies were shaped by the opportunities and limits of world food

> markets. These gave little reason to question the dominant ideologies—capitalist and socialist; modernization and dependency—which all encouraged states to downplay agriculture except as a contribution to industrial development.

In response to the initial perceived failures of GATT by countries in the Global South, subsequent rounds of GATT negotiations attempted to address the inequality institutionalized into the GATT agricultural provisions. Nevertheless, these negotiations also favored countries in the Global North (Raju 2008). In particular, like the outcomes of PL480, GATT increased the reliance of some poorer countries on food imports, which had to play by free trade rules. This ultimately meant that low supplies of food and high food prices harmed low-income countries in the Global South, as their populations were more likely to suffer from food shortages (Ritchie 1988). And, while GATT prohibited the "dumping" of most traded goods (i.e., exporting goods into the global market below their normal value), this was never the case for agricultural products, as many food items such as grain and dairy products were often traded by countries in the Global North at a fraction of their cost. Thus, US State subsidies that allowed for this type of agricultural trade helped to transfer wealth to transnational food organizations. which were amassing incredible amounts of power. Even when the dumping of food was addressed, only some forms were prohibited (Friedmann 1982).

Global Food Trade Post-1970

As Xu (2019:9) observes, "the very mechanism that constructed the post-war solution to the food problem also contained the seeds of its destruction." The destruction came in the form of a global food crisis in 1973–1974. An unusual shortfall in crop production in major producing countries, combined with high demand, especially for meat production, and rising populations in developing countries, combined with higher prices associated with increases in energy costs tied to fossil fuels necessary for the US model of global food systems, led to a severe food shortage. In addition, the global market in grain trade was exploited by Russia, who reacted to shortfalls by purchasing a significant amount of overproduced and subsidized grain from the US, in what has been described by historians as the "great grain robbery" (Rankin 1980). Finally, and important to note, food dependency in the Global South created under PL480 aid and GATT undoubtedly contributed to this problem (Sanderson 1975). However, the global food crisis of 1973–1974 would not be the last global food crisis in the century (see Lang 2010).

Since GATT was created, agriculture trade policy within the Agreement was controversial and changed little over various rounds of trade negations. It was not until the Uruguay Round, the disbanding of GATT, and the creation of the WTO that more serious regulation over agricultural trade, tariffs, and subsidies was considered (Tangermann 1996). New trade policies were organized under the WTO's authority and included converting non-tariff barrier practices into tariff barrier practices, reducing tariffs, and firming up commitments to reduce export subsidies, especially among developed nations. However, again, the Global South was required to adhere to free trade policies, while the Global North found loopholes in the system. As Clapp (2015:107) has pointed out, the Uruguay negotiations were

> mediated through the power dynamics of the negotiating countries [and] resulted [in] demanded market-opening measures in developing countries, while at the same time allowing industrialized countries to continue to protect their own markets through a range of domestic support measures.

This was accomplished through the classification of countries into subsidies by categories (by the colors amber, blue, and green); those tariff policies which were defined as least distorting to neoliberal policies were in categories occupied by countries with the most power in the negotiations, or those in the Global North, while those policies which were defined as most distorting to neoliberal polices were in categories occupied by the least powerful countries, or those in the Global South. Thus, McDougall's legacy continues to plague the global food system through institutionalized forms of empire trade at a global level, where the destructive power of neoliberal trade policies harms the least powerful nations. As one West African official pleaded during a United Nations conference, "If the developed countries can't do more to help us, they could try to avoid hurting us" (cited in Jones 1973:161).

The most recent round of global negotiations during the Doha Round under the WTO and its 164 member countries affirms these agricultural trade principles, which continue to aim to reduce tariffs and subsidies, especially correcting what are viewed as unfair trade practices in developed countries (Margulis 2020). As global food policy continues to develop; however, the US and other powerful countries continue to hold an advantage in defining what counts as a subsidy (Hopewell 2022). Moreover, agro-food corporations are gaining more power in the global marketplace, shaping trade policy, including pressure to reduce tariffs while maintaining national subsidies. In short, the Global South remains subordinate to the Global North when it comes to trade in agricultural goods.

An Introduction to the Concept of Food Security

Modern global food shortages have led to changes in the way food is discussed at global, national, and local levels. One of the objectives of the FAO's 1973–1974 World Food Conference was to address the impending global food crisis (Shaw 2007). As Shaw (2007) notes, the concept of "food security" was first used during the 1973–1974 World Food Conference to depict global food shortages. This new thinking about food shortages is important because it went beyond the physical pains of hunger and malnutrition to include emotional distress caused by worrying about future meals. As noted in Chapter 1, the link between deprivation and food security is obvious and exists in all definitions of food security, of which we are aware. What is less obvious is the connection between food insecurity and future expectations about the ability to access food. Thus, the threat or fear of being unable to eat at some point in the future is also important to understanding food insecurity and aligns with Bourdieu's (1962) concept of a divided habitus, where individuals experience internal conflict and tension as they worry about what lies ahead. Food insecurity has the potential to sever the social relations that form the basis of a stable, coherent habitus, as one is forced to focus on making ends meet at the expense of maintaining social ties that are beneficial in the long term. Insecurity makes it difficult to project oneself into the future, which is necessary for the very types of rational calculations required by the neoliberal subject (Bourdieu 1998:83). Short-term concerns over food are simply overwhelming. Indeed, rapid changes in the global economic system can quickly change how people interact with food systems, causing them to worry greatly about how and where they can obtain enough food to eat. The 1974 *UN World Food Conference* took up this issue and stated in the 1975 report of that conference,

> food security is the joint responsibility of the entire international community ... [and that] agricultural production, import requirements, export availabilities, livestock health, inputs and trade [are needed to meet] the requirements of world food security' [and ensure] that within a decade no child will go to bed hungry, that no family will fear for its next day's bread, and that no human being's future capacities will be stunted by malnutrition.
>
> *(United Nations 1975:13, 64)*

The factors that were viewed as responsible for the absence of food security (i.e., food insecurity) are described throughout the UN report and focused on issues of production, trade, and aid, with a renewed emphasis on ensuring equality in global trade. However, it was not until 1983 that the FAO, who aided in organizing the 1974 Conference, begain focusing more on the issue of food access, suggesting that food insecurity could exist even when there were enough food supplies within a country to adequately feed the population. This new way of looking at food security therefore recognized both availability and access to food within the definition of food security. As welfare economist and Nobel Prize winner Amartya Sen (1982) famously pointed out, "starvation is the characteristic of some people not having enough food to eat. It is not a characteristic of there not being enough food to eat." The FAO broadly defined food security stating that "the ultimate objective of world food security is to ensure that all people at all times have both physical and economic access to the basic food that they need" (FAO 198314). However, it was not until 1996 that the FAO finally defined food security at the World Food Summit (FAO 1996). This 1996 definition of food security was slightly modified by the FAO in 2012, as follows:

> A situation that exists when all people, at all times, have physical, social and economic access to sufficient, safe and nutritious food that meets their dietary needs and food preferences for an active and healthy life (FAO 2012:57).

It is this conceptual definition of food security that endures today, and the one we adopt in this book. Building from our general definition of insecurity in Chapter 1, food insecurity refers to the inability to predict a stable future with consistent access to healthy food that meets one's dietary needs and preferences.

Dimensions of Food Security

There are six dimensions of food security, including availability, access, utilization, stability, agency, and sustainability. The first four dimensions, also known as the pillars of food security, were described in detail by the FAO in 2013 (see also FAO 1996) in *State of Food Insecurity in the World*. The remaining two dimensions were introduced by Clapp et al. (2022). We address each dimension in turn.

First, food availability, as described by the FAO (2008), refers to the supply side of food security and involves having enough healthy and nutritious food. Food availability is largely generated from agricultural production but can also be generated from existing food stocks. As previously noted, the world produces enough food to feed everyone in the world. Table 3.4 shows the rising global surplus of food over the past 60 years. In general, the availability of calories from food has steadily increased across the globe between 1961 and 2021, and is now approaching 3,000 calories per person.

Given that average adults need somewhere between 2,000 and 2,500 calories per day, this level of production suggests that there is more than enough food available to feed everyone in the world. Of course, food availability does not always translate to access to food. Wealthy people in wealthy countries possess more economic capital to access food and may be more likely to waste food, while others experience food insecurity because they cannot access enough food to meet even the basic caloric requirements. Moreover, the availability of food says little about the quality of food available.

TABLE 3.4 Total Kilocalories Available per Person 1961–2021

Year	*Kilocalories*
1961	2181.25
1965	2277.64
1970	2357.15
1975	2366.76
1980	2458.61
1985	2550.86
1990	2584.99
1995	2617.24
2000	2669.08
2005	2689.63
2010	2798.40
2015	2872.43
2020	2940.42
2021	2949.11

Source: Roser, Max, Hannah Ritchie, and Pablo Rosado. 2013. "Food Supply." *Our World in Data*. https://ourworldindata.org/food-supply.

Low-income individuals are more likely to have access to sources of food that are unhealthy (i.e., ultra-processed foods).

The second dimension of food security is access (FAO 2025). As we have noted elsewhere, access to food is largely a political economic activity that occurs through aid, trade, and markets. Access can be limited by several factors, including the inability to purchase food that results from poverty. Access can also be reduced by a lack of infrastructure, such as the ability to transport food during times of war, or even by policies that limit the distribution of food during times of crisis (i.e., food aid during periods of austerity). Social and political inequality also play a significant role in determining access to food. For instance, as we have shown, at the global level, trade policies encourage the overproduction of food in many countries in the Global North, while countries in the Global South are dependent on the North for cheap food. At the individual level, the poorest people living in nearly all countries are unable to access enough food to meet their nutritional needs, primarily because they are unable to afford it or face restricted access to food, even with various types of government welfare policies in place.

Utilization is the third dimension of food security. It is not enough to have access to food, but the body must utilize that food (FAO 2025). Not all food is utilized by the body in the same way, and processed foods that are high in sugar do not provide sufficient nutrients the body needs to function. As a result, the way food is utilized not only depends on things like diet diversity and food preparation but also on access to appropriate spaces to store, prepare, and clean food. This too varies by cultural capital, and individuals who possess more of this capital through nutritional education and family socialization surrounding food choices may be more likely to utilize food in ways that increase food security. Moreover, economic capital helps provide access to clean water to wash food, as well as aids in accessing energy services (discussed in Chapter 4) that can increase utilization through food storage and preparation.

The fourth dimension of food security is stability (FAO 2025). Having consistent and predictable access to food is an important aspect of food security. Events that impact this stability include loss in production caused by severe weather, loss of income from unemployment, and/or the lack of food-related infrastructure to transport food to distribution points. For instance, in small UK villages, independent food shops often serve as an important source of food for the community. Recently, these food shops have struggled to secure a stable source of food supply because, as *The Guardian* notes, the food giant Tesco has limited deliveries to village shops by taking control of major food suppliers, such as Booker Inc. (Butler 2024). After the purchase of Booker by Tesco, food supplies dwindled as the food industry became more concentrated (Collins and Lee 1968). One well-placed food industry source said, "It's harder and harder to get a delivery" to my shop (Butler 2024). The end of this type of stable food delivery means that many village stores are less able to serve as a stable source of food for those villagers who do not have the ability or means to access food elsewhere. Such monopolistic food industry practices may also be partly responsible for the creation of food deserts, or communities where residents do not have access to food (Bitto et al 2002; Smith and Thompson 2022).

Agency is a fifth dimension of food security and refers to the idea that citizens can exercise control over food systems that they are part of, providing input into food policy (Clapp et al. 2022). This idea highlights the ability of all people's voices to be heard and to change food systems, for example, to reduce forms of social inequality. Clapp et al. point out that agency is closely related to the food sovereignty social movement that opposed the domination of transnational corporations and neoliberal food policies over local and national production. These movements have therefore pushed for policies and politicians that support food sovereignty over dependency. As we have discussed, at the global level, there has been strong opposition to socially unjust food policies and neoliberal policies that are often applied to only the most vulnerable countries. However, food movements have been fighting against these policies. It is increasingly clear that as large companies tighten their control of the food system, they put financial pressure on other organizations within the food system, such as small retail sellers and family farms (Clarke and Banga, 2010).

The sixth and final dimension of food security is sustainability, which ensures that current practices of food production, distribution, and consumption do not threaten the food needs of future generations. This notion of sustainability must, according to Clapp et al. (2022:5), be focused on "Ecological systems [because they] deserve special attention in relation to food systems as they provide the material foundation for food production and dietary diversity, including biodiversity in ecosystems, which provides the basis for nutritional adequacy." In short, various components of food security are linked through sustainability.

Empirical Measures of Food Security

Food security has been measured since the concept emerged (Lambie-Mumford and Dowler 2015). However, the United Nations' call to promote health and well-being among all people put pressure on governments and other organizations to measure the concept of food insecurity. With respect to food, the UN has suggested that one sustainable development goal is for all people to have consistent, sufficient, and safe access to nutritious food by 2030 (UN DESA 2023). To monitor this goal, a measure of food security (and food insecurity) is necessary. And, while many measures of food security exist (Cafiero 2019), we mainly focus on the FAO's measurements in the chapter, as these are the most widely reported and comparable indicators of food insecurity (Jones et al. 2013). Moreover, the FAO measures of food security discussed below are most consistent with Sen's (1983) basic thesis that most food insecurity is a result of a lack of access to food.

The FAO uses two indicators of food security: an aggregate-level measure and a household-level measure. Both indicators focus on 'access' to food as a dimension of food insecurity. At the aggregate level, the FAO estimates undernourishment – defined as the proportion of people in a country that can't access minimum food energy requirements (UN DESA 2013). This estimate of food security is sometimes described as measuring "hunger," with data on the indicator available for more than 100 countries and published annually since 1974 (De Haen et al. 2011). The measure is based on total calories available in a country, a country's population, the calorie intake for the country, and variation in consumption of those calories (UN DESA 2015). To calculate caloric intake, the amount of food available in a country is used as an indicator of calories available to the population, which is then divided by the population to determine the per capita dietary energy supply in kilocalories per day. This estimate of calories per person is then adjusted by variation in calorie uptake across different populations, using food expenditures from household surveys in that country (or neighboring countries).

Undernourishment estimates cannot provide information about food insecurity within a country, and measurement of food insecurity has been

TABLE 3.5 Trends in Undernourishment across the Globe, 2005 and 2023

Year	*% Undernourishment*
2005	12.2
2010	8.7
2015	7.7
2016	7.1
2017	7.1
2018	7.2
2019	7.5
2020	8.5
2021	9.0
2022	9.1
2023	9.1

Source: FAO, IFAD, UNICEF, WFP and WHO. 2024. *The State of Food Security and Nutrition in the World 2024 – Financing to End Hunger, Food Insecurity and Malnutrition in All Its Forms.* Rome. https://doi.org/10.4060/cd1254en.

criticized for containing systematic measurement error in estimates of average dietary energy supplies (De Haen et al. 2011). Moreover, it is unclear whether estimates of the minimum calories accurately reflect different populations within a country even while the FAO adjusts for these calories. Nevertheless, undernourishment is one of the only measures of food insecurity that can be consistently examined across countries. And, while other national measures of food insecurity exist (i.e., surveys of consumption and anthropometry), they are not as easy to compare over time because they are not consistently administered across countries. While the calculation of undernourishment may not always provide accurate estimates of the levels of food insecurity, they can be used to examine trends in undernourishment. Finally, the FAO undernourishment estimate, while not perfect, can be reasonably assumed to provide us with some insight into differences in food insecurity between countries (Saint Ville et al. 2019).

Table 3.5 provides estimates of trends in the undernourished world population over the last 18 years (2005–2023). While there were some initial reductions in the prevalence of undernourishment since the 2000s, this trend has since reversed. For instance, in 2016 and 2017, the prevalence of undernourishment was at an all-time low, with 7.1% of the global population facing undernourishment. Since 2017, however, the prevalence of undernourishment has increased steadily, and in 2023, nearly 1 in 10 global citizens (or approximately 735 million people) were estimated to be undernourished. This global rate of undernourishment is the highest it has been in nearly a decade. As a result, trends in global malnutrition do not appear to be substantially decreasing.

The second measure of food security created by the FAO serves as an alternative to the prevalence of undernourishment. This measure is called the *Food Insecurity and Experiences Scale* (FIES) and is survey-based data that examines the concept at the individual or household level, thus allowing for the prevalence of food insecurity to be calculated for various populations and subpopulations in a wide assortment of administrative units. FIES was created in the late 1980s at Cornell University to identify various dimensions of hunger among people who experienced that condition (Swindale and Bilinsky 2006). The Cornell researchers discovered that food insecurity encompasses a range of experiences. For instance, food insecurity can be (1) mild in the case of people who are uncertain about their ability to get food in the future, (2) moderate where it may impact the quality or quantity of nutritious food, or (3) severe where people experience hunger because they have no access to food (Cafiero et al. 2018). Importantly, these experiences of food insecurity are determined to be similar around the globe and are therefore consistent among households in a variety of different situations (Cafiero et al. 2018). The data obtained from FIES surveys are used by the FAO to calculate the proportion of the population that find it difficult to obtain sufficient quality or quantity of food. The FIES questionnaire was adopted by the FAO in 2013 under the *Voices of the Hungry* project and consists of eight questions that ask about experiences during the previous 12 months. The survey was first administered by Gallup, Inc., in 2014 as part of its Gallup World Poll, which is conducted annually among households in 150 countries (Saint Ville et al. 2019).

Table 3.6 shows the eight questions used to estimate food insecurity among individuals or households (if people are selected to answer on behalf of their households). Importantly, these questions can be self-administered. Question

TABLE 3.6 Eight Questions Used by the FAO to Measure Food Insecurity

	During the Last 12 Months, Was There a Time When, Because of Lack of Money or Other Resources:
1	You were worried you would not have enough food to eat?
2	You were unable to eat healthy and nutritious food?
3	You ate only a few kinds of foods?
4	You had to skip a meal?
5	You ate less than you thought you should?
6	Your household ran out of food?
7	You were hungry but did not eat?
8	You went without eating for a whole day?

Source: Food and Agriculture Organization (FAO). 2025. *Food Insecurity Experience Scale (FIES)*. FAO Statistics. Retrieved from http://www.fao.org/in-action/voices-of-the-hungry/fies/en/.

1 measures the potential emotional state of the respondent by examining future food insecurity; questions 2 and 3 examine the potential quality of a diet; and questions 4 to 8 examine the quantity of food a respondent can access. Results from the FIES questions are measured on a continuum of severity that ranges from mild to severe based on the total number of positive responses (a 'yes' response is scored as '1,' while a 'no' response is scored '0') to the eight questions. Households are determined to be 'food secure' if they score '0,' 'mildly food insecure' if they score between 1 and 3, 'moderately food insecure' if they score between 4 and 6, and 'severely food insecure' if they score 7 or 8. As already noted, FIES estimates of food insecurity can also be aggregated up to various administrative units and used to monitor global food security (De Haen, et al. 2011; Hossain, Long, and Stretesky 2021). For instance, the FAO estimates the percentage of a country's population that experience at least moderate food insecurity. People who are moderately food secure often eat low-quality diets and/or may reduce the quantity of food they eat during periods of food scarcity. FAO also estimates the percentage of a country's population that is severely food insecure. People in households that are severely food insecure often go entire days without eating due to lack of financial (or other) resources. The consequences of food security are significant and can worsen physical, mental, and social well-being (Long et al. 2021a, 2021b; Stretesky et al. 2020).

As noted, the FIES can be used to track the level of food insecurity within and across countries to (1) identify those populations that are vulnerable to food insecurity, (2) monitor the effects of interventions, and (3) isolate the causes and consequences of food insecurity. Importantly, FIES is standardized across countries so that it can be compared by using means and standard deviations obtained from the items in the scale (FAO, 2025). The FAO's estimates of food insecurity across the globe are presented in Table 3.7 for the years 2015–2023.

TABLE 3.7 Trends in Food Insecurity across the Globe, 2015–2023

Year	*% Severe*	*% Moderate*	*% Total*
2015	7.5	14.0	21.5
2017	8.2	15.7	23.9
2019	9.1	15.9	25.0
2020	10.6	18.2	28.8
2021	11.1	18.0	29.1
2022	10.8	18.1	28.9
2023	10.7	18.2	28.9

Source: FAO. 2024. *The State of Food Security and Nutrition in the World 2024 – Financing to End Hunger, Food Insecurity, and Malnutrition in All Its Forms*. Rome. https://doi.org/10.4060/cd1254en.

Trends in Table 3.7 reveal that across the globe, levels of severe / moderate food insecurity have increased between 2015 and 2023. Today, nearly 2.3 billion people face moderate or severe food insecurity, which represents nearly 28.9% of the global population. These trends suggest that over the past ten years, food insecurity has increased substantially. Finally, while malnutrition, hunger, and food insecurity are problems all countries face, they do not affect all countries equally. Different countries have different levels of food insecurity, hunger, and malnutrition. In the following section, we examine these inequalities in food insecurity in the Global South and Global North.

Food Insecurity in the Global South

As previously noted, Sen (1982:1) suggested that starvation and hunger are not a characteristics of food availability, but of food accessibility. This inequality in access to food today can be traced back through history and colonial practices, as countries around the globe were subjected, often through the military might of the world's most dominant powers, to both economic and political control (Ypi 2013). These colonial practices were often for the purpose of the extraction of natural resources and agricultural products. Moreover, many countries were colonized by Great Britain, who, according to Khilnani (2022:1), represented an "island smaller than Kansas [that] controlled roughly a quarter of the world's population and landmass." Britain for its part promoted the cultivation of agricultural products to be shipped back to England to help keep food prices low for labor needed to fuel the Industrial Revolution (Banerjee 2022) or sold in the global market. This was accomplished by claiming agricultural land in colonized countries and forcing the colonized agricultural population to abandon traditional agricultural practices in exchange for growing cash crops (often though monocropping) such as vegetable oil, tea, coffee, cocoa, and sugar (Hodge 2007; Munro 1984). This type of exploitation occurred well into the 1950s, creating a peasant class that could not compete with the Green Revolution's level of production in the Global North, while also putting much of the Global South in a subordinate position as trade liberalization took hold (Munro 1984). Today, many countries in the Global South face high levels of food insecurity, even though global food surpluses exist. In addition, colonialism still occurs through corporate theft of Indigenous agricultural knowledge, which is reproduced on a large scale (Shiva 2016). As we have already discussed, global variation in food insecurity persists, at least in part, because of the way global food systems have developed in contemporary times. Today, the struggle to access available food is still a plague in much of the Global South (e.g., see Sommerville, Essex and Le Billon 2014; Warnock 2019). Over the past 75 years, for instance, powerful countries have been able to protect their agricultural production by avoiding trade liberalization, while simultaneously demanding that low-income countries adopt such liberalization policies. Alongside these liberalization policies, patterns of global income inequality also appear to be intensifying over time. For instance, inequality in neocolonial capitalism has increased since the 1980s, and is no different today than in early forms of colonialism (Chancel and Piketty 2021).

Modern trade policies draw upon historical exports of raw products under colonialism in the South, while demanding open markets for finished products in the North in what has been described as "unequal terms of trade" (Emmanuel 1972). These uneven trade policies were aided by loans, often through the IMF and World Bank (Bretton Woods Institutions), with support from the WTO; these policies allow wealthy countries to remain self-reliant in their production of food, while shipping food surpluses through trade or aid to low-income countries, who are forced to adopt liberalization polices in their historically exploited agricultural industries. These distorted liberalization policies only further entrenched food insecurity and dependency in the Global South. Research shows that, even today, export-driven economies, typical of the Global South, tend to have lower food supplies than non-export-driven economies (Bradshaw et al. 1993). Moreover, countries that are attempting to develop their economies are, as we have already discussed, more dependent on food imports and "specialized" food exports; therefore, working-class populations are more likely to be negatively impacted by food insecurity when the global price of food rises on the world market. As a result, spikes in the price of food often lead to significant levels of food insecurity in the Global South (Otero, Pechlaner, and Gurcan 2013). In short, the current global food system is unequal, unsustainable, and increasingly based on global capitalism and neoliberal solutions for poor countries.

Table 3.8 shows the outcomes of global food policies in terms of the prevalence of undernourishment in the Global South between 2005 and 2023.

While estimates of levels of undernourishment computed by the FAO (FAO 2023) have decreased across the globe between 2005 and 2023 (from 12.1% of the population to 9.2% of the population), much of these gains have occurred in North America and Europe, which have a low prevalence of undernourishment (i.e., less than 2.5% of the population). However, areas of Africa, which have the highest levels of undernourishment in the world, have experienced increased undernourishment over the past two decades. For instance, countries in Northern Africa (i.e., Algeria, Egypt, Libya, Morocco, Sudan, and Tunisia) have experienced small increases in the prevalence of undernourishment (from 6.2% to 7.5% of the population), while the prevalence of undernourishment in sub-Saharan Africa has remained unchanged (at nearly 22.5% of the population in 2005 and 2023), with nearly 1 in 3 people experiencing undernourishment in Eastern Africa (i.e., Burundi, Comoros, Djibouti, Eritrea, Ethiopia, Kenya, Madagascar, Malawi,

TABLE 3.8 Prevalence of Undernourishment by Region, 2005–2023

	Africa	*Asia*	*Latin American and The Caribbean*	*Oceania*	*Northern America and Europe*
2005	19.9	13.9	8.9	6.9	<2.5
2010	15.9	9.3	6.1	7.3	<2.5
2015	16.0	7.5	5.2	6.9	<2.5
2016	16.6	7.5	6.1	6.1	<2.5
2017	16.7	6.3	5.8	6.8	<2.5
2018	16.6	7.1	5.9	7.1	<2.5
2019	17.4	6.6	5.6	7.0	<2.5
2020	18.8	7.8	6.5	6.7	<2.5
2021	19.5	8.2	6.9	7.5	<2.5
2022	19.7	8.2	6.6	7.1	<2.5
2023	20.4	8.1	6.2	7.3	<2.5

Source: FAO, IFAD, UNICEF, WFP, and WHO. 2024. *The State of Food Security and Nutrition in the World 2024 – Financing to End Hunger, Food Insecurity, and Malnutrition in All Its Forms*. Rome. https://doi.org/10.4060/cd1254en.

Mauritius, Mozambique, Rwanda, Seychelles, Somalia, South Sudan, Tanzania, Uganda, Zambia, and Zimbabwe) and Middle Africa (i.e., Cameroon, Central African Republic, Chad, Congo, Democratic Republic of the Congo, Equatorial Guinea, Gabon, and Sao Tome and Principe). Other areas in the world also have relatively high levels of undernourishment, such as countries located in Western and Southern Asia, as well as those in the Caribbean. Some of the biggest reductions in undernourishment have occurred in South Asia (Afghanistan, Bangladesh, Bhutan, India, Maldives, Nepal, Pakistan, and Sri Lanka), Central Asia (i.e., Kazakhstan, Kyrgyzstan, Tajikistan, Turkmenistan, and Uzbekistan), and Latin America. These reductions in undernourishment have been credited to a green revolution in these areas that "exceeded even the progress seen in high income countries a generation or two earlier" (Barrett 2021:10). Moreover, rising incomes, the opening of markets, and the creation of protective subsidies for agricultural industries have all been reported to have helped reduce undernourishment in these regions (Burkitbayeva et al. 2021; Sun and Zhan 2021). Unfortunately, these positive reports do not align with the current trends in the data, as the processes of global capitalism and the lingering effects of colonialism in international trade policies remain pervasive. Neoliberal food policies have become deeply entrenched around the globe.

Worldwide levels of moderate and severe food insecurity have also been increasing since the concept has been measured. For instance, as indicated in Table 3.9, the prevalence of moderate food insecurity has increased from 21.7% to 29.6% between 2015 and 2023, while the prevalence of severe food insecurity has increased from 7.8% to 11.3% during the same time.

Most of these increases in prevalence rates are due to large increases in food insecurity in the Global South. In Africa, moderate levels of food insecurity have increased from 45.0% to 58.0%, meaning that nearly six in ten people in Africa, or 854 million people on that continent alone (based on population estimates from the World Bank), live in conditions of at least moderate food insecurity. Moreover, the prevalence of both severe and moderate food insecurity has increased in Asia and Latin America, even as the prevalence of undernourishment is declining.

Importantly, while estimates of undernourishment have shown success in combating this issue, these indicators do not fully capture (as previously noted) all aspects of food insecurity in a country in the Global South. That is, undernourishment estimates do not necessarily capture differences in populations within a country even when the FAO attempts to adjust estimates of calories. As a result, economic policies that appear to decrease undernourishment may simultaneously increase food insecurity. Such a condition is strengthened by data collected across the Global South, using FEIS.

As Table 3.8 shows, some gains in reductions in undernourishment appear to have occurred in the Global South. However, food insecurity is, above all, a function of global capitalism and drives the changing nature of food production from agriculture aimed at feeding people to agriculture aimed at feeding livestock. These changes create threats to global food prices and food availability, which result from new land use policies of exporting countries in the Global North that may not be captured in undernutrition data (Yawson 2020). Thus, the rising food insecurity, reported in Table 3.9, is not unexpected, as food insecurity is about much more than access to calories in households. Moreover, the dependency of many former colonies in the Global South continues to have impacts on food security for people living there. Thus, for many countries in the South, little has changed since McDougall's calls for "empire trade" (McDougall 1925). These underlying problems of the global food system were made even more clear during the COVID-19 pandemic when many countries in the South were unable to get adequate agricultural supplies such as seeds, fertilizers, and farming equipment needed to maintain food production (Crush and Si 2020).

As the world locked down during the spread of the COVID-19 pandemic, the food system illustrated how entangled global food supply chains are and how changes in one country can create food insecurity in other countries. As Zurayk (2020) notes, during COVID-19, global food supply chains were reduced as land and air shipping was disrupted, and some food-producing countries implemented trade restrictions on food commodities, which increased the price of food on the global market, impacting food accessibility in food-importing countries. Given all these problems in the global trade relationships between the North and the South, the periodic scarcity of food and agricultural products, shifts in food production from grain to

TABLE 3.9 Prevalence of Food Insecurity by Region, 2005–2023

Year	*Africa*			*Asia*			*Latin American and The Caribbean*			*Northern America and Europe*		
	Severe	*Moderate*	*Total*	*Severe*	*Moderate*	*Total*	*Severe*	*Moderate*	*Total*	*Severe*	*Moderate*	*Total*
2015	16.7	28.3	45.0	6.6	11.2	17.8	6.5	17.9	24.4	1.3	7.7	9.0
2017	20.0	31.5	51.5	6.5	12.4	18.9	9.7	23.3	33.0	1.2	7.2	8.4
2019	19.1	33.1	52.2	8.3	13.1	21.4	8.6	20.3	28.9	0.9	6.0	6.9
2020	20.7	33.3	54.0	9.8	16.0	25.8	11.1	23.5	34.6	1.1	6.5	7.6
2021	21.6	35.7	57.3	10.2	15.0	25.2	12.1	22.2	34.3	1.4	6.1	7.5
2022	21.7	36.2	57.9	9.7	15.0	24.7	11.0	20.4	31.4	1.5	7.0	8.5
2023	21.6	36.4	58.0	9.8	25.0	24.8	8.7	19.5	28.2	1.6	7.1	8.7

Source: FAO, IFAD, UNICEF, WFP and *WHO. 2024. The State of Food Security and Nutrition in the* World 2024 – *Financing to End Hunger, Food Insecurity, and Malnutrition in All Its Forms*. Rome. https://doi.org/10.4060/cd1254en.

livestock, and unsustainable agricultural practices, it is questionable whether food demands in the South can be satisfied in the coming decades (Ingram 2011). Patterns in global food insecurity observed in the data certainly do not paint an optimistic picture of food security for the Global South in the coming years.

Food Insecurity in the Global North

While high levels of inequality threaten food security in the Global South, there is also a considerable amount of food insecurity in the North. Many wealthy nations produce (and import) more food than their populations need even though some people in these nations are undernourished and experience food insecurity. There are two reasons for this situation. First, the level of income inequality in many wealthy countries of the North is immense and continues to increase. This inequality is intensified by cuts to state welfare programs under neoliberal policies (Harvey 2005). For instance, the current income inequality measures in the US suggest that in 2023, the top 10% of US individuals controlled approximately 67% of the wealth, while 50% controlled only 2.5% (Kent and Ricketts 2024). In the UK, 1% of the population controls more wealth than 70% of the wealth (Oxfam 2023a). The second reason for high levels of food insecurity in the North are neoliberal policies adopted by governments in the US, the UK, and Western European countries. These policies withdraw State support for food aid, placing the blame for food insecurity on individuals who are left to be looked after by the third-sector (non-profit) organizations. In the case of food benefits, neoliberal ideology associated with the retrenchment of social welfare policies has also come to characterize the UK. Garthwaite (2011) notes that the people in need of food aid are often characterized as deviant—a condition that has been made more visible during the UK's recent welfare reforms. Moreover, food aid in the North is often distributed based on efforts to determine how 'deserving' recipients are, which ultimately makes it more difficult to access this type of aid (Shildrick 2018). Even with these efforts at identifying those worthy of aid, neoliberal ideology has come to dominate food aid policies. This neoliberal food ideology has led Wells and Caraher (2014:1436) to conclude that neoliberal politicians have perpetuated the idea that people in need of food aid are "freeloaders [who are] opportunistically taking advantage of the burgeoning network [of organizations] offering free food." These modern political populist ideological attacks highlight the threat of those who are insecure as deviants, blaming them for food insecurity because they refuse to participate in the global economy (Shildrick 2018). As a result of this neoliberal ideology, the public has come to see food aid in their own countries as a wasted resource for the undeserving poor. The combination of this individualistic mentality with cuts in social benefits to reduce taxes fits well with a limited government intervention approach to food aid. Neoliberalism's biggest political supporters, such as Reagan in the US and Thatcher in the UK, pursued a mandate for small government. Thus, the problem of food insecurity was down to individual responsibility, with a call for increased voluntarism in civil society to help those individuals in need. Thus, ordinary citizens, not the government, should help feed the less fortunate in society.

This is a clear example of the "symbolic violence" (Bourdieu 1991, 2000) of neoliberalism. Structural inequality in access to food is misrecognized as the result of individual moral failings, which makes those experiencing food insecurity undeserving of government support. In turn, failure to recognize the structural roots of food insecurity serves the economic and political interests of elites, as neoliberal policies continue to garner support and help officials win elections and remain in office. The dominated interpret success or failure within the terms established by the dominant in the neoliberal competition within the food space, which obfuscates the wielding of symbolic power and makes it far more effective than the use of physical force (Bourdieu 2000).

Together, income inequality and neoliberal policies to aid the poor are unsustainable and contribute to conditions of food insecurity, especially among the most disadvantaged subpopulations in countries such as the US and UK. In fact, in 2023, data from the US Census Bureau's Household Pulse Survey found that 12.5% of all US adults (i.e., 28 million people) were living in a household where they said they did not always have enough to eat (U.S. Census 2024. However, this level of food insecurity was much higher for Black households (22.4%) and Hispanic households (20.8%) (Rabbitt et al. 2023). Moreover, households with single parents have some of the highest levels of food insecurity in the US. For instance, 33.1% of households headed by single female mothers are food insecure (Rabbitt et al. 2023). These food insecurity statistics are incredible for one of the richest nations in the world and show how the poor in the North may face similar conditions to those in the South.

The US is not alone in its elevated levels of food insecurity. Figure 3.1 lists the percentage of moderate and severe food insecurity among 21 countries in the North, according to FAO data for the year 2023. These data demonstrate that food insecurity exists in many countries of the North, and it is even very high in several countries (i.e., New Zealand, Finland, Australia, and Portugal). Moreover, across all countries, the estimates of food insecurity rarely dip below 5% of the population, suggesting that the US is typical of other countries in the Global North (FAO 2023).

More recent data show that even while some countries appear to have low levels of food insecurity, this condition can change quickly. For instance, in the UK, the Department of Work and Pensions surveys its population, using questions similar to those used by the FAO, and estimates that the percentage of people living in food-insecure households (over the past 30 days) has

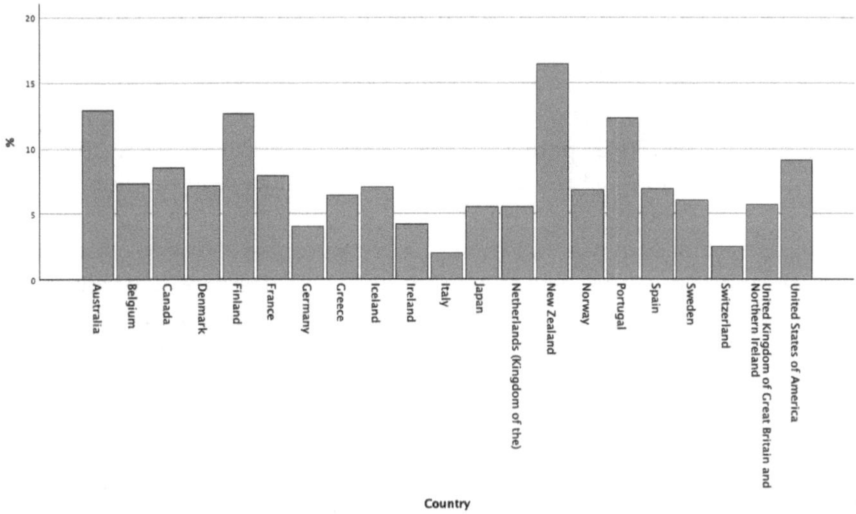

FIGURE 3.1 Prevalence of Moderate and Severe Food Insecurity among 21 Countries, 2023

increased dramatically since 2020, and increased from 7% in 2021 to 11% in 2023, with single-parent households experiencing food security at levels near 23% (House of Commons Library 2024; Department of Work and Pensions 2023). Thus, simply living in a country in the North is no guarantee that you will be food secure.

The Role of Agrobusiness

While food insecurity is a major problem for much of the world, the largest food companies are making record profits. For instance, Oxfam (2023b) found that a total of eight food and beverage companies made a combined $14 billion in profits in 2021/2022. This level of profit is aided by the neoliberal restructuring of agriculture, enabling companies to gain greater levels of monopoly control over agriculture. As Clapp (2022:48) notes, "corporate concentration has become a dominant feature of the modern industrial food system." This corporate monopoly over the food system has been occurring in all food system markets, from the genetic engineering of seeds to retail sales. Clapp (2022) notes that the present consolidation is driven by three factors. First, there are the financial incentives where agriculture companies seek to ensure corporate profits for major shareholders. When agricultural commodity prices fell after record-breaking profits during the recent world food crisis, which occurred between 2008 and 2012, many large companies were pressured by investors, who threatened to take their investments elsewhere, to ensure profits remained high. This pressure led directly to restructuring and mergers in the agricultural industry. In 2017, for example, the Dow Chemical Company merged with DuPont in a deal worth approximately $130 billion; Ed Breen, CEO of DuPont at the time, said the merger "unlocked higher value and greater opportunity" (Dow-Dupont 2017, para 7). Second, Clapp (2022) points out that mergers are also influenced by technological innovations. This was particularly evident as biotechnology developed and seed firms merged with chemical companies to form agrochemical giants. These companies could then ensure that crops grown from their seeds were resistant to the pesticides and herbicides used to boost productivity (e.g., Roundup Ready Seed). Or, more recently, John Deer's merger with Blue River Company introduced artificial intelligence in "precision" agriculture systems to improve the targeted application of fertilizer and herbicides. As John Deere notes,

> Blue River has created and fielded real-time autonomous agricultural robots. Their "see and spray" robotics platform uses computer vision to recognize plants, and sprays herbicide on weeds and fertilizer on crops with similar precision to inkjet printers.
>
> *(DCVC 2017)*

In short, better horizontal and/or vertical integration through mergers or acquisitions of companies in the food system is becoming increasingly common and is viewed as profitable for shareholders. Finally, Clapp (2022) notes that as regulations governing agriculture patents changed, there were suddenly more incentives for agricultural companies to merge with, or acquire, research and development firms to ensure patents were protected and could be used to gain higher profits in the markets. These mergers have become so common that marketplace concentration across the food system is a well-known issue in the literature. For instance, MacDonald, Dong, and Fuglie (2023) have recently estimated trends in market ownership for three industries in the food system: (1) seed, (2) meatpacking, and (3) food retailing. They found that companies such as Monsanto increased its market share of corn sales, from 11.2% in the early 2000s to 33.3% in 2018, after its merger with the German company Bayer. The top five producers (Monsanto, DuPont Pioneer, AgReliant, Syngenta, Dow Chemical) of corn seed increased their market share of sales, from 59.5% of the global market in 2000 to 83.9% of the market in 2020. Similar trends have occurred for other seed products in the global market. Moreover, according to MacDonald et al. (2023), four food retail chains hold at least 34% of the market in the US, with an even higher concentration of retailers in urban areas. In the UK, food retail chains are even more concentrated, with three retailers (Tesco, Sainsbury's, and ASDA) holding nearly 60% of the consumer market (UK CMA 2023).

TABLE 3.10 Ten Largest Agricultural Companies in the World by Revenue, 2021

Name	*Annual Revenue (in Millions)*	*Headquarters*
Cargill Inc.	$134,400	USA
BASF	$92,938	Germany
Archer Daniels Midland	$85,249	USA
Wilmar International	$65,794	Singapore
Bunge Global	$9,152	USA
Bayer	$2,124	Germany
CHS	$38,448	USA
Nutrien	$27,712	Canada
BayWa AG	$23,459	Germany
Associated British Foods	$17,807	UK

Source: Global Data. n.d. "Top 10 Agricultural Products Companies in the World in 2021 by Revenue." Retrieved from https://www.globaldata.com/companies/top-companies-by-sector/agriculture-forestry/global-agricultural-products-companies-by-revenue/.

Annual profits by corporations involved in the food system are incredible and even surpass the national budgets of most governments. Table 3.10 lists the ten largest global agricultural companies by annual revenue. Together, these companies employ 690,743 people and generate $597,083,000,000 (almost $600 billion) in annual revenue, with an average annual revenue growth rate of 25.9%

As these agribusinesses take on greater shares of the global marketplace, they can also have an impact on food security. As industrial organization theorists recognized 45 years ago, "firm numbers and the distribution of market shares among firms are important determinants of industry prices and profits" (Lamm 1981:67, more recently see MacDonald et al. 2023).

When a small number of corporations control markets, they can use their power to accumulate wealth for shareholders rather than seek to do what is in the best interests of global society. Large companies operating in a concentrated food system can therefore use prices and profits in two ways, which have implications for food insecurity. First, they can increase food insecurity by increasing the costs of agricultural products, especially when those products are in high demand. Unfortunately, high demand usually comes during food shortages when countries and populations are most food insecure and can least afford higher food prices. Second, companies often demand that food suppliers charge less for their goods. Thus, farmers may be paid less for their products, as there are few other buyers in a concentrated market (Sivramkrishna and Jyotishi 2005). This may be especially problematic for smaller farmers in the Global South, especially those that are financially squeezed. However, this also occurs in countries in the North, where small producers have been increasingly forced out of business as they lack bargaining power in the market and are often forced to sign exploitative contracts (i.e., contract farming) with buyers. This is especially the case with meat-packing plants (Stretesky et al. 2003).

In short, the increased concentration of agrobusiness sales has continued to increase profits by lowering prices paid for materials and labor, while simultaneously increasing prices for consumers. At the same time, these agrobusiness are shifting dietary patterns by focusing production on meat, which is more energy-intensive, diverting grain production away from feeding people; they also promote processed foods that are often harmful to human health and linked to diet-related diseases. More recently, there has been a rapid growth in highly profitable processed foods and beverages in the Global South (Scrinis 2015:137). Such practices, while good for corporate profits, do not necessarily help achieve food security or provide for a sustainable food system that can withstand global shocks to production, making global food shortages more likely.

Example: Neoliberalism and Food Insecurity, 2014–2021

Data and Method

In this section, we examine the association between food insecurity and neoliberalism between 2014 and 2021. Data come from countries that report food insecurity survey results using the FIES and from countries that have calculated scores on the *Economic Freedom of the World* (EFW) index, as estimated by the Fraser Institute. Recall that FIES was first administered by Gallup, Inc., in 2014, as part of its Gallup World Poll, which is conducted annually among households in various countries. For a review of the items used to calculate food insecurity, see Table 3.6. We use FIES to examine the estimated percentage of households in each country that are classified as "moderately" or "severely" food insecure. These results are released in *The State of Food Insecurity in the World* reports. Here, we use data from the first release in 2014, and from subsequent releases in 2016, 2018, and 2021. The indicator of neoliberalism we examine, known as the EFW index, comes from the Fraser Institute. The EFW index is created from data derived from multiple sources, including the IMF, World Bank, World Economic Forum, and the United Nations (see Gwartney et al. 2023). Each country receives a score on a scale from 0 to 10, which is frequently used to measure neoliberalism (e.g., Dixon 2020, 2022; Gwartney et al. 2023; Long et al. 2024; McLean et al. 2019; Tracy et al. 2010). A higher score on the EFW index represents more national-level neoliberal policies and practices.

We begin our analyses by presenting descriptive statistics for FIES and EFW in Table 3.11. We include means and standard deviations for the years 2014, 2016, 2018, and 2021. However, we also present data on the five-year change (%) in the EFW index, which can be interpreted as an indicator of

TABLE 3.11 Descriptives for Macro-Level Measures of Food Insecurity and Economic Freedom for Countries in the North and South

	2014		2016		2018		2021	
	Mean	*SD*	*Mean*	*SD*	*Mean*	*SD*	*Mean*	*SD*
% Population in Moderate and Severe Food Insecurity								
North	11.8	10.1	12.0	10.1	13.1	14.9	15.0	15.6
South	34.9	21.1	38.9	22.1	39.6	22.0	43.0	23.1
Economic Freedom World Index								
North								
Current Score	7.34	0.63	7.71	0.62	7.65	0.69	7.40	0.72
Five-Year % Change	4.05	3.46	2.08	3.89	1.52	3.05	–2.27	2.42
South								
Current Score	6.32	0.88	6.34ds	0.84	6.37	0.84	6.20	0.78
Five-Year % Change	4.16	9.87	4.75	7.50	1.68	4.71	–2.15	5.70

Source: Food Insecurity Data Come from the 2014, 2016, 2018, and 2021. *The State of Food Insecurity in the World*. Data on economic freedom come from the Fraser Institute (fraserinstitute.org).

short-term neoliberalization (i.e., the process of neoliberal restructuring). For example, in 2014, the "5-Year % Change" represents the percent change in EFW index scores between 2009 and 2014. We calculate this increase according to the following formula: $\% \Delta EFW = [(EFW(t) - EFW(t-5)) / |EFW(t-5)|] \times 100$, where t represents the time period, or year, under investigation. For example, Liberia's $\% \Delta EFW$ in 2014 is 22.91%, which was calculated as follows: $[(6.33 - 5.15) / 5.15] \times 100$, where 6.33 is the EFW score in 2014, and 5.15 is the EFW score in 2009. We include these short-term changes in the rate of neoliberalization, as we believe they have greater impact on insecurity than static EFW scores.

In the Global North, the percentage of households experiencing moderate or severe food insecurity, on average, increased from 11.8% in 2014 to 15.0% in 2021, while in the Global South, the percentage of households experiencing moderate or severe food insecurity, on average, increased from 34.9% in 2014 to 43.0% in 2021. It is, however, important to keep in mind that the number of countries in the samples increased from $n = 88$ in 2014 to $n = 121$ in 2021. Thus, the changing nature of the sample could impact these average trends in food insecurity over time. Unlike food insecurity scores, which have increased consistently, scores for the EFW have remained, on average, relatively stable. Overall, EFW scores increase slightly in the Global North and the Global South in 2014, 2016, and 2018. However, EFW scores declined slightly in 2021.

One thing to keep in mind when viewing EFW is that neoliberalism may have already reached a high point by 2014, the first year in this analysis. For instance, the average EFW score in the Global North was 7.34 in 2014, and 7.40 in 2021. These average EFW scores are relatively high; indeed, the highest neoliberalism score for any country in the entire data set is 8.58 for Hong Kong in 2021. Thus, average EFW score is already nearly 85% of the maximum global EFW score for any country. Thus, short-term changes in EFW scores are likely to be relatively small if they could be compared to changes decades earlier. In particular, the average short-term increase in neoliberalization in the North was 4.05% in 2014, 2.08% in 2016, and 1.52% in 2018. In the South, these increased from 4.16% in 2014, 4.75% in 2016, and 1.68% in 2018. It was only in 2021 that the neoliberal scores decreased by −2.27% in North and −2.15% in the South. Thus, it is hard to draw any definitive conclusions about the linear correlation between food insecurity and neoliberalism from Table 3.11, as the FIES scores increase, while EFW scores increase and then decrease.

As an alternative to Table 3.11, we explore individual EFW and FIES scores in more detail for each year in Tables 3.12–3.15. In 2014, the largest food insecurity scores (i.e., the percentage of households that are moderately or severely food insecure) occur in Liberia (79.7%), Malawi (78.1%), Sierra Leone (75.8%), Chad (67.9%), and Uganda (66.3%). These five countries

TABLE 3.12 Cross-National Differences in Food Insecurity and Economic Freedom in 2014

Country	*Food Insecurity*	*EFW Score*	*EFW % Δ*
Liberia	79.7	6.33	22.91
Malawi	78.1	5.34	-4.98
Sierra Leone	75.8	5.92	-4.98
Chad	67.9	4.95	2.70
Uganda	66.3	6.86	1.18
Zimbabwe	64.7	5.30	25.89
Togo	60.4	5.95	7.99
Ethiopia	56.2	5.08	-5.05
Benin	55.0	5.96	4.38
Dominican Republic	54.2	7.38	3.22
Namibia	53.2	6.19	2.48
Kenya	50.7	6.74	2.12
Cameroon	49.9	5.61	.18
Cambodia	48.9	6.75	18.84
Jamaica	48.3	7.33	3.82
Botswana	46.5	6.70	7.89
Guatemala	42.7	7.64	5.09
El Salvador	42.2	7.39	-1.34
Honduras	41.6	7.08	.28
Senegal	39.0	6.11	3.91
Albania	38.8	7.56	4.85
Ghana	38.3	6.11	-8.53
Peru	37.2	7.55	.00
Nigeria	34.7	6.25	13.64
Côte d'Ivoire	34.1	5.81	2.47
Bangladesh	32.2	5.75	-3.69
Georgia	31.8	7.87	11.16
Nepal	29.5	6.35	9.86
Libya	29.1	4.23	23.68
Mauritania	26.3	5.77	-1.54
Mexico	24.9	7.03	3.08
Algeria	22.9	4.85	-2.41
Ecuador	20.7	5.76	-4.79
Colombia	20.0	6.57	.00
Ukraine	19.8	5.64	8.05
Romania	19.3	7.86	5.65
Argentina	19.2	4.50	-23.21
Tajikistan	19.1	5.90	27.43
Tunisia	18.2	6.17	-.80
Malaysia	17.4	7.31	15.12
Greece	15.8	7.00	.29
Lithuania	15.3	8.02	6.65
North Macedonia	15.1	7.18	2.87

(*Continued*)

TABLE 3.12 (Continued)

Country	*Food Insecurity*	*EFW Score*	*EFW % Δ*
Bulgaria	14.9	7.50	3.31
Portugal	14.7	7.72	5.90
Seychelles	14.3	7.41	25.81
Pakistan	14.1	5.72	1.78
Brazil	13.3	6.36	-.78
Mauritius	13.0	7.96	-1.00
Montenegro	12.6	7.33	12.08
Kuwait	12.6	6.57	-2.09
Slovenia	12.3	7.30	.55
Costa Rica	12.2	7.62	4.53
Serbia	11.4	6.79	7.95
Hungary	11.3	7.53	2.03
Israel	11.0	7.50	3.31
Australia	10.8	8.23	.37
Chile	10.8	7.98	-.87
New Zealand	10.0	8.82	2.68
Latvia	9.9	8.04	3.47
Bosnia and Herzegovina	9.6	6.72	5.16
Estonia	9.5	8.10	1.76
Finland	9.3	8.01	.00
Ireland	8.9	8.27	5.48
Poland	8.9	7.41	8.02
Paraguay	8.3	6.96	.58
Russian Federation	8.2	6.16	10.99
Spain	7.1	7.79	3.18
France	6.8	7.75	-.13
Croatia	6.5	7.19	10.96
Iceland	6.4	7.50	8.54
Indonesia	6.0	6.85	4.74
Denmark	5.9	8.17	2.51
Azerbaijan	5.9	5.97	7.96
Sri Lanka	5.9	6.44	6.98
Czechia	5.8	7.95	4.47
Malta	5.8	8.00	.76
Austria	5.5	7.93	1.02
Norway	4.8	7.90	2.46
Switzerland	4.8	8.51	-.12
Luxembourg	4.7	8.14	3.30
Sweden	4.5	7.99	2.57
Germany	4.1	8.08	2.15
Singapore	2.8	8.77	-.68
Japan	2.6	7.94	1.15

Source: Food insecurity data come from the 2014 *The State of Food Insecurity in the World*. Data on economic freedom come from the Fraser Institute (fraserinstitute.org).

TABLE 3.13 Cross-National Differences in Food Insecurity and Economic Freedom in 2016

Country	*Food Insecurity*	*EFW Score*	*EFW % Δ*
Sierra Leone	83.0	5.70	-1.89
Liberia	81.0	6.18	22.38
Malawi	80.3	5.58	-4.94
Uganda	76.0	6.88	4.24
Chad	74.7	5.22	10.36
Zimbabwe	67.0	5.16	12.17
Angola	66.5	5.04	7.46
Benin	66.3	5.97	2.58
Togo	61.8	5.94	9.39
Guinea-Bissau	61.7	5.32	8.13
Kenya	60.9	6.62	1.69
Ethiopia	59.4	5.27	6.90
Cameroon	58.0	5.60	-2.10
Papua New Guinea	57.3	6.04	-6.21
Namibia	55.3	6.13	1.49
Dominican Republic	54.4	7.38	2.07
Botswana	53.4	6.81	3.81
Niger	50.0	5.89	4.62
Jamaica	46.9	7.53	6.51
Cambodia	44.9	6.90	6.48
Ghana	43.8	6.22	-4.45
Guatemala	43.5	7.67	4.50
Peru	42.9	7.63	.26
Nigeria	42.8	6.42	7.90
El Salvador	41.6	7.39	.82
Honduras	41.1	7.06	-.14
Burkina Faso	38.9	5.99	3.45
Albania	38.6	7.68	5.21
Cabo Verde	37.7	7.19	8.77
Côte d'Ivoire	37.0	6.13	13.73
Senegal	35.8	6.10	7.39
Georgia	35.5	7.95	7.29
Libya	33.2	4.12	40.14
Argentina	32.3	5.50	-1.61
Mauritania	32.3	6.10	4.99
Nepal	31.6	6.35	5.48
Bangladesh	31.5	5.75	-.86
Tajikistan	29.6	5.92	3.68
Ecuador	26.2	6.18	3.69
Mali	25.9	5.73	-.35
Colombia	24.9	6.59	-.75
Mexico	23.0	7.02	1.74

(*Continued*)

TABLE 3.13 (Continued)

Country	*Food Insecurity*	*EFW Score*	*EFW % Δ*
Ukraine	21.5	5.61	–.88
Tunisia	20.0	6.06	1.51
Algeria	19.8	4.96	.81
Mauritius	18.5	8.03	1.13
Armenia	17.1	7.41	.54
Greece	16.6	6.75	-5.06
Paraguay	15.6	7.07	1.73
Brazil	15.5	6.54	–.30
Malaysia	15.1	7.44	13.59
Romania	14.7	7.90	6.33
North Macedonia	14.3	7.16	2.29
Seychelles	14.3	7.29	17.01
Chile	13.7	8.03	–.50
Costa Rica	13.7	7.73	1.18
New Zealand	13.3	8.84	3.03
Pakistan	12.8	5.86	.69
Australia	12.7	8.29	1.47
Serbia	12.5	6.98	8.39
Israel	12.3	7.52	1.62
Kuwait	12.3	6.58	1.39
Lithuania	12.2	8.06	4.95
Bulgaria	12.0	7.73	5.17
Montenegro	12.0	7.33	4.27
Portugal	11.6	7.76	3.60
Slovenia	11.2	7.41	2.92
Latvia	9.4	8.04	4.42
Hungary	8.8	7.59	1.47
Bosnia and Herzegovina	8.7	6.79	2.57
Azerbaijan	8.5	6.43	16.49
Finland	8.3	7.97	-1.73
Estonia	8.2	8.16	1.87
Russian Federation	7.9	6.42	6.12
Croatia	7.8	7.29	3.55
Indonesia	7.6	7.06	4.13
Spain	7.5	7.84	1.42
Iceland	6.8	8.03	13.10
Ireland	6.6	8.29	2.85
Sri Lanka	6.5	6.62	6.09
France	6.3	7.71	.52
Denmark	5.4	8.21	2.24
Sweden	5.4	7.95	.89
Poland	5.3	7.32	5.02

(Continued)

TABLE 3.13 (Continued)

Country	*Food Insecurity*	*EFW Score*	*EFW % Δ*
Malta	5.1	8.01	1.01
Canada	5.0	8.25	2.87
Norway	4.8	7.89	.90
Austria	4.4	7.88	-.13
Singapore	4.1	8.79	1.38
Czechia	3.9	8.01	3.49
Germany	3.6	8.09	1.00
Luxembourg	3.3	8.07	2.15
Japan	3.2	8.03	1.90
Switzerland	3.1	8.53	.12
Kazakhstan	2.1	6.80	3.98

Source: Food Insecurity Data Come from the 2016. *The State of Food Insecurity in the World.* Data on economic freedom come from the Fraser Institute (fraserinstitute.org).

TABLE 3.14 Cross-National Differences in Food Insecurity and Economic Freedom in 2018

Country	*Food Insecurity*	*EFW Score*	*EFW % Δ*
Sierra Leone	85.3	5.64	-3.42
Haiti	82.7	6.08	-.98
Central African Republic	81.3	4.94	-2.56
Liberia	80.6	5.70	2.70
Malawi	79.9	5.63	6.03
Chad	75.9	5.49	12.96
Angola	73.5	4.34	-10.33
Uganda	73.1	7.01	2.94
Zimbabwe	69.8	4.71	-9.07
Kenya	67.7	6.76	1.20
Benin	64.0	6.28	8.09
Guinea-Bissau	62.0	5.19	-1.89
Madagascar	59.6	6.06	-2.73
Namibia	57.6	6.15	-.32
Papua New Guinea	57.3	6.03	-3.98
Cameroon	56.4	5.73	.70
Ethiopia	56.3	5.35	3.08
Togo	56.3	6.32	9.53
Dominican Republic	55.0	7.41	1.65
Botswana	54.0	6.84	.74
Timor-Leste	53.7	6.10	2.18
Nigeria	53.5	6.62	6.43
Lesotho	52.0	5.94	.51
Niger	50.1	5.79	5.66

(*Continued*)

TABLE 3.14 (Continued)

Country	*Food Insecurity*	*EFW Score*	*EFW % Δ*
Guatemala	49.6	7.61	–.52
Jamaica	48.4	7.50	1.49
Peru	47.8	7.78	2.23
Cambodia	46.6	6.98	6.24
Honduras	45.6	7.05	–.28
El Salvador	45.1	7.30	–.27
Philippines	42.7	7.10	–2.20
Mauritania	41.2	6.06	6.50
Georgia	39.7	7.95	1.92
Burkina Faso	39.5	5.96	3.29
Côte d'Ivoire	39.5	6.09	7.98
Belize	39.0	6.30	–.32
Ghana	38.2	6.36	–3.20
Libya	37.4	4.06	–9.78
Nepal	36.4	6.40	2.56
Argentina	35.8	5.59	14.55
Cabo Verde	35.1	7.59	15.00
Albania	33.8	7.65	3.52
Senegal	33.3	6.23	2.30
Ecuador	32.7	6.47	8.56
Bangladesh	31.9	5.84	1.04
Tajikistan	28.7	6.05	4.31
Colombia	28.5	6.66	–.45
Mexico	25.3	7.07	2.02
Tunisia	25.0	5.88	–3.61
Pakistan	24.3	5.92	.00
Mauritius	24.2	8.16	2.13
Paraguay	24.0	7.16	1.70
Mali	23.9	5.80	1.58
Myanmar	22.2	5.41	4.44
Lebanon	21.1	6.61	–2.07
Ukraine	19.9	5.86	–2.50
South Africa	18.2	6.62	–3.92
North Macedonia	17.7	7.17	.70
Algeria	17.6	4.80	–2.83
Chile	17.3	8.08	.50
Brazil	15.8	6.68	3.25
Costa Rica	15.3	7.67	.26
Malaysia	14.9	7.63	5.83
Fiji	14.3	6.08	–1.46
New Zealand	14.0	8.74	.34
Uruguay	14.0	7.18	–1.64
Romania	13.9	7.71	–.13
Israel	13.7	7.58	2.29

(*Continued*)

TABLE 3.14 (Continued)

Country	*Food Insecurity*	*EFW Score*	*EFW % Δ*
Montenegro	13.5	7.39	-1.73
Bulgaria	13.2	7.68	2.13
Australia	12.3	8.29	1.10
Kuwait	12.3	6.55	-1.80
Serbia	12.0	7.03	5.71
Armenia	11.7	7.65	4.65
Portugal	11.5	7.74	.65
Lithuania	11.3	8.06	2.03
Croatia	11.0	7.31	3.39
Latvia	10.2	7.84	-2.24
Bosnia and Herzegovina	10.0	6.87	3.78
Sri Lanka	8.9	6.71	1.67
Azerbaijan	8.8	6.44	9.71
Spain	8.8	7.81	1.69
Greece	8.6	6.96	1.31
Hungary	8.6	7.41	-.54
Ireland	8.3	8.20	.37
Slovenia	8.2	7.41	4.37
Finland	8.0	8.01	.75
Estonia	7.9	8.09	.75
Mongolia	6.8	7.37	4.54
Iceland	6.6	7.98	9.17
Russian Federation	6.0	6.56	4.46
Canada	5.8	8.11	.37
France	5.8	7.60	-.65
Indonesia	5.8	7.11	4.56
Poland	5.8	7.20	-.96
Thailand	5.4	6.96	5.30
Sweden	5.3	7.81	-1.26
Denmark	5.0	8.25	1.60
Singapore	4.5	8.81	2.09
Malta	4.3	8.00	.63
Czechia	4.2	7.98	1.40
Norway	4.1	7.86	.00
Belgium	3.7	7.63	-.39
Germany	3.4	7.99	-.25
Japan	3.4	8.03	.63
Luxembourg	3.1	8.09	.87
Austria	3.0	7.87	.13
Kazakhstan	2.6	7.14	5.15
Switzerland	2.0	8.54	1.07

Source: Food Insecurity Data Come from the 2018. *The State of Food Insecurity in the World.* Data on economic freedom come from the Fraser Institute (fraserinstitute.org).

TABLE 3.15 Cross-National Differences in Food Insecurity and Economic Freedom in 2021

Country	*Food Insecurity*	*EFW Score*	*EFW % Δ*
Sierra Leone	88.6	5.77	1.23
Haiti	82.8	5.88	-4.23
Malawi	81.7	5.77	3.41
Central African Republic	81.3	4.88	.83
Liberia	81.0	5.87	-5.02
Comoros	79.7	5.61	N/A
Somalia	79.7	5.94	N/A
Angola	79.2	5.17	2.58
Chad	76.6	5.15	-1.34
Nigeria	73.9	6.44	.31
Kenya	72.8	6.75	1.96
Uganda	71.2	6.65	-3.34
Burundi	70.8	5.43	-6.06
Zimbabwe	70.7	3.77	-26.94
Madagascar	68.6	5.97	-2.13
Benin	63.3	6.23	4.36
Guinea-Bissau	62.5	5.38	1.13
Mauritania	61.2	6.00	-1.64
Guatemala	59.8	7.45	-2.87
Cameroon	59.6	5.68	1.43
Ethiopia	59.0	5.15	-2.28
Papua New Guinea	57.3	6.04	.00
Togo	57.0	6.20	4.38
Namibia	56.8	6.08	-.82
Lesotho	56.7	5.90	-.17
Honduras	56.0	6.89	-2.41
Eswatini	55.9	5.26	-2.95
Jamaica	55.1	7.40	-1.73
Botswana	54.8	6.74	-1.03
Timor-Leste	53.7	5.88	-.34
Peru	51.7	7.43	-2.62
Cambodia	50.5	6.76	-2.03
Niger	50.3	5.74	-2.55
Djibouti	49.2	6.41	
El Salvador	46.9	7.12	-3.65
Dominican Republic	46.1	7.21	-2.30
Belize	45.5	5.95	-4.95
Pakistan	44.9	5.85	-.17
Philippines	44.1	6.93	-4.28
Trinidad and Tobago	43.3	6.64	-5.95
Ghana	42.4	6.35	2.09
Burkina Faso	40.7	6.06	1.17

(*Continued*)

TABLE 3.15 (Continued)

Country	*Food Insecurity*	*EFW Score*	*EFW % Δ*
Lebanon	40.1	5.26	-22.30
Côte d'Ivoire	39.4	5.87	-4.24
Libya	37.9	4.63	12.38
Nepal	37.0	6.26	-1.42
Ecuador	36.9	6.39	3.40
Argentina	36.1	4.55	-17.27
Suriname	35.8	5.35	-7.92
Cabo Verde	34.3	7.35	2.23
Georgia	32.4	7.59	-4.53
Albania	32.2	7.58	-1.30
Myanmar	32.0	5.08	-5.22
Mauritius	31.2	7.74	-3.61
Barbados	31.1	6.73	.90
Ukraine	31.0	6.06	8.02
Colombia	30.7	6.55	-.61
Bangladesh	30.5	5.76	.17
Senegal	29.4	6.13	.49
Fiji	29.2	5.92	-2.47
Tajikistan	28.0	6.28	6.08
Tunisia	26.7	5.98	-1.32
Paraguay	26.2	6.53	-7.64
Guyana	25.5	5.46	-12.64
Mexico	20.7	7.00	-.28
North Macedonia	20.2	6.99	-2.37
Mali	20.0	5.71	-.35
South Africa	19.4	6.58	.15
Romania	19.1	7.62	-3.54
Algeria	18.9	4.77	-3.83
Brazil	18.4	6.47	-1.07
Chile	17.6	7.52	-6.35
Malaysia	16.7	7.44	.00
New Zealand	16.4	8.43	-4.64
Costa Rica	16.2	7.74	.13
Uruguay	15.7	6.93	-3.08
Hungary	15.0	7.31	-3.69
Bulgaria	14.8	7.47	-3.36
Seychelles	14.3	6.66	-8.64
Bosnia and Herzegovina	13.3	6.40	-5.74
Serbia	13.0	6.86	-1.72
Australia	12.9	8.00	-3.50
Finland	12.6	7.80	-2.13
Montenegro	12.3	7.45	1.64
Portugal	12.3	7.53	-2.96

(Continued)

TABLE 3.15 (Continued)

Country	*Food Insecurity*	*EFW Score*	*EFW % Δ*
Azerbaijan	12.2	6.12	-4.82
Israel	12.2	7.49	-.40
Sri Lanka	11.4	6.04	-8.76
Latvia	10.2	7.68	-4.48
Czechia	10.0	7.78	-2.87
United Arab Emirates	10.0	7.30	3.40
Estonia	9.3	7.91	-3.06
Kuwait	8.7	6.51	-1.06
Canada	8.5	7.93	-3.88
Malta	8.2	7.74	-3.37
Croatia	7.9	7.21	-1.10
France	7.9	7.38	-4.28
Slovenia	7.9	7.21	-2.70
Armenia	7.8	7.52	1.48
Singapore	7.7	8.53	-2.96
Belgium	7.3	7.42	-2.62
Thailand	7.2	7.02	1.74
Denmark	7.1	8.10	-1.34
Iceland	7.0	7.84	-2.37
Spain	6.9	7.51	-4.21
Norway	6.8	7.63	-3.30
Greece	6.4	6.88	1.93
Lithuania	6.1	7.92	-1.74
Sweden	6.0	7.77	-2.26
Japan	5.5	7.86	-2.12
Poland	5.4	7.07	-3.42
Mongolia	5.3	6.94	.14
Austria	4.9	7.67	-2.66
Indonesia	4.9	6.94	-1.70
Russian Federation	4.6	6.23	-2.96
Ireland	4.2	8.12	-2.05
Germany	4.0	7.70	-4.82
Luxembourg	2.6	7.92	-1.86
Switzerland	2.5	8.47	-.70
Kazakhstan	2.2	7.01	3.09
Italy	2.0	7.22	-4.87

Source: Food Insecurity Data Come from the 2021. *The State of Food Insecurity in the World.* Data on economic freedom come from the Fraser Institute (fraserinstitute.org).

are in the Global South and are among the most food insecure countries each year.

It is notable that EFW scores among the top ten food insecure countries in Table 3.12 are below average for the Global South (i.e., 6.32 in 2014). There are only three exceptions to this trend, including Liberia, which has an

EFW score of 6.33, Uganda with an EFW score of 6.86, and the Dominican Republic with an EFW score of 7.38. It is also interesting to note that % Δ *EFW* scores do not follow the same pattern as EFW scores for the most food insecure counties in 2014. There are three % Δ *EFW* scores in the top ten most food insecure countries that are negative, meaning neoliberalization was decreasing five years prior to 2014. However, Liberia and Zimbabwe have some of the highest % Δ *EFW* scores in the data set, exceeding by 20%, which suggests rapid short-term neoliberalization (i.e., 2009–2014). Other countries in Table 3.12 that became neoliberal quickly and had % Δ *EFW* scores over 20% are Tajikistan (27.4%), Seychelles (25.8%), and Libya (23.7%).

Table 3.13 shows FIES and EFW scores for 2016. The highest food insecurity countries were once again Sierra Leone (83.0%), Liberia (81.0%), Malawi (80.3.8%), Uganda (76.0%), and Chad (74.7%).

It is notable that again EFW scores among these top food insecure countries are below average for the Global South in 2016 (i.e., 6.34). Out of the top ten food insecure countries, there are only two exceptions to this trend in high food insecurity and low neoliberalism – Uganda and the Dominican Republic – with both having higher EFW scores than the average country. However, we again find only two of the top ten most food insecure countries that have negative % Δ *EFW* scores (Sierra Leone with a score of –1.89, and Malawi with a score of –4.91). Liberia, again, had one of the highest % Δ *EFW* scores in the data set, exceeding 20% between the years 2011 and 2016. The only other countries in Table 3.13 to have a high % Δ *EFW* score was Libya, which had a % Δ *EFW* score of 40.1%. Despite this rather large change in neoliberalization, Libya's food FIES score was 33.2%, less than half of the most food insecure countries in the Global South.

Table 3.14 shows FIES and EFW scores for 2016. The highest food insecurity countries changed slightly from 2016, and were Sierra Leone (85.3%), Haiti (82.7%), Central African Republic (81.3%), Liberia (80.6%), and Malawi (79.9%). However, both Uganda and Chad remain among the top ten most food insecure countries in the world.

It is notable that only Uganda has an EFW score that is above the average EFW score in 2018 (i.e., 7.01 vs. 6.37). A significant departure from the 2014 and 2016 data set is that several of the top ten most food insecure countries have negative % Δ *EFW* scores, suggesting that short-term increases in neoliberalism lead to lower levels of food insecurity in Sierra Leone (–3.24%), Haiti (–0.98%), Central African Republic (–2.56%), Angola (–10.33%), and Zimbabwe (–9.07%). In short, half of the top ten food insecure countries in 2018 became less neoliberal, according to the EFW, between 2013 and 2018.

Finally, we turn to Table 3.15, which shows FIES and EFW scores for 2021. The top five countries with the highest food insecurity did not change from 2018, and included, Sierra Leone (88.6%), Haiti (82.8%), Malawi (81.7%), Central African Republic (81.3%), Liberia (81.0%).

Only Nigeria has an EFW score that is above the average EFW score in 2021 (i.e., 6.44 vs. 6.20). Again, three of the top ten most food insecure countries have negative % Δ *EFW* scores, suggesting that short-term increases in neoliberalism lead to lower levels of food insecurity in Haiti (–.23%), Liberia (-5.02%), and Chad (–1.34%).

When it comes to EFW changes, very few individual countries experience significant changes in EFW scores. For instance, only a handful of countries in Tables 3.12–3.15 have short-term EFW change scores above 20%. For instance, in 2021, only Libya had short-term changes in EFW above 20%. However, there appears to be a clear pattern among the countries with the largest FIES scores, where the % Δ *EFW* scores are positive, except in 2018. Moreover, larger % Δ *EFW* scores seem to be associated with countries that have higher levels of food insecurity, as is evidenced in FIES. In short, descriptive results reveal that rapid neoliberalization may indeed be associated with somewhat higher levels of food insecurity in at least some instances.

As Table 3.11 makes clear, and as previously noted, the average pace of neoliberalization slowed down considerably between 2016 and 2021, while food insecurity continued to rise. Thus, these results suggest that slight drops in the EFW do not appear to produce lower levels of food insecurity. For instance, Zimbabwe, Lebanon, and Argentina all had significant drops (greater than 20%) in EFW scores between 2016 and 2021. Despite these large EFW drops, nearly seven in ten Zimbabwean households were still food insecure in 2021 (ranking Zimbabwe the 14th most food insecure country out of 121 countries in the dataset), 40.1% of Lebanese households were food insecure in 2021 (ranking Lebanon 43 of 121 countries), and 36.1% of Argentinian households were food in insecure in 2021 (ranking Argentina 46 of 121 countries). Thus, these food insecurity scores are still moderate to relatively high despite large, short-term drops in EFW scores.

Given the large number of countries, years and trends in FIES, EFW, and % Δ *EFW* in Tables 3.11, 3.12, 3.13, 3.14, and 3.15, we present scatterplots for the relationship between % Δ *EFW* and FIES scores in 2014, 2016, 2018, and 2021. Figure 3.2 displays those scatterplots. We include the regression lines for the scatterplots that summarize the relationship between neoliberalization and food insecurity for the Global North and the Global South, given their different neoliberal paths as noted earlier in this chapter. In each graph, the solid line represents the relationship in the Global North, and the dashed line represents the relationship in the Global South.

The results in Figure 3.2 indicate that there is a persistent tendency for short-term increases in neoliberalization to correspond with slightly greater levels of food insecurity in the Global North in 2014, 2016, 2018, and 2021. The relationship between neoliberalization and food insecurity is strongest

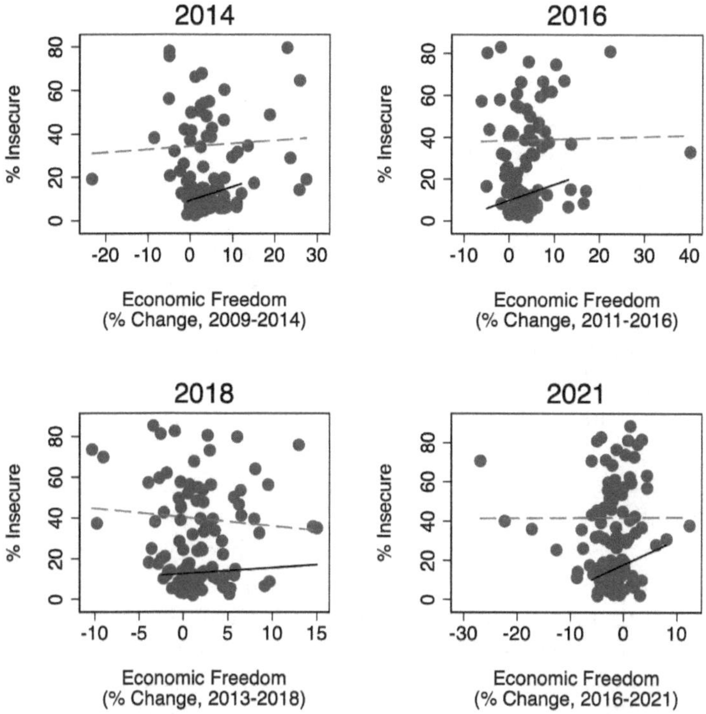

FIGURE 3.2 Food Insecurity (FIES) as a Function of Short-Term Neoliberalism (EFW% Δ) in the Global North and Global South, 2014, 2016, 2018, and 2021

among the 47 Global North countries in 2021. A 1-point increase in neoliberalization (i.e., % Δ EFW) between 2016 and 2021 was associated with a 1.3% increase in household food insecurity in 2021. The correlation is weakest in 2018, where a 1-point increase in *% Δ EFW* corresponds to a 0.3% increase in household food insecurity. Despite these differences, increasing neoliberalization, as measured by *% Δ EFW*, is correlated with the percentage of food-insecure households as measured by FIES. That is, at the structural level, changes in neoliberalism appear to be consistently correlated with food insecurity in the Global North between 2009 and 2021.

Figure 3.2 also summarizes the relationship for the Global South. Again, there is a tendency for short-term increases in neoliberalization to correspond with slightly higher levels of food insecurity in the Global South in 2014, 2016, and 2021. The relationship is strongest among the 53 countries in the Global South in the 2014 scatterplot. A 1-point increase in neoliberalization (i.e., % Δ *EFW*) was associated with a 0.1% increase in household food insecurity in 2014. The correlation is weakest in the 2021 scatterplot, where a 1-point increase in neoliberalization between 2016 and 2021 corresponds to a 0.02% increase in household food insecurity in 2021. Moreover, in 2018, the association between % Δ *EFW* and FIES is negative, suggesting that across countries in the Global South, neoliberalization leads to *lower* levels of food insecurity (i.e., a 1-point increase in % Δ *EFW* is associated with a drop in food insecurity of about –0.41%). This finding is contradictory to our theoretical perceptive, but it is also an outlier compared to the overall pattern, which suggests that, in most years, neoliberalization leads to more food insecurity in both the Global North and Global South.

The scatterplots shown in Figure 3.2 lead us to suggest that it is the process of neoliberalization, rather than the current level of neoliberalism, that appears to translate into greater insecurity; therefore, studies of neoliberalism need to pay attention to years under investigation and to the geographic parameters of the study (i.e., North vs. South). Critically, cross-national studies typically involve a relatively small number of countries, focusing on a single year or a short span of years. The temporal and geographic limits of the study will play an important role in shaping the findings regarding neoliberalism's consequences for food insecurity. While seven of the scatterplots show evidence of a positive correlation between short-term changes in EFW scores and FIES scores, the correlation is still relatively weak in the Global South. However, because FIES was not developed until 2014, it is not clear how the relationship between EFW and FIES was prior to 2014. As a result, alternative analyses of the association between neoliberalism and food insecurity are needed. We suggest just such an analysis in Chapter 7 of this book.

Conclusion

As we noted at the beginning of this chapter, one person dies from hunger every few seconds (United Nations 2002:15). Moreover, there are hundreds of millions of global citizens who are living with some amount of food insecurity. While there have been calls to rid the world of this social problem, it is unlikely that any progress can be made if the global food system is dominated by unequal exchange between countries in the North and South, and if the system is dominated by increasingly monopolized markets. In short, even while there is enough food to ensure that no one need be food insecure, the global nature of the food system itself is dominated by powerful actors who are, themselves, protected from the devastating forces of global capitalism and neoliberal policies and ideology. As we have shown, these forces produce untold social harm. As trade agreements remain unequal and large agribusinesses continue to dominate the global food system, it is unlikely that food security will increase anytime soon. In fact, unless the food system changes, the opposite is likely to occur, and food insecurity is likely to increase as a result. Unfortunately, food insecurity is but one of the many forms of insecurity people may face during their lifetime.

To illustrate the hypothesized relationship between neoliberalism and food insecurity, we used existing data that measure these concepts at the national level. Food insecurity was measured using FIES, and short-term changes in neoliberalism were accessed using EFW scores. These scores allowed us to examine how the process of neoliberalization is related to food insecurity at the macro-level, and if that relationship has changed over time and is different in the Global North and the Global South. While the lack of data is a weakness in the current analyses, we find that food insecurity tends to be highest in countries experiencing rapid, short-term neoliberalization. While these findings provide evidence of the intersection between insecurity and neoliberalism, additional research is needed given the limitations of these data. Moreover, while our study of insecurity has begun with food, we are not only concerned with food insecurity. We also set out to examine energy insecurity and job insecurity. We therefore continue the investigation of neoliberalism and insecurity in the next chapter, where we examine another type of insecurity: energy insecurity.

References

Alexander, Richard J. (2024). Is Cargill Inc. Really the Answer to World Hunger? Grosvenor House Publishing.

Banerjee, Arindam. 2022. "Locating Agrarian Labour within the Contours of Imperialism." Pp. 285–294 in *The Oxford Handbook of Economic Imperialism*, edited by Zak Cope and Immanuel Ness. New York: Oxford University Press.

Barrett, Christopher B. 2021. "Overcoming Global Food Security Challenges through Science and Solidarity." *American Journal of Agricultural Economics* 103(2): 422–447. https://doi.org/10.1111/ajae.12160.

Barrett, Christopher B. and Daniel G. Maxwell. 2004. "PL480 Food Aid: We Can Do Better." *Choices* 9(3): 53–57.

Bauerly, Brad. 2016. *The Agrarian Seeds of Empire*. Leiden, The Netherlands: Brill.

Bitto, Ella Annette, Lois Wright Morton, Mary Jan Oakland, and Mary Sand. 2003. "Grocery store access patterns in rural food deserts." *Journal for the Study of Food and Society* 6(2):35–48.

Bradshaw, York, Rita Noonan, Laura Gash, and Claudia Sershen. 1993. "Borrowing Against the Future: Children and Third World Indebtedness." *Social Forces* 71: 629–656.

Brannan, Charles F. 1951. "Problems of Agricultural Production." *The ANNALS of the American Academy of Political and Social Science* 278(1): 119–125.

Bourdieu, Pierre. 2000. *Pascalian Meditations*. Stanford, CA: Stanford University Press.

Bourdieu, Pierre. 1998. *Acts of Resistance: Against the Tyranny of the Market*. New York: The New Press.

Bourdieu, Pierre. 1991. *Language & Symbolic Power*. Cambridge, MA: Harvard University Press.

Burkitbayeva, Saule, William Liefert, and Johan Swinnen. 2021. "Agricultural Development and Food Security in Eastern Europe and Central Asia." Pp. 233–276 in *Agricultural Development: New Perspectives in a Changing World*, edited by Keijiro Otsuka and Shenggen Fan. Washington D.C.: International Food Policy Research Institute.

Butler, Sarah. 2024. "Tesco Accused of Using Cash and Carry Arm Booker to Squeeze Village Stores out of Business." *The Guardian*, March 22. Available at: https://www.theguardian.com/business/2024/mar/22/tesco-accused-of-using-cash-and-carry-arm-booker-to-squeeze-village-stores-out-of-business.

Cafiero, Carlo. 2019. "Measuring Food Insecurity." Pp. 169–205 in *Food Security Policy, Evaluation and Impact Assessment*, edited by Sheryl L. Hendriks. London: Routledge.

Cafiero, Carlo, Sara Viviani, and Mark Nord. 2018. "Food Security Measurement in a Global Context: The Food Insecurity Experience Scale." *Measurement* 116:146–152.

Chancel, Lucas and Thomas Piketty. 2021. "Global Income Inequality, 1820–2020: The Persistence and Mutation of Extreme Inequality." *Journal of the European Economic Association* 19(6):3025–3062. https://doi.org/10.1093/jeea/jvab047.

Cheek, Bruce M. 1958. *United States Loans Repayable in Local Currencies*. International Bank for Reconstruction and Development. Report No. EC-65a. https://documents1.worldbank.org/curated/pt/714551468142477048/pdf/multi-page.pdf.

Clapp, Jennifer. 2022. "The Rise of Big Food and Agriculture: Corporate Influence in the Food System." Pp. 45–66 in *A Research Agenda for Food Systems*, edited by A. Research Agenda. Cheltenham, UK: Edward Elgar Publishing.

Clapp, Jennifer. 2020. *Food*. London: Polity Press.

Clapp, Jennifer. 2015. "Food Security and Contested Agricultural Trade Norms." *Journal of International Law and International Relations* 11: 104–116.

Clapp, Jennifer, William G. Moseley, Barbara Burlingame, and Paolo Termine. 2022. "The Case for a Six-Dimensional Food Security Framework." *Food Policy* 106: 102–164.

Clarke, Ian and Sunil Banga. 2010. "The Economic and Social Role of Small Stores: a Review of UK Evidence. " *The International Review of Retail, Distribution and Consumer Research* 20(2): 187–215.

Collins, Norman R. and Lee E. Preston. 1968. *Concentration and Price-cost Margins in Manufacturing Industries*. Berkeley, California: University of California Press.

Conservative and Unionist Film Association. 1934. *Empire Trade*. Great Britain. Retrieved from http://www.colonialfilm.org.uk/.

Crush, Jonathan and Zhenzhong Si. 2020. "COVID-19 Containment and Food Security in the Global South." *Journal of Agriculture, Food Systems, and Community Development* 9(4): 149–151.

Davis, Joseph S. 1960. "Food for Peace." *Food Research Institute Studies* 1(2): 135–149.

DCVC – Data Collective Venture Capital. 2017. *John Deere Acquires Blue River Technology for $305 Million, Bringing Full Stack AI to Agriculture*. Retrieved from https://www.dcvc.com/news-insights/john-deere-acquires-blue-river-technology-for-305-million-bringing-full-stack-ai-to-agriculture/#:~:text=Congratulations%20to%20Blue%20River%20Technology,leading%20manufacturer%20of%20agricultural%20equipment.

DeBlois, Eleanor N. 1967. *Twelve Years of Achievement under Public Law 480*. Washington, DC: 19 Economic Research Service.

De Haen, Hartwig, Stephan Klasen, and Matin Qaim. 2011. "What Do We Really Know? Metrics for Food Insecurity and Undernutrition." *Food Policy* 36(6): 760–769. https://doi.org/10.1016/j.foodpol.2011.08.003.

Department of Work and Pensions. 2023. "*Family Resources Survey, Table 9.2: Household Food Security Status by Household Composition* [Note 4], 2021 to 2022, United Kingdom." Available at https://assets.publishing.service.gov.uk/media/641b00a5e90e0769f5bb4e5c/c9-household-food-security.xlsx.

Dow-DuPont. 2017. *Dow-DuPont Merger Complete.* 8 September 2017. https://www.paintsquare.com/news/dowdupont-merger-complete#:~:text=%E2%80%9CFor%20shareholders%2C%20customers%20and%20employees,chief%20executive%20officer%20of%20DowDuPont.

Dixon, Jeffrey C. 2020. "Understanding Perceived Worker Insecurity in Europe, 2002–2016: Economic Freedom and Neoliberalism as Alternative Theories?" *Sociological Perspectives* 63: 5–28.

Dixon, Jeffrey C. 2022. "Where are the Neoliberals? Examining Economic Freedom, Perceived Freedom, and Free Market Values." *Comparative Sociology* 21: 142–197.

Emmanuel, Arghiri. 1972. *Unequal Exchange.* Vol. 197, No. 2. New York: Monthly Review Press.

FAO [Food and Agriculture Organization]. 2025. *Food Insecurity Experience Scale (FIES).* FAO Statistics. Available at https://www.fao.org/in-action/voices-of-the-hungry/fies/en/. Accessed February 14, 2025.

FAO [Food and Agriculture Organisation]. 2024. *The State of Food Security and Nutrition in the World 2024 – Financing to End Hunger, Food Insecurity and Malnutrition in All Its Forms.* Rome, Food and Agricultural Agency of the United Nations. Available at https://doi.org/10.4060/cd1254en. Accessed 24 June 2024.

FAO [Food and Agriculture Organization]. 2023. *The State of Food Security and Nutrition in the World 2023: Urbanization, Agrifood Systems Transformation and Healthy Diets across the Rural–Urban Continuum.* Rome, Food and Agricuture Organisation of the United Nations. https://doi.org/10.4060/cc3017en. Accessed February 14, 2025.

FAO [Food and Agriculture Organization]. 2021. *The State of Food and Agriculture.* Rome, Food and Agriculture Organization of the United Nations. Available at https://openknowledge.fao.org/items/552896c3-03be-4b36-a8aa-0cffc2bfc70d. Accessed June 24, 2024.

FAO [Food and Agriculture Organisation]. 2013. *The State of Food Insecurity in the World: The Multiple Measures of Food Security.* Rome, Food and Agriculture Organisation of the United Nations. Available at https://www.fao.org/3/i3434e/i3434e.pdf. Accessed June 24, 2024.

FAO [Food and Agriculture Organisation]. 2012. *The State of Food Insecurity in the World: Economic growth is necessary but not sufficient to accelerate reduction of hunger and malnutrition.* Rome, Food and Agriculture Organisation of the United Nations. Available at https://www.fao.org/4/i3027e/i3027e.pdf. Accessed June 24, 2024.

FAO [Food and Agriculture Organisation]. 2008. *The State of Food Insecurity in the World: High Food Prices and Food Security-Threats and Opportunities.* Rome, Food and Agriculture Organisation of the United Nations. Available at https://www.fao.org/4/i0291e/i0291e00.htm. Accessed June 24, 2024.

FAO [Food and Agriculture Organization]. 1996. *The State of Food and Agriculture*. Rome, Food and Agriculture Organisation of the United Nations. Available at https://www.fao.org/4/w1358e/w1358e00.htm. Accessed June 24, 2024.

FAO [Food and Agriculture Organisation]. 1985. Part II. *Report of the Eighth Session of the Committee on World Food Security, 13–20 April*. Rome, Food and Agriculture Organisation of the United Nations. Available at https://www.fao.org/4/AK626E/ak626e08.htm. Accessed February 14, 2025.

FAO [Food and Agriculture Organization]. 1983. *The State of Food and Agriculture: .The situation in Sub-Saharan Africa; Women in Developing Agriculture*. Rome, Food and Agriculture Organisation of the United Nations. Available at https://www.fao.org/4/ap663e/ap663e.pdf. Accessed June 24, 2024.

FAO [Food and Agriculture Organization]. 1948. *The State of Food and Agriculture*. United States, Washington D.C., Food and Agriculture Organisation of the United Nations. Available at https://doi.org/10.18356/eb42e417-en. Accessed June 24, 2024.

Friedmann, Harriet. 1993. "The Political Economy of Food: A Global Crisis." *New Left Review* 197: 29–57.

Friedmann, Harriet. 1987. "International Regimes of Food and Agriculture Since 1870." *Peasants and Peasant Societies* 2: 247–258.

Friedmann, Harriet. 1982. "The Political Economy of Food: The Rise and Fall of the Postwar International Food Order." *American Journal of Sociology* 88: 248–286.

Garthwaite, Kayleigh. 2011. "'The Language of Shirkers and Scroungers?' Talking About Illness, Disability and Coalition Welfare Reform." *Disability & Society* 26(3): 369–372. https://doi.org/10.1080/09687599.2011.560420.

Gauld, William S. 1968. "The Green Revolution: Accomplishments and Apprehensions." *AgBioWorld*. Retrieved August 8, 2011 (https://www.agbioworld.org/biotech-info/topics/borlaug/borlaug-green.html).

Gwartney, James, Robert Lawson, and Ryan Murphy. 2023. *Economic Freedom of the World 2023 Annual Report*. https://www.fraserinstitute.org/sites/default/files/economic-freedom-of-the-world-2023.pdf.

Hamblin, Jacob D. 2012. "The Vulnerability of Nations: Food Security in the Aftermath of World War II." *Global Environment* 10: 42–65.

Harvey, David. 2005. *A Brief History of Neoliberalism*. Oxford and New York: Oxford University Press.

Hodge, Joseph M. 2007. *Triumph of the Expert: Agrarian Doctrines of Development and the Legacies of British Colonialism*. Athens, OH: Ohio University Press.

Hopewell, Kristen. 2022. "Heroes of the Developing World? Emerging Powers in WTO Agriculture Negotiations and Dispute Settlement." *The Journal of Peasant Studies* 49(3): 561–584. https://doi.org/10.1080/03066150.2021.1873292

Hossain, Md Belal, Michael A. Long, and Paul B. Stretesky. 2021. "Welfare State Spending, Income Inequality and Food Insecurity in Affluent Nations: A Cross-National Examination of OECD Countries." *Sustainability* 13: 324. https://doi.org/10.3390/su13010324.

House of Commons Library. 2024. "*Who Is Experiencing Food Insecurity in the UK?*" Retrieved from https://commonslibrary.parliament.uk/who-is-experiencing-food-insecurity-in-the-uk/#:~:text=The%20number%20of%20people.

Ingram, John. 2011. "A Food Systems Approach to Researching Food Security and Its Interactions with Global Environmental Change." *Food Security* 3: 417–431. https://doi.org/10.1007/s12571-011-0149-9.

Jones, Brendan. 1973. "Developing Africa Stresses Self-Reliance." *The New York Times*, February 4. https://www.nytimes.com/1973/02/04/archives/developing-africa-stresses-selfreliance-developing-africa-seeks.html.

Johnson, Sherman E. 1945. "Agricultural Production after the War." *Journal of Farm Economics* 27(2): 261–280.

Jones, Andrew D., Francis M. Ngure, Gretel Pelto, and Sera L. Young. 2013. "What Are We Assessing When We Measure Food Security? A Compendium and Review of Current Metrics." *Advances in Nutrition* 4(5): 481–505.

Khilnani, Sunil. 2022. "The British Empire Was Much Worse Than You Realize." *The New Yorker*. Available at https://www.newyorker.com/magazine/2022/04/04/the-british-empire-was-much-worse-than-you-realize-caroline-elkinss-legacy-of-violence.

Kneen, Brewster. 2006. "The Invisible Giant: Cargill and Its Transnational Strategies." Pp. 443–448 in *A Reader in Ecology, Culture and Sustainable Living*, edited by Nora Haenn and Richard Wilk. New York: New York University Press.

Kent, Ana Hernandez and Lowell Ricketts. 2024. "The State of U.S. Wealth Inequality." U.S. Federal Reserve Bank. Available at https://www.stlouisfed.org/institute-for-economic-equity/the-state-of-us-wealth-inequality.

Krausmann, Fridolin and Ernst Langthaler. 2019. "Food Regimes and Their Trade Links: A Socio-Ecological Perspective." *Ecological Economics* 160: 87–95. https://doi.org/10.1016/j.ecolecon.2019.02.011.

Laaksonen, Mikko. 2023. *Food for Leverage*. Thesis. Tampere University. Available at https://trepo.tuni.fi/bitstream/handle/10024/152988/LaaksonenMikko.pdf?sequence=2.

Lambie-Mumford, Hannah and Elizabeth Dowler. 2015. "Hunger, Food Charity and Social Policy–Challenges Faced by the Emerging Evidence Base." *Social Policy and Society* 14(3): 497–506. https://doi.org/10.1017/S1474746415000172.

Lamm, R. McFall. 1981. "Prices and the Concentration in the Food Retailing Industry." *Journal of Industrial Economics*. 30(1): 67–78.

Lang, Tim. 2010. "Crisis? What Crisis? The Normality of the Current Food Crisis." *Journal of Agrarian Change* 10(1): 87–97. https://doi.org/10.1111/j.1471-0366.2009.00250.x.

Lang, Tim. 1999. "The New GATT Round: Whose Development? Whose Health?" *Journal of Epidemiology and Community Health* 53(11): 681.

Long, Michael A., Margaret Anne Defeyter, and Paul B. Stretesky. 2021a. *Holiday Hunger in the UK: Local Responses to Childhood Food Insecurity*. Abingdon, Oxon, UK: Routledge.

Long, Michael A., Paul B. Stretesky, Eilish Crilley, Zeb Sattar, and Margaret Anne Defeyter. 2021b. "Examining the Relationship between Child Holiday Club Attendance and Parental Mental Wellbeing." *Public Health in Practice* 2: 100122.

Long, Michael A., Michael J. Lynch, Md Belal Hossain, and Paul B. Stretesky. 2024. "Neoliberalism, World System Position, and Biodiversity Loss: A Cross-National Examination of Threatened Species." *Sociology of Development* 10: 335–365.

MacDonald, James M., Xiao Dong, and Keith Fuglie. 2023. *Concentration and Competition in U.S. Agribusiness*. Report No. EIB-256. U.S. Department of Agriculture, Economic Research Service. https://doi.org/10.32747/2023.8054022.ers.

Margulis, Matis E. 2020. "The World Trade Organization between Law and Politics: Negotiating a Solution for Public Stockholding for Food Security Purposes." Pp. 169–186 in *Transnational Food Security*, edited by Emily Webster, Ankita Gupta, and Ruth Ambros. Routledge.

Margulis, Matis E. 2017. "The Forgotten History of Food Security in Multilateral Trade Negotiations." *World Trade Review* 16(1): 25–57.

McDougall, Frank L. 1951. "Food and Population." *International Conciliation* 29: 539 https://heinonline.org/HOL/LandingPage?handle=hein.journals/intcon29&div=27&id=&page=.

McDougall, Frank L. 1925. *Sheltered Markets: A Study of the Value of Empire Trade*. London: J. Murray.

McDougall, Frank L. n.d. *The McDougal Memoranda: Some Documents Relating to the Origins of FAO and the Contribution Made by Frank L. McDougall*. Food and Agriculture Organisation of the United Nations. Available at https://www.fao.org/fileadmin/templates/library/docs/mcdougall_memoranda.pdf

McHenry, Donald F. and Kai Bird. 1977. "Food Bungle in Bangladesh." *Foreign Policy* 27: 72–88.

McLean, Craig, Michael A. Long, Paul B. Stretesky, Michael J. Lynch, and Steve Hall. 2019. "Exploring the Relationship between Neoliberalism and Homicide: A Cross-National Perspective." *International Journal of Sociology* 49: 53–76.

McMichael, Philip. 2000. "The Power of Food." *Agriculture and Human Values* 17: 21–33.

Mercy Corps. 2020. "*The Facts: What You Need to Know About Global Hunger*." Retrieved April 5, 2024. https://www.mercycorps.org/blog/facts-global-hunger.

Munro, John Ford. 1984. "The 'Peasant' Economies." Pp 40–50 in *Britain in Tropical Africa, 1880–1960*, edited by John Ford Munro. London: Palgrave. https://doi.org/10.1007/978-1-349-06172-3_5.

O'Brien, John B. 2000. "FL McDougall and the Origins of the FAO." *Australian Journal of Politics & History* 46(2): 164–174. https://doi.org/10.1111/1467-8497.00091.

Otero, Gerardo, Pechlaner, Gabriela, and Gürcan, Efe Can. 2013. "The Political Economy of 'Food Security' and Trade: Uneven and Combined Dependency." *Rural Sociology* 78(3): 263–289.

Oxfam. 2023a. *The Richest 1% Grab Nearly Twice as Much New Wealth as the Rest of the World Put Together*. Retrieved from https://www.oxfam.org.uk/mc/ar8thi/.

Oxfam. 2023b. *Corporation Windfall Profits Rocket to $1 Trillion a Year*. Oxfam, July 6, 2023. https://www.oxfam.org.uk/mc/9ano9s/.

Phillips, Ralph W. 1983. *FAO: Its Origins, Formation and Evolution 1945–1981*. Retrieved from https://www.fao.org/3/p4228e/P4228E00.htm#TOC.

Quinn, Kenneth M. 2008. "Dr. Norman E. Borlaug: Twentieth Century Lessons for the Twenty-First Century World." *Advances in Agronomy* 100: 1–13.

Rabbitt, Matthew P., Laura J. Hales, Michael P. Birke, & Alisha Coleman-Jensen. 2023. *Household Food Security in the United States in 2022* (Report No. ERR-325). U.S. Department of Agriculture, Economic Research Service.

Raju, K. D. 2008. *World Trade Organization Agreement on Anti-Dumping*. Alphen aan den Rijn, The Netherlands: Kluwer Law International.

Rankin, P. Jeffery. 1980. "The Grain Embargo." *The Washington Quarterly* 3(3): 141–153.

Rietkerk, Aaron D. 2015. "'The Constructive Use of Abundance': The UN World Food Programme and the Evolution of the International Food-Aid System during the Post-War Decades." *The International History Review* 38(4): 788–813. https://doi.org/10.1080/07075332.2015.1038844.

Ritchie, Mark. 1988. *Impact of GATT on World Hunger*. Minnesota, US: Institute for Agriculture and Trade Policy. Available: https://www.iatp.org/sites/default/files/GATTFOODSECURITY.pdf.

Robin, Marie-Monique. 2010. *The World According to Monsanto: Pollution, Corruption, and the Control of the World's Food Supply*. New York: The New Press.

Sanderson, Fred H. 1975. "The Great Food Fumble." *Science* 188(4188): 503–509. https://doi.org/10.1126/science.188.4188.503.

Saint Ville, Arlette, June Yee Tsun Po, Akankasha Sen, Anh Bui, and Hugo Melgar-Quiñonez. 2019. "Food Security and the Food Insecurity Experience Scale (FIES): Ensuring Progress by 2030." *Food Security* 11: 483–491.

Scrinis, Gyorgy. 2015. "CRFA-Big Food Corporations and the Nutritional Marketing and Regulation of Processed Foods." *Canadian Food Studies* 2(2): 136–145.

Sen, Amartya. 1982. *Poverty and Famines: An Essay on Entitlement and Deprivation*. Oxford and New York: Oxford University Press.

Sethi, A. (2018). *The Framing of a Famine: A Case Study of Ethiopia*. Department of Development Studies, Uppsala University.

Shaw, D. John. 2007. "World Food Board Proposal." Pp. 15–31 in *World Food Security*, edited by David J. Shaw. London: Palgrave Macmillan. https://doi.org/10.1057/9780230589780_3.

Shildrick, Tracy. 2018. *Poverty Propaganda: Exploring the Myths*. Bristol, United Kingdom: Policy Press.

Shiva, Vandana. 2016. *Biopiracy: The Plunder of Nature and Knowledge*. Berkeley, CA: North Atlantic Books.

Singh, Tejinder P. 2017. "World Food Trade and Food Security: A Sociological Analysis of Dependency Framework in the Globalized Era." *Smart Moves Journal* V(X): 565–577.

Sivramkrishna, Sashi and Amalendu Jyotishi. 2005. *Monopsonistic Exploitation in Contract Farming: Articulating a Strategy for Grower Cooperation*. Gujarat Institute of Development Research. https://doi.org/10.1002/jid.1411.

Stevenson, James R., Nelson Villoria, Derek Byerlee, Timothy Kelley, and Mywish Maredia. 2013. "Green Revolution Research Saved an Estimated 18 to 27 Million Hectares from Being Brought into Agricultural Production." *Proceedings of the National Academy of Sciences* 110(21): 8363–8368. https://doi.org/10.1073/pnas.1208065110.

Stirling, Alfred. 1986. "McDougall, Frank Lidgett (1884–1958)." *Australian Dictionary of Biography*, National Centre of Biography, Australian National University. (accessed April 5, 2024). https://adb.anu.edu.au/biography/mcdougall-frank-lidgett-689/text12753

Stretesky, Paul B., Margaret Anne Defeyter, Michael A. Long, Liesel A. Ritchie, and David A. Gill. 2020. "Holiday Hunger and Parental Stress: Evidence from Northeast England." *Sustainability* 12(10): 4141. https://doi.org/10.3390/su12104141.

Stretesky, Paul B., Janis E. Johnston, and Jeremy Arney. 2003. "Environmental Inequity: An Analysis of Large-Scale Hog Operations in 17 States, 1982–1997." *Rural Sociology* 68(2): 231–252. https://doi.org/10.1111/j.1549-0831.2003.tb00136.x.

Sun, Zhiwei and Defeng Zhang. 2021. "Impact of Trade Openness on Food Security: Evidence from Panel Data for Central Asian Countries." *Foods* 10(12): 3012. https://doi.org/10.3390/foods10123012.

Swindale, Anne and Paula Bilinsky. 2006. "Development of a Universally Applicable Household Food Insecurity Measurement Tool: Process, Current Status, and Outstanding Issues." *The Journal of Nutrition* 136(5): 1449S–1452S. https://doi.org/10.1093/jn/136.5.1449S.

Schwenger, Robert B. 1958. "Synthesis of Trade and Agricultural Policy in GATT." *Journal of Farm Economics* 40(2): 238–248.

Smith, Dianna and Claire Thompson. 2022. *Food Deserts and Food Insecurity in the UK: Exploring Social Inequality*. Abingdon: Routledge.

Sommerville, Melanie, Jamey Essex, and Philippe Le Billon. 2014. "The 'Global Food Crisis' and the Geopolitics of Food Security." *Geopolitics* 19(2): 239–265. https://doi.org/10.1080/14650045.2013.811641.

Tangermann, Stefan. 1996. "Implementation of the Uruguay Round Agreement on Agriculture: Issues and Prospects." *Journal of Agricultural Economics* 47(1–4): 315–337. https://doi.org/10.1111/j.1477-9552.1996.tb00696.x.

Taylor, Kenneth. 1926. "Sheltered Markets: A Study of the Value of Empire Trade." *The Canadian Historical Review* 7(1): 78–79. https://doi.org/10.3138/chr-07-01-br17.

Thackeray, David and Richard Toye. 2018. "What Was a British Buy? Empire, Europe and the Politics of Patriotic Trade in Britain, c. 1945–1963." Pp. 133–157 in *Imagining Britain's Economic Future, c. 1800–1975: Trade, Consumerism, and Global Markets*, edited by David Thackeray, Andrew Thompson, Richard Toye. Cham: Palgrave Macmillan.

Tracy, Melissa, Margaret E. Kruk, Christine Harper, and Sandro Galea. 2010. "Neo-Liberal Economic Practices and Population Health: A Cross-National Analysis, 1980–2004." *Health Economics, Policy and Law* 5: 171–199.

UK Competition and Markets Authority. 2023. *Competition, Choice and Rising Prices in Groceries*.https://assets.publishing.service.gov.uk/media/64b80adaef5371000d7aeefb/Competition__choice_and_rising_prices_in_groceries.pdf.

UN DESA [United Nations Department of Economic and Social Affairs]. 2023. *The Sustainable Development Goals Report 2023: Special Edition* – July 2023. New York: UN DESA. https://unstats.un.org/sdgs/report/2023/.

United Nations. 2023. "'Outrageous a Person Dies of Hunger Every Few Seconds', Secretary-General Declares in Message on World Food Day, Calls for Crisis to Be Top of Global Agenda." SG/SM/21980, October 6, 2023. United Nations Press Release. https://press.un.org/en/2023/sgsm21980.doc.htm.

United Nations. 2002. "'Anyone Dying from Hunger Was Dying from Murder' Special Rapporteur Tells Third Committee, as Discussion on Human Rights Continues." United Nations Press Release, November 11, 2002. https://www.ohchr.org/en/press-releases/2009/10/anyone-dying-hunger-was-dying-murder-special-rapporteur-tells-third.

United Nations. 1975. "Report of the World Food Conference." Report No. E/CONF.65/20. Rome 5–16. Available at https://digitallibrary.un.org/record/701143/files/E_CONF.65_20-EN.pdf?ln=en. Accessed February 14, 2025.

United Nations General Assembly. 1948. "Universal declaration of human rights" (217 [III] A). Paris. Available at https://www.refworld.org/legal/resolution/unga/1948/en/11563. Accessed June 24, 2024.

United States Census Household Pulse Survey. 2024. *Food Insecurity*. https://www.census.gov/data-tools/demo/hhp//.

Vansteenkiste, Jennifer. 2017. *Food Insecurity in Haiti: A Gendered Problem* (Doctoral dissertation, University of Guelph).
von Braun, Joachim, Kaosar Afsana, Louise Fresco, Mohamed Hassan, and Maximo Torero. 2023. "Food System Concepts and Definitions for Science and Political Action." in *Science and Innovations for Food Systems Transformation*, edited by von Braun, Joachim, Kaosar Afsana, Louise Fresco, and Mohamed Hassan. Cham, CH: Springer-Verlag.
Warnock, John W. 2019. *The Politics of Hunger: The Global Food System*. Abingdon, Oxon, UK: Routledge.
Watkins, Kevin. 1991. "Agriculture and Food Security in the GATT Uruguay Round." *Review of African Political Economy* 18(50): 38–50.
Way, Wendy. 2013. *A New Idea Each Morning: How Food and Agriculture Came Together in One International Organisation*. Canberra: Australian National University Press. https://library.oapen.org/bitstream/handle/20.500.12657/33541/459941.pdf?sequence=1.
Wells, Rebecca and Martin Caraher. 2014. "UK Print Media Coverage of the Food Bank Phenomenon: From Food Welfare to Food Charity?" *British Food Journal* 116(9): 1426–1445. https://doi.org/ 10.1108/BFJ-03-2014-0123.
Wood, Robert E. 1986. *From Marshall Plan to Debt Crisis: Foreign Aid and Development Choices in the World Economy*. Berkeley, CA: University of California Press.
World Food Programme. 2021. "In World of Wealth, 9 Million People Die Every Year from Hunger, WFP Chief Tells Food System Summit." September 24, 2021. Available at https://www.wfp.org/news/world-wealth-9-million-people-die-every-year-hunger-wfp-chief-tells-food-system-summit#:~:text=%E2%80%9CThere%20is%20400%20trillion%20dollars,die%20per%20day%20from%20hunger.
Xu, Zhun. 2019. "Food Dependency and Global Food Crisis." *International Critical Thought* 9(2): 269–281. https://doi.org/10.1080/21598282.2019.1613920.
Yawson, David O. 2020. "Climate Mitigation and Hidden Vulnerabilities: Widening the Food Gap between the Global North and South." *Environmental Justice* 13(6): 210–221. https://doi.org/10.1089/env.2020.0029.
Ypi, Lea. 2013. "What's Wrong with Colonialism." *Philosophy & Public Affairs* 41(2): 158–191.
Zurayk, Rami. 2020. "Pandemic and Food Security: A View from the Global South." *Journal of Agriculture, Food Systems, and Community Development* 9(3): 17–21. https://doi.org/10.5304/jafscd.2020.093.01.

4

THE POLITICAL ECONOMY OF ENERGY AND ENERGY INSECURITY

Introduction

Without a reliable supply of energy, civilization would cease to exist. And, while renewable energy provides some of the energy we need to survive, we still rely heavily on fossil fuels such as oil, gas, and coal. Thus, as the global population increases, and production intensifies, we continue to consume more non-renewable energy. However, the production and consumption of renewable and non-renewable energy are both complicated and contested. As a result, energy availability, stability, efficiency, impact, and distribution are often called into question by citizens, states, and non-state actors (Sovacool and Dworkin 2014; Steffen et al. 2015). These issues often frame debates about "energy security" and "energy insecurity," which make up the basis of this chapter.

The concept of energy security is nothing new, and it has been used frequently since about the middle of the twentieth century to address the need for a sufficient oil supply, which was critical to the expansion of petroleum-based production (Hubbert 1934; 1949; Lubell 1961; for a brief history of energy security, see Cherp and Jewell 2011). After WWII, US geologists worked on providing more accurate estimates of local and global oil reserves (Hubbert 1949). However, a disputed, but growing, perspective suggested that countries such as the US were likely to experience a decline in oil production, which would increase production costs and limit economic growth. Marion King Hubbert, a geologist from the University of Chicago, was at the forefront of this argument. Hubbert (1934, 1949) believed the earth's resources could not satisfy continuous economic growth. Hubbert aligned himself with social scientists, such as Thorstein Veblen (2001 [1899]), to

DOI: 10.4324/9781003326892-4

assert that irrational production and consumption (especially conspicuous consumption) posed a threat to energy reserves and created an unnecessary and distorted social order. Hubert (1949) noted that oil production, just like any other fossil fuel, would rise to a peak, and then decline to zero. This peak – between the rise and fall of oil production – is defined as 'peak oil' and thought to mark a fundamental shift in the interaction between society and the environment due to resource scarcity (see also Schnaiberg 1980).

Hubbert's predictions about peak oil were realized in 1970 when US oil production began to decline, and the price of oil quadrupled (see also Bardi 2009; 2019; for opposing evidence of peak oil, see Deming 2023). This 1970 oil shortage led to significant inflation in Western economies and highlighted the importance of a stable energy supply, which was unreliable at the time, given the increasing dominance of OPEC and the global conflict in the Middle East. Hence, Hubbert advocated for restraint in production and consumption to delay peak oil and believed that a new social structure – governed by "fundamentals of energy ... with an accounting system based on physical relations, thermodynamics ... rather than a monetary system" – was necessary (Doel 1989: para 31). While Hubbert's emphasis on thermodynamics as an organizing principle of exchange never gained traction, his emphasis on technological innovations has, ironically, come to align with neoliberalism, embedding the discourse of technological solutions to inequality and environmental harm (Huesemann 2001). This is especially relevant to contemporary energy insecurity, as the limits of non-renewable resources are increasingly recognized. Importantly, alternative sources of energy are emerging and becoming more focal to global energy security, as there are some who believe that the world's production in oil has peaked. Matthew Simmons, the former chair of Simmons & Company International, one of the largest global energy investment banks, stated:

> Based on the best information we have on global oil supply, there is growing evidence that global production of crude oil peaked in 2005, and for the past three years has struggled to remain at an undulating plateau of some 73 to 74 million barrels a day. Since the world's total petroleum consumption is about 88 million barrels per day, we currently bridge this gap through the intensive use of liquefied natural gas, refining processing gains and tapping into the world's oil inventory.
>
> *(cited in Simmons 2008:22)*

As Simmons suggests, energy scarcity is imminent, and, if Hubbert is correct, peak oil will fundamentally alter the interaction between society and the environment. As a result, energy security is one of the most pressing issues facing the world today. As global energy demands increase, non-renewable energy from fossil fuels, such as oil, coal, and gas, will continue to play a major role in the global energy supply but may only cover global energy needs until 2070 (Le and Park 2021). Nevertheless, and as we point out, sources of energy have changed (or diversified to include renewable energy sources), and domestic energy in several nations across the globe is no longer coming from the same sources as in the past (Trifonov et al. 2021; for a theoretical discussion of importance of diversification, see Ranjan and Hughes 2014). Nevertheless, fossil fuels still dominate energy production and therefore shape energy security across the globe.

Today, researchers who study energy scarcity often approach it as a form of energy insecurity. Energy insecurity is a situation that occurs when households or states don't have access to affordable, reliable, or sufficient energy to meet needs that support a healthy lifestyle (see, for instance, the importance of these concepts in Ang, Choong, and Ng 2015). For households, energy insecurity is associated with an inability to obtain things such as heating, cooking, lighting, the powering of appliances, and security (Jain 2010). Indeed, Sustainable Development Goal 7 is to "ensure access to affordable, reliable, sustainable and modern energy for all" (United Nations 2024: para 1). Moreover, the World Health Organization (2006:6) points out that "energy is essential to meeting our basic needs: cooking, boiling water, lighting and heating. It is also a prerequisite for good health – a reality that has been largely ignored by the world community." Consistent with food insecurity examined in Chapter 3, individuals who suffer from energy insecurity often struggle to pay for energy and must often choose between the basic needs (i.e., 'heat or eat' – see Snell, Lambie-Mumford, and Thomson 2018). In this chapter, we examine energy insecurity. We do this by first examining the way energy insecurity is measured. We then examine energy insecurity in the Global North and Global South, followed by a discussion of energy insecurity as a function of political economy that is dominated by global corporate actors. We conclude by investigating the association between neoliberalism and three indicators of energy insecurity (dependency on foreign sources of energy, energy affordability, and clean energy).

Measuring Energy Insecurity

Multiple definitions of energy security exist (Hernandez 2016; Le and Park 2021). Moreover, the way people think about energy in security has changed over time (Sovacool and Mukherjee 2011). For instance, the earliest conception of energy security focused on national defense. However, over time, energy security was redefined to measure energy insecurity at the household level and focused more on the lack of clean energy (i.e., energy that comes from zero-emission sources) to power important household services. For this reason, we divide our discussion of energy insecurity into national definitions and household-level definitions.

Energy Insecurity at the National Level

As previously noted, energy security has been studied as an issue for nation-states since the beginning of the twentieth century. The focus on security, however, intensified after WWII (Papascoma and Heiss 2016). Importantly, post-WWII, definitions of energy security were largely connected to the concept of national defense. Even today, energy resources are viewed as critical to the distribution of power in world politics, and there are numerous examples of this in recent history. For instance, David Harvey (2005) has pointed out that the 1973 oil embargo by Saudi Arabia, Kuwait, and Abu Dhabi (capital of the United Arab Emerites) was viewed as such a large threat that the US government created plans to invade these countries to increase access to oil to bring down high oil prices. More recently, Richard Pearl's (1981) declassified Memorandum for Assistant to the President for National Security Affairs states:

> I have reviewed the Department of State's paper on oil and gas equipment and technology export controls and have a number of serious reservations about its recommendations. [To protect national defense the U.S. must] reduce the Western stake in Soviet energy production [and] aim for the broadest possible denial of equipment and technology derived from U.S. sources, including U.S. subsidiaries, licensees and manufacturing associates.

Pearle feared that Russia could develop their own oil market, which would undermine US energy security and ideological interests in Eastern Europe. These national security concerns are still reflected in definitions of energy security. For instance, the International Energy Agency (2024a) defines energy security as the "uninterrupted availability of energy sources at an affordable price."

Despite the strong ties between energy security and national security, a variety of more contemporary definitions of energy security have emerged. The concept of national energy security now includes hundreds of indicators, including those that measure energy reserves, import dependence, diversification, decentralization, innovations, investment, access, reliability, literacy, resilience, justice, and environmental quality (Sovacool 2011: 7476–7477). In addition, national energy security can be threatened in both the short and the long terms (Kosai and Unesz 2020). Short-term threats to energy security can include natural disasters, extreme weather, malicious events, and/or technological failures, while long-term threats to energy security include increasing demand, the depletion of energy sources, and environmental impacts.

Measures of energy security at the national level include the Sustainable Energy Security Index, Energy Sustainability Index, and the Energy Security Index (Brown and Sovacool 2007; Mainali et al. 2014; Narula and Reddy

2016). The *Global Energy Institute* (https://www.globalenergyinstitute.org/), for instance, has created the 'International Energy Security Risk Index.' The index is made up of 37 variables that measure several different types of energy risk at the national level (i.e., global fuels, fuel imports, energy expenditures, price and market volatility, energy use intensity, electric power sector, transportation sector, environmental, and basic science and energy research and development) for each year after 1970. Lower energy index scores represent lower energy security risk (the baseline risk was set at 100 in 1980 for the US energy security index, and 1000 in 1980 for the international energy security risk index that is composed of the Organisation for Economic Co-operation and Development member countries).

Figure 4.1 captures that trend in the US energy security index between the years 1970 and 2020 (where lower scores refer to more energy security). While the US energy security index has fluctuated significantly over the past 50 years, it is now at an all-time low. This situation changed, however, with a renewed focus on fossil fuels.

However, in 2010, energy security in the US began to decline when greater domestic oil supplies were realized through the shale gas revolution. As the Global Energy Institute 2020a:6) states:

> The importance of the U.S. shale revolution in driving these remarkable improvements [in energy security since 2011] cannot be overstated. The application of hydraulic fracturing, horizontal drilling, and advanced seismic imaging has unlocked a tremendous oil and gas resource, turning energy scarcity into abundance.

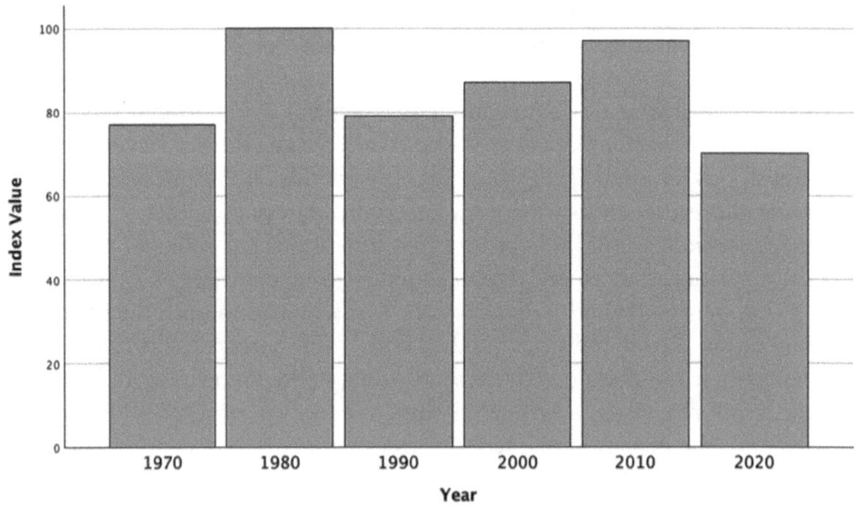

FIGURE 4.1 US Energy Security Risk Index, 1970–2020

It is notable that the US share of global oil and gas production is expected to continue to grow significantly due to its unconventional shale gas, with production levels estimated to double between 2005 and 2025 (International Energy Administration 2023). The role of shale gas, as a domestic source of energy, is likely to contribute to the overall levels of energy insecurity in the US compared to the rest of the world. At the national level, the US has one of the lowest levels of energy insecurity. Table 4.1 ranks the largest 25 OECD (Organization for Economic Co-operation and Development) countries by their level of energy insecurity, from the most secure to the least secure (Global Energy Institute 2020a).

Table 4.1 shows that, in 2018, the last year for which the levels of energy insecurity were calculated by the *Global Energy Institute*, the mean level of energy insecurity was 884 (below the 1980 baseline of 1000). The US had, for the first time, the lowest level of energy insecurity of any of the largest

TABLE 4.1 Energy Security Risk Scores for Largest 25 Countries, 2018

Country	*Risk Score*	*Rank*
US	727	1
New Zealand	757	2
Canada	802	3
Australia	805	4
Denmark	864	5
Norway	869	6
Russia	875	7
OECD	884	
China	912	8
Indonesia	932	9
UK	944	10
Mexico	966	11
Poland	967	12
Brazil	1,059	13
Germany	1,085	14
France	1,128	15
India	1,144	16
Netherlands	1,147	17
South Africa	1,156	18
Spain	1,189	19
Italy	1,240	20
Turkey	1,267	21
Japan	1,281	22
Thailand	1,396	23
South Korea	1,453	24
Ukraine	1,463	25

Source: Global Energy Institute. 2020. *Index of U.S. Energy Security Risk*. U.S. Chamber of Commerce. https://www.uschamber.com/assets/documents/gei/IESRI-Report_2020_4_20_20.pdf

OECD countries (Energy Insecurity Score = 727). Moreover, seven countries, fall below the global mean energy security score of 884 (i.e., New Zealand, Canada, Australia, Denmark, Norway, and Russia), while 18 countries have energy security scores above the mean (i.e., China, Indonesia, UK, Mexico, Poland, Brazil, Germany, France, India, Netherlands, South Africa, Spain, Italy, Turkey, Japan, Thailand, South Korea, and Ukraine). Many of those countries at the bottom of the list suffered from higher levels of energy insecurity because they relied on energy imports (Global Energy Institute 2020b). For instance, the meltdown of the Fukushima Daiichi nuclear power plant in 2011 led to a decrease in Japan's energy diversity, increasing its reliance on oil and gas imports. As a result of the Fukushima disaster, Japan faced a rapid decrease in energy security, and the country ranked 22 of 25 on the 2018 Energy Security Risk Score. It is also important to note that most countries in the world rely on energy imports in the form of fossil fuels, while few countries (i.e., 15 to 20) export non-renewable forms of energy (Le and Park 2021). Most fossil fuel-importing countries have fast growing economies, such as those in Asia, which drive global energy demand (Stretesky and Lynch 2009). Table 4.2 lists the largest fossil fuel energy (in quadrillion British thermal units or quad BTUs) import and export countries across the globe. At the top of the list is China, which consumes more energy than it produces, meaning it must find alternative energy from other parts of the world. The US, which occupies the second spot on the list, produces more energy than it consumes. But this is a recent phenomenon, associated with the shale gas revolution, which has increased energy production to some of the highest levels ever recorded in US history. As Table 4.2 suggests, many large consumer countries must rely on energy imports from other parts of the world to meet their energy needs. In particular, many countries produce less than they consume.

Finally, as the dominance of fossil fuels persists, it has a significant impact on the Energy Security Risk Score, because it reduces energy diversity. Oil, for instance, makes up 32% of world energy consumption, with coal at 27%, gas at 22%, biomass at 10%, and electricity at 9% (Enerdata 2024). Moreover, natural gas production is now growing rapidly, and the big fossil fuel producers remain Saudi Arabia, the US, Iran, and Russia. As previously noted, these countries have a disproportionate impact on the global energy outlook. For example, Figure 4.2 shows the rapid increase in three energy sources: (1) natural gas, (2) new forms of renewable energy, and (3) liquid biofuels. At the same time, liquid oil and gas (petroleum and other liquids), as well as coal, have remained relatively stable over time, with petroleum and natural gas projected to remain dominant well into the future.

As noted, energy security at the national level is often focused on the amount of energy that is produced and consumed, and on its diversity and distribution. And while energy security at the national level is often focused on national security, the same is not true of energy security at the household level.

TABLE 4.2 Largest 25 Energy Consumers and Producers, 2022

Rank	*Country*	*Consumption*	*Rank*	*Country*	*Production in quadrillion BTUs*
1	China	173.964	1	China	137.828
2	US	94.791	2	US	98.526
3	India	35.791	3	Russia	59.936
4	Russia	32.541	4	Saudi Arabia	29.651
5	Japan	16.89	5	India	21.890
6	Iran	13.502	6	Canada	21.550
7	Canada	12.266	7	Australia	17.824
8	South Korea	12.204	8	Iran	17.636
9	Saudi Arabia	11.429	9	Indonesia	16.502
10	Germany	11.093	10	United Arab Emirates	10.883
11	Brazil	10.766	11	Brazil	10.824
12	Indonesia	9.102	12	Iraq	10.022
13	France	8.290	13	Qatar	9.958
14	Mexico	7.563	14	Norway	8.907
15	UK	6.735	15	Kazakhstan	7.715
16	Australia	6.174	16	Kuwait	7.126
17	Turkey	6.025	17	Algeria	6.719
18	Italy	5.806	18	South Africa	6.030
19	South Africa	5.721	19	Mexico	5.921
20	Spain	5.048	20	Nigeria	4.452
21	Thailand	5.016	21	UK	4.267
22	Taiwan	4.920	22	Malaysia	4.185
23	United Arab Emirates	4.686	23	Egypt	3.890
24	Poland	4.055	24	Colombia	3.773
25	Egypt	4.047	25	Oman	3.753

Source: Energy Information Administration (EIA) (n.d). https://www.eia.gov/international/rankings/world?pa=12&u=2&f=A&v=none&y=01%2F01%2F2022.

Energy Insecurity at a Household Level

Energy security at the household level means household members can access "household energy services," such as heating, air conditioning, refrigerating, lighting, and cooking through a variety of energy sources such as electricity, oil, natural gas, propane, coal, wood, and charcoal. The scarcity of fuel combined with high energy prices increase the likelihood that households will be energy insecure. Building on our general definition of insecurity from Chapter 1, we define energy insecurity as the inability to predict a stable future in terms of the consistency of one's access to basic household energy services, such as heating, cooling, and cooking.

Scholars measure household energy insecurity in a variety of ways. For instance, Hernández (2016) suggests there are three dimensions to energy

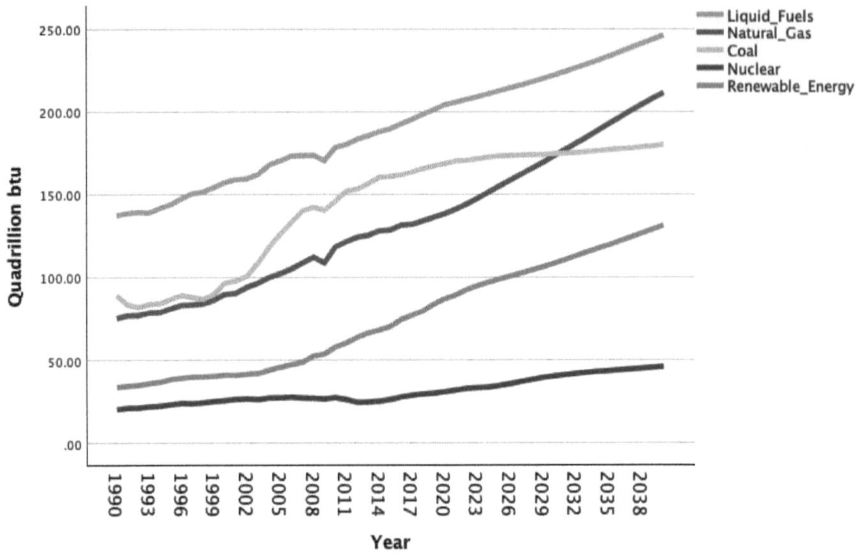

FIGURE 4.2 World Fuel Consumption and Fuel Projections, 1990–2040

insecurity. The first dimension is economic, that is, the inability to pay for energy utility bills due to low income and competing expenses. The second dimension is the inefficient use of energy by households and household energy services. This physical inefficiency can increase energy needs and costs. The final dimension of energy security involves the coping behaviors that household members adopt in response to economic insecurity and energy inefficiencies. These coping mechanisms often mean cutting back on other costs, such as those associated with housing, food, health, and paying other bills (Hernández 2016).

One of the more popular sources of information about household energy insecurity in the US comes from the *Residential Energy Consumption Survey* (RECS) produced by the US Energy Information Administration. The energy insecurity questions were first administered to a sample of US households in 2015–2016, and then again in 2020–2021 (https://www.eia.gov/consumption/residential/data/2015/). The RECS questionnaire asks a representative sample of households across the US population about situations that limit their ability to access energy services in their households, such as being unable to afford to pay for fuel or being confronted with decisions about whether to heat/cool their home or go without medical care or food as a coping mechanism. Importantly, households are asked a set of closed-ended questions that measure the extent to which they are energy insecure. Table HC11.1 of that report summarizes the results of five of the energy insecurity questions. Most recently, the energy insecurity questions in the RECS survey have been slightly redesigned for the next round of data collection, using the questions in Table 4.3, "recoded for statistical analyses."

TABLE 4.3 Residential Energy Consumption Survey (RECS) 2024 Household Survey Questionnaire (Form EIA-457A) Programming Specification

Energy Assistance and Security Questions

In the past year, how many months did your household reduce or forego expenses for basic household necessities, such as medicine or food, in order to pay an energy bill?
1. Almost every month
2. Some months
3. 1 or 2 months
0. Never

In the past year, how many months did your household keep your home at a temperature that you felt was unsafe or unhealthy?
1. Almost every month
2. Some months
3. 1 or 2 months
0. Never

In the past year, how many times was your household unable to pay an energy bill or unable to pay the full bill amount?
1. Almost every month
2. Some months
3. 1 or 2 months
0. Never

In the past year, how many months did your household receive a disconnection notice, shut off notice, or nondelivery notice for an energy bill?
1. Almost every month
2. Some months
3. 1 or 2 months
0. Never

When you received that notice, did your household apply for and receive home energy assistance to help pay your energy bill?
1. Yes
0. No

In the past year, was there ever a time your household was unable to use your main source of heat because any of the following events happened? Please select all that apply.

Your heating equipment was broken and you couldn't afford to pay for the repair or replacement [NOHEATBROKE]
You couldn't pay for electricity and it was disconnected [NOHEATEL]

(*Continued*)

TABLE 4.3 (Continued)

Energy Assistance and Security Questions

You couldn't pay for natural gas and it was disconnected [NOHEATNG]
You ran out of fuel oil, propane, wood, or pellets because you couldn't afford a delivery
[NOHEATBULK]
None of these happened [NOHEATNONE]

About how many days was your household without heat?
_______ days

When that happened, did your household apply for and receive home energy assistance to help restore your heating?
1. Yes
0. No

In the past year, did anyone in your household need medical attention because your home was too cold?
1. Yes
0. No

In the past year, was there ever a time your household was unable to use your air conditioner or other cooling equipment because any of the following events happened? Please select all that apply.

Your air conditioning equipment or other cooling equipment was broken and you couldn't afford to pay for the repair or replacement [NOACBROKE]
You couldn't pay for electricity and it was disconnected [NOACEL]
None of these happened [NOACNONE]

About how many days was your household without air conditioning?
_______ days

When that happened, did your household apply for and receive home energy assistance to help restore your cooling?
1. Yes
0. No

In the past year, did anyone in your household need medical attention because your home was too hot?
1. Yes
0. No

(*Continued*)

TABLE 4.3 (Continued)

Energy Assistance and Security Questions
Including times when you received assistance for heating and cooling bills, has your household participated in a home energy assistance program that helps to pay energy bills or fix broken equipment? 1. Yes 0. No (https://www.eia.gov/survey/form/eia_457/RECS%20457%20A_Questionnaire%20Content.pdf)

As Table 4.3 indicates, these questions are focused on two dimensions of energy insecurity: (1) the ability of people to pay for access to household energy services, and (2) coping mechanisms when the households can't afford energy. The survey also examines if households receive any type of energy assistance. Researchers such as Konisky et al. (2022:3) have examined energy assistance when exploring the problem of energy insecurity in the US during the COVID-19 pandemic. Konisky et al. (2022) used three indicators of energy assistance, including the "the inability to pay an energy bill," "receipt of a shutoff or service termination notice," and the "disconnection from an energy service."

Another important measure of household energy insecurity is based on household energy expenditures in proportion to the overall household budget (Barnes, Khandker, and Samad 2010). When a household's expenditures on energy are substantial (typically more than 10% of their monthly disposable income, see Chandler 2016) then the household is defined as being energy insecure (Steele and Bergstrom 2021). This approach has been used in multiple high-income countries to measure energy insecurity (Brown et al. 2020; Heflin 2016). However, as previously noted, the ratio of expenditures to income doesn't necessarily account for household energy efficiency or behavior.

Another approach to examining household energy insecurity is to focus on "worry" or "concern" about access to household energy services. As food security research teaches us, constantly worrying about the ability to access energy services can create a strain on both mental and physical well-being (Demski et al. 2018). In the UK, for example, research in 2024 by the National Associations of Citizens Advice Bureau (André-Paul et al. 2024) suggests that approximately 9 in every 20 energy bill payers (or around 11 million households) are "concerned," or "very concerned," that they will be unable to pay their energy bills during the upcoming winter. Moreover, changes to the energy assistance eligibility could mean that nearly 3 million additional households across the countries could be food insecure. Nevertheless, concern about energy insecurity changes how people may interact with energy in their households, causing them to sometimes put themselves and other household members at risk by limiting sufficient access to energy (Ambrose et al. 2021). Ambrose et al. (2021), for instance, reports that of the 28,300 excess deaths during the UK winter, around 30% are likely the result of cold homes (see Guertler and Smith 2018). Worries and concern about energy insecurity are sometimes, but not often, measured in household surveys. The Department for Business, Energy and Industrial Strategy (BEIS [2023]) specifically measures energy security by focusing on how much people "worry" about their energy bills and what steps they take to cope or "mitigate" these worries in their "Public Attitudes Tracker." The questions in the Public Attitudes Tracker, included in Table 4.4, follow the approach we take in measuring insecurity in the present research.

As the questions in Table 4.4 recognize, measures of energy insecurity are subjective, that is, people are asked about their own experiences. In the case of energy insecurity, this approach has an advantage over more objective measures of energy insecurity, which often require hard-to-obtain information about income, energy use, home energy efficiency, disconnections from energy needed to supply services, and energy assistance, which can carry a stigma or vary, depending on government and energy company policies. As a result of the difficulties of using objective measures of energy security, there has been an increase in the use of subjective measures (Jahedi and Méndez 2014). For example, the BEIS survey begins by asking households whether they are "concerned" about energy price increases and "worried" about paying their energy bills. Respondents who are worried are then asked how they cope with any energy concerns. In particular, the survey asks whether they reduce their use of energy services in the household by lowering heating even when it is uncomfortable, use less energy to bathe, turn out lights, or change the way they prepare food. Research on these issues suggests that people who are more worried about their ability to pay for energy do all these things in greater frequency than those who are not worried about energy payments. Unfortunately, energy insecurity coping mechanisms, whether necessary or not, can increase other forms of household insecurity, such as food insecurity, which can impact health and well-being (Fry et al. 2023). The intersection of insecurities, which we have mentioned more than once, impacts many individuals' lives.

Subjective measures of energy insecurity are also important because they are rooted in objective positions within the social space (Bourdieu 1984). As our mapping of the US space of neoliberal capitalism will show in Chapter 7, worries over energy use are not simply thoughts in one's head, disconnected from the world. They are the result of an internalization of one's position within the national space of neoliberal capitalism, thus reflecting the reality

TABLE 4.4 BEIS Public Attitudes Tracker: Heat and Energy in the Home Spring 2022, UK

How much attention do you pay to the amount of energy you use to heat/cool your home?

None at all
Hardly any
A little
A fair amount
A lot

[Option 1] You said that you pay [a lot/a fair amount] of attention to the amount of energy you use to heat/cool your home. What is the main reason for this?

To minimize the money, spend on energy
To make sure my home is comfortable
To minimize the environmental impact of energy used for heating/cooling
To keep control over the amount of heat/cooling used
Other reason
Don't know

[Option 2] You said that you pay [only a little/hardly any/no] attention to the amount of heat/cool your home. What is the main reason for this?

I use as much energy as needed to be comfortable
I set controls at a level I'm comfortable with then don't need to adjust
I don't feel I can control the amount of energy used to heat/cool my home
I'm just not interested in the amount of energy used to heat/cool my home
Other
Don't know

Over the last twelve months, how worried, if at all, have you been about paying for energy bills (gas/electricity)?

Very worried
Fairly worried
Not very worried
Not at all worried
Not applicable/Don't know
Prefer not to say

You said you were more worried about paying for energy bills compared with food and other household essentials, or transport. Why are you more worried about energy bills? Please select all that apply

Concerned that prices will go up compared to what I have paid in the past
Energy prices have increased more than other outgoings
Energy bills are/will be more expensive than other outgoings
Cannot easily go without energy like I can for some other outgoings
I have less control over energy bills
Don't know how much energy bill will cost in advance so harder to budget
Other reason

(*Continued*)

TABLE 4.4 (Continued)

Don't know

During the past 12 months did your household cut back on fuel use at home in any of these ways listed below, because you could not afford the costs?

	Yes	*No*	*Prefer not to say*
Turned heating/cooling down or off, even though it was uncomfortable in the house/flat	Checkbox	Checkbox	Checkbox
Only heated/cooled part of the house	Checkbox	Checkbox	Checkbox
Cut the number of hours that heating/cooling was on to reduce fuel costs	Checkbox	Checkbox	Checkbox
Used less hot water than I/we need to reduce fuel costs	Checkbox	Checkbox	Checkbox
Turned out more lights in my home than I/we needed to try and reduce the electricity bill	Checkbox	Checkbox	Checkbox
Had fewer hot meals or hot drinks that I/we needed to reduce fuel costs	Checkbox	Checkbox	Checkbox

Source: BEIS Public Attitudes Tracker, Spring 2022. https://assets.publishing.service.gov.uk/media/6406f2cd8fa8f527f110a3ca/BEIS_PAT_Spring_2022_Questionnaire.pdf.

of a precarious social and economic standing; in such circumstances, restricting energy use and worrying about it becomes an understandable, albeit unfortunate response given the consequences it has for individuals and their families. Objective and subjective measures of energy insecurity are inextricably linked, and by including subjective measures of energy insecurity, we also learn more about its objective side as well. They are two sides of the same neoliberal coin.

Energy Insecurity in the Global North

Countries in the Global North are now investing in renewable energy to reduce dependence on fossil fuels (Saravanan et al. 2022). However, as previously noted, energy insecurity is still pervasive across the globe – including in the Global North. A recent study by Ipsos (2023) surveyed more than 20,000 people in 24 high-income countries about their energy security concerns. Ipsos found that energy "self-sufficiency" and reducing dependency on foreign energy sources are concerns for many citizens in the Global North. For instance, in Table 4.5, several of the countries in the Global North are concerned that their country relies too heavily on foreign sources of energy (i.e., the first column). For instance, the oil boom in Norway, and the shale

TABLE 4.5 Concern about Energy by Country, Sorted by Energy Security, 2023

Country	*Energy Security*	*Affordability*	*Cleaner Energy*	*Other*
South Africa	44%	33%	33%	21%
Norway	42%	28%	25%	20%
Sweden	41%	27%	21%	23%
Poland	36%	35%	31%	24%
Italy	36%	32%	31%	20%
Hungary	35%	30%	30%	26%
Turkey	35%	28%	33%	23%
France	34%	33%	23%	18%
U.S.	33%	25%	26%	18%
Malaysia	32%	17%	25%	21%
Canada	31%	28%	25%	19%
Saudi Arabia	25%	21%	22%	16%

Source: Venditti, Bruno. 2023. "Visualizing the Top Energy Priorities of Major Countries" https://www.visualcapitalist.com/visualizing-the-top-energy-priorities-of-major-countries/.

Note: Energy security is "how concerned are you about the reliance on foreign energy sources?" It is energy insecurity in the orthodox sense. Table can be created from link above to list security on all indicators for all 25 countries and combined into one table.

gas revolution in the US, have increased energy independence within both countries. Indeed, and as noted in Table 4.2, both countries produce more energy than they consume. Nevertheless, the citizens of both countries are disproportionately concerned about reliance on foreign energy.

Citizens of Norway, for example, rank 2nd among all countries in worry, and 44% of its citizens believe there is too much dependence on foreign energy sources. Likewise, in the US, 33% of residents worry that the country is too reliant on foreign energy sources, and it ranks 9th on the list of 25 countries. Messages about energy affordability also dominate political discourse. For instance, in the 2024 US presidential elections, both candidates favored the development of shale gas as a strategy to keep energy costs low (Lefebvre 2024). In the case of Vice President Kamala Harris, this position was a reversal of her earlier policy position – that fracking should be banned in the US. Moreover, energy affordability was the primary concern of many European countries, as indicated in Table 4.6. As discussed in Chapter 2, the neoliberal policies that increase economic insecurity among many residents across European countries, and especially in the UK (which ranks 2nd among all 25 countries in the Ipsos survey), have spilled over into concern about various aspects of life, including high energy prices. This concern may be intensifying in Europe, for instance, where many of the more polluting forms of energy production, associated with coal plants, are expanding to alleviate

TABLE 4.6 Concern about Energy by Country, Sorted by Affordability, 2023

Country	*Energy Security*	*Affordability*	*Cleaner Energy*	*Other*
Belgium	33%	43%	17%	21%
Great Britain	38%	41%	25%	24%
Australia	31%	37%	23%	18%
Germany	28%	34%	23%	15%
Netherlands	30%	33%	20%	23%
Spain	27%	32%	26%	20%

Source: Venditti, Bruno. 2023. "Visualizing the Top Energy Priorities of Major Countries" https://www.visualcapitalist.com/visualizing-the-top-energy-priorities-of-major-countries/.

high energy prices exacerbated by the war between Russia and Ukraine (Bordoff and O'Sullivan 2023).

The issue of affordability stands in sharp contrast to countries in the Global South, which tend to be more concerned with cleaner energy (discussed later). Indeed, this may be a result of the reliance of these countries on exporting natural resources to wealthy nations. Or, in the case of Japan, it is more concerned about clean energy than any other nation, perhaps because of the technological risks associated with the Fukushima Daiichi disaster and because of the increased reliance on dirty fossil fuels that replaced nuclear energy.

The data on public concerns about energy security and affordability also appear to play out among countries in the Global North, with increasing regularity. A recent analysis of government data collected by YouGov found that 37% of all UK households spend more than 10% of their income on heating their homes (Topham, 2024). As previously discussed, this level of energy expenditure is an indicator of household energy insecurity. Moreover, energy insecurity was highest among low-income households. For instance, 77% of single-parent households were likely to face energy insecurity during the winter months because energy was simply not affordable. And, importantly, nearly 50% of all British adults are now planning to ration their energy use during the colder months (Topham 2024). This level of coping with energy insecurity has been followed closely by a statement from the Energy Crisis Commission, suggesting that the UK is 'dangerously underprepared' for the coming winter and too reliant on foreign sources of natural gas (Ambrose 2024).

The consequences of energy insecurity in high-income countries of the Global North are now studied with regularity (Boateng et al. 2020; Hernández 2016; Memmott et al. 2021). Moreover, research on household energy insecurity among countries in the Global North shows that individuals in households that do not have adequate access to energy services are more likely to experience depression, anxiety, physical discomfort, and even premature death than those who do have access (Cook et al. 2008; Corman et al. 2016; Rehfuess 2006; Siegel et al. 2024; Simes, Khan, and Hernández 2023; Snyder and Baker, 2010). By way of example, the lack of access to air conditioning was identified as one major contributing factor in an estimated 70,000 deaths during the 2003 European summer heat wave (Bouchama et al. 2007, Robine 2007). Thus, the Global North is not immune to energy insecurity, and the most economically disadvantaged populations in countries in the Global North may easily suffer from ill-health effects associated with energy insecurity. Finally, many poor people who live in the Global North often occupy dwellings with insufficient energy efficiency, which makes them likely to have to pay more for their energy usage (Memmott et al. 2021). As previously noted, elevated energy costs can lead to other forms of insecurity, such as food insecurity, covered in Chapter 3 (Coleman-Jensen, Rabbitt, Gregory and Singh, 2015, Power 2006). Racial and ethnic inequality are often strong predictors of energy insecurity in the Global North (Lewis, Hernández, and Geronimus 2020). And, marginalized populations, disproportionately made up of racial and ethnic minorities, are more likely to have their utilities disconnected and face long-duration outages (Pradhan and Chan 2024).

Energy Insecurity in the Global South

As Ortzi et al. (2017: 18046) shrewdly state, "energy consumption is totally unfair between different countries." Energy insecurity in the Global South is more prevalent than in the Global North. There are a variety of reasons for this situation, but differences between the North and the South follow general trends in inequality, which are reinforced by neoliberal globalization, as discussed in previous chapters (Mohanty 2018). The most recent US Energy Information Administration (2024b) report on affordable and clean energy estimates around 750 million people in the Global South lack access to electricity, and at least 2 billion people can't access clean energy needed to prepare meals. Studies of individual countries in the Global South also show this is a significant problem. Boateng et al. (2020) found, for instance, that approximately 56% of households in Ghana and Nigeria frequently did not have access to clean energy for cooking (and instead used charcoal, wood, wood chippings, and dung), while 43% of households said they were unable to work because they could not access energy services (Boateng et al. 2020). People in the Global South also worry about accessing clean energy.

Table 4.7 shows that when it comes to clean fuels, several countries in the Global South dominate the top of the list for the 24 countries in the Ipsos

TABLE 4.7 Concern about Energy by Country, Sorted by Cleaner Energy, 2023

Country	*Energy Security*	*Affordability*	*Cleaner Energy*	*Other*
Japan	21%	17%	40%	26%
Argentina	33%	23%	38%	30%
New Zealand	34%	33%	36%	21%
Chile	30%	25%	35%	24%
Colombia	24%	26%	33%	28%
Peru	22%	22%	31%	25%
Mexico	29%	23%	31%	20%

Source: Venditti, Bruno. 2023. "Visualizing the Top Energy Priorities of Major Countries" https://www.visualcapitalist.com/visualizing-the-top-energy-priorities-of-major-countries/.

(2022) survey. As previously noted, Japan, a country in the Global North, is ranked as most concerned about clean energy, likely because of the Fukushima Daiichi disaster. But other countries also worry about clean energy, including Argentina, Chile, Columbia, Peru, and Mexico. Concerns about dirty energy in countries in the Global South are consistent with the health impacts these countries face. Consistent with that concern are estimates that suggest that each year, there are 3.7 million premature deaths (mainly in Asia and sub-Saharan Africa) caused by the burning of solid fuels that increase the concentration of particulate matter in the air (Conibear et al. 2018; see also International Energy Agency 2023). The misery and death related with this dimension of energy insecurity are tied to the global movement of capital associated with neoliberal polices. Saravanan et al. (2022) note that financial institutions operating in developing countries, such as Asia, are less likely to invest in clean (i.e., renewable) energy, as it is viewed as a risky business. This is because financial investors ask for higher rates of return on energy investments in developing economies to offset perceptions that those investments are riskier. The result is that countries in the Global South adopt non-renewable energy to power their economy, which tends to threaten health and is also, as a result, more expensive in the long run (Energy Information Administration 2024).

While a disproportionate number of people in the Global South suffer from problems associated with energy insecurity, the oil production in those countries is a major source of energy used for powering household energy services. The Persian Gulf (i.e., countries that are often considered part of the Global South, such as Iran, Iraq, and Bahrain, and Oman, along with countries considered part of the Global North, such as Kuwait, Saudi Arabia, Qatar, and the United Arab Emirates) supplies over half of the oil in the world. Even though these countries provide energy to the world, they are not more energy secure. Mayer (2022) recently found that nations in the Global South that specialize in fossil fuel production are not any more energy secure than non-specializing countries. At the same time, energy insecurity is increasing in countries such as Bangladesh, China, India, Indonesia, Malaysia, Nepal, Pakistan, Saudi Arabia (usually defined as part of the Global North), Sri Lanka, Thailand, and Vietnam, while it fluctuates considerably in countries such as Iran, Iraq, Jordan, Kazakhstan, Lebanon, and Tajikistan (Le et al. 2019).

The unequal distribution of energy resources also influences violent conflicts in the Global South (Bonds 2013; see also Williams 2006. For instance, social scientists believe that the need for fossil fuel energy sources is one factor that contributes to conflict and war in oil-rich regions, such as such as the 2003 invasion of Iraq (Bonds 2013). Some conflicts rely on funding derived from energy extraction and sales on the global market and put significant pressure on those countries that are rich in natural resources, often propping up non-democratic regimes (See Colgan 2013). Oil has even been found to play a role in the recent conflict between Russia and Ukraine. Rosneft, one of Russia's largest energy companies, not only supplies oil to the Russian army to support their war against Ukraine but also sells oil to companies such as British Petroleum (BP). These BP sales indirectly help fund the war (Bout 2022). As Mansson (2014:6) notes, "it is widely recognized that the presence of some fossil fuels and their transport routes can affect the risk of conflict." Research by Greenpeace (2021) found over 50% of all EU military missions were focused on ensuring security for the production and transportation of oil and gas.

Many countries in the South are the most vulnerable when it comes to problems associated with fossil fuels, such as climate change, decreased life expectancy, and food insecurity (Wilkinson et al. 2007). Even more striking is that over the last few years, the energy security rift between the Global North and Global South has increased. At the same time, countries in the South have rejected requests to reduce their use of fossil fuel to build their economies, arguing that it is hypocritical for governments in the North to expect such energy reductions when those very governments have built their own country's wealth and power using these very same fossil fuel energy sources.

Energy Companies and the Political Economy

Both State and private sector energy companies are central actors in the production and distribution of energy across the globe. As a result, corporations play a major role in the shape and distribution of energy insecurity. This contemporary situation is heavy influenced by developments that have occurred since World War II in the oil sector (De Graaff 2012). At the end of the WWII, 85% of all global oil and gas reserves were controlled by massive multinational oil companies, which were dominated by US firms (Najm 2022). These oil and gas giants included Standard Oil Company of New Jersey, Standard Oil Company of New York, Standard Oil Company of California, Texas Oil Company, Gulf Oil, Anglo-Persian Oil Company, and Shell (Odell 2013). The global economic and political power these postwar energy companies possessed was so immense that Italy's state oil director and politician Enrico Mattei referred to them collectively as the "seven sisters" (Najm 2022; White 1976). Mattie recognized the need for energy to build Italy's economy and believed that powerful oil companies at the time had formed an oligopoly that was blocking Italy and, indeed, many non-Western countries from realizing economic prosperity. In response, Mattie helped broker partnerships between State-run oil companies in Italy and the Soviet Union and made inroads into gaining access to and developing oil reserves in countries such as Tunisia, Morocco, Iran, Egypt, and Algeria. In Mattei's own words, in a speech on June 10, 1960, in Tunisia, he contended:

> I am here to respond to your call to invest and to help you in your struggle against underdevelopment. I am not afraid of the War in Algeria. I am not afraid of decolonization. I believe in decolonization not only for moral reasons to do with human dignity, but for economic reasons to do with productivity. Colonial condition exists when a hegemonic power—also a private one of a monopoly or oligopoly—tampers with the play of supply and demand for a vital raw material. In the petroleum sector, this hegemonic-monopolistic power is the cartel. I am fighting against the cartel not only because it is oligopolistic, but also it is Malthusian—and Malthusian [in a way that] damages the [oil-]producing countries as well as the consumer countries.
>
> *(Wilson Center Digital Archives 2022)*

Mattie was killed in a plane crash on October 27, 1962 (New York Times 1962). Nevertheless, the legacy of Mattie's energy politics lives on, and on October 27, 2023, the current Italian Prime Minister Giorgia Meloni (2023) said, the "'Mattei formula' is still deeply relevant… energy is a key part of the model for cooperation on an equal footing that we intend to build together with our partners, starting with African nations."

The power of the original seven sisters waned over time, especially with the oil crisis in the 1970s. After World War II, US oil and gas companies directed oil revenues through oil-producing nations in the Middle East. During this time, global oil production expanded, and the oil company, Standard Oil, dominated the international petroleum industry (Pratt 2012). However, political revolutions in the Middle East, combined with conflicts in Israel and peak oil production in the US, led to the declining global power of American oil companies in that part of the world. As Painter (2012:35) explains:

> After a difficult decade [the 1970s], the United States was able to reassert its influence through a strategy that included permitting higher prices to induce more efficient use of oil, replacing oil with other energy sources (particularly in electricity generation), and reducing imports from OPEC producers by increasing production elsewhere [i.e., other than the Middle East]. Despite losing their concessions, the oil companies managed to retain an important role in the world oil economy and remained among the largest and most profitable corporations in the world.

The decline in US dominance over global oil in the Middle East, as described by Painter, is sometimes linked with the rise of new forms of global financial power that increase not only energy insecurity but also other forms of insecurity as well (see Chapter 3 and 5). For instance, US companies began focusing on increasing the global reliance on international credit, which supports neoliberal policies and the movement of capital across the globe, This helps companies to maintain profits through production of commodities by using cheap labor, while simultaneously avoiding costly environmental regulations (Harvey 2005; Jorgenson 2016). At the same time, financial and banking institutions began increasing domestic consumer debt though credit and deficit financing to ensure high levels of consumption (Foster et al. 2021). Despite these shifts, US oil and gas companies continue to remain important, albeit less powerful, actors in global politics and economics.

Today, State-owned energy companies in Asia and Saudi Arabia, which are also dominated by fossil fuels, have among the largest annual revenues among all global companies. There are currently four State-owned energy companies on Global Fortune's list of the top ten companies (State Grid, Saudi Aramco, Sinopec, and China National Petroleum). State Grid, for instance, a State-owned electric company, is the third largest company in the world, and generates over $500 billion in annual revenue. Private sector international and transnational corporations, reminiscent of the "seven sisters," still rank near the top of Global Fortune's list, according to annual revenue, and include companies such as ExxonMobil, Shell, BP, Total Energy, and ConocoPhillips. Nearly all modern energy companies employ neoliberal free trade ideology in the pursuit of economic profits associated with oil and gas production and extraction. Most energy companies exploit global political-economic networks that give them the ability to shape other types of security across the globe. Moreover, these companies are protected by the State, which can nurture their economic power so that they can derive profit from both upstream extraction practices and downstream sales of electricity.

An example of this situation is Sinopec, a Chinese state-owned and independent corporation listed on several stock exchanges, with over 100 subsidiary companies operating in countries around the world. Recently, Sinopec has focused on obtaining oil and gas from African countries (Alves 2008), in particular, Gabon's Loango National Park. China's friendly political connections with Gabon helped establish a relationship through China's support to construct the Sino-Gabonese Friendship Stadium, where the African Cup of Nations could be held. However,

> At the same time [China] started to get more interested in the extraction of Gabon's rich natural resources, particularly oil, timber and iron ore, and involved in its economic development plan. Two large deals were signed, the first one to guarantee a minimum supply of crude oil to China, the second one between Unipec, a subsidiary of Sinopec, and Total Gabon for oil exploration and refining in Gabon.
>
> *(Cabestan 2014:6)*

The relationship between China's energy companies and African nations, however, is not invariant. When Sinopec was unable to gain access to natural resources in Nigeria, for example, the company resorted to giving payments to government elites. Sinopec was recently investigated for bribing the Nigerian government, using $100 million to gain tax breaks and special access to energy reserves (Whistleblower Layer Team 2017). The company has already paid a fine of $32 million for engaging in deviant activities related to these criminal charges (Whistleblower Lawyer Team 2017).

As the history of global energy development suggests, the Sinopec case is only one recent example of the way oil and gas companies operate in a global market to gain access to oil and gas reserves, especially in the Middle East and Africa, even while other global actors have changed. Moreover, the dominance of oil and gas companies in the world energy scene will continue. As Guo et al. (2023) suggest, oil and gas companies are not getting rid of fossil fuels. Instead, many of these countries change their behavior in small ways by investigating other energy sources. Nevertheless, even the most radical changes simply focus on energy diversification rather than on the total elimination of fossil fuels from a company's portfolio (Guo et al. 2023).

Large energy companies have therefore remained closely tied to the development of oil and gas across the globe, continuing to be associated with global conflicts and environmental destruction (Månsson 2014). However, increased concerns over climate change are a long-term threat to oil and gas companies and are not going away (Guo et al. 2023). At present, however, renewable energy sources do not appear to be significantly diminishing the share of the world's energy that comes from oil and gas. Moreover, in 2025, the US Energy Information Administration (2024) expects that the production of liquid fuels will increase by 2 million barrels per day, while the consumption of liquid fuels will increase by 1.3 million barrels per day. Some countries, like the US, are expected to set new oil production records for the country in 2025 (Tank 2024).

As is evident in many high-income countries in the Global North, there is a renewed corporate interest in developing sources of fossil fuels with a combined nationalistic flavor of protectionism (e.g., as former and current US President Donald Trump has stated numerous times, "under my Administration, we are no longer beholden to foreign powers or domestic radicals. We are powering our Nation on our own terms"). This nationalistic pursuit of fossil fuels to solve energy insecurity can be linked to a backlash against neoliberal policies that espouse free markets. However, these nationalistic policies do little to rearrange energy security at the international or household level, as energy companies, whether State or private, seem to remain indifferent to marginalized countries and communities.

Example: Neoliberalism and Energy Insecurity in 2022

Data and Method

In this section, we examine the association between energy insecurity and neoliberalism, using data from the *Context Energy Survey* (CES) collected by Ipsos (2023) and data from the *Economic Freedom of the World* (EFW) index collected by the Fraser Institute. The CES, conducted in the Fall of 2022, asked 24,000 people in 28 countries about different aspects of energy security. CES indicators represent the percentage of a country's population concerned about (1) dependency of foreign sources of energy, (2) the affordability of energy, and/or (3) adequate access to clean energy. As noted in Chapter 3, EFW data are used to measure neoliberalism and come from the Fraser Institute. Recall that EFW index is scored from 0 to 10, and is often used to measure neoliberalism (e.g., Gwartney et al. 2023; Tracy et al. 2010; McLean et al. 2019; Dixon, 2020, 2022; Long et al. 2024). Higher EFW scores are associated with more neoliberal policies and practices. We also measure short-term neoliberalization, using the five-year change (%) in the EFW index. In the current example, the "5-Year % Change" represents the percent change in EFW scores between 2017 and 2022. We calculate this increase according to the following formula: $\% \Delta EFW = [(EFW(t) - EFW(t - 5)) / |EFW(t - 5)|] \times 100$, where t represents the time period, or year, under investigation.

Table 4.8 contains descriptive statistics for the three CES indicators, the EFW index, and the five-year % change score for countries in the Global North and the Global South. In Global North countries, the average percent of the population concerned about too much reliance on foreign energy is

TABLE 4.8 Descriptives for Macro-Level Measures of Energy Insecurity and Economic Freedom for Countries in the North and South

	2022	
	Mean	SD
% Population Concerned about Energy Dependence		
North	33.2	5.1
South	29.1	6.4
% Population Concerned about Affordable Energy		
North	32.4	4.9
South	23.8	4.3
% Population Concerned about Clean Energy		
North	26.7	5.9
South	29.9	5.2
Fraser Economic Freedom Index		
North		
Current score	7.5	0.6
Five-Year % change	–4.2	3.2
South		
Current score	6.7	0.9
Five-Year % change	–2.8	7.0

Source: Energy Insecurity data come from the Ipsos the *Context Energy Survey* (CES). Data on economic freedom come from the Fraser Institute (fraserinstitute.org).

33.2%, the average percent of the population concerned about affordability is 32.4%, and the average percent of the population concerned about clean energy is 26.7%. In the Global South, 29.1% of the population, on average, is concerned about reliance of foreign energy, the average percent of the population concerned about affordable energy is 23.8%, and the average percent of the population concerned with clean energy is 29.9%. It is clear, as previously discussed, that clean energy is more of a concern in the Global South than in the Global North. However, energy dependency and affordable energy are more of a concern in the Global North. Importantly, neoliberalization is decreasing among the 28 countries in the sample between 2017 and 2022, in both the Global South (i.e., % Δ *EFW* =-2.8%) and the Global North (% Δ *EFW* =-4.2%).

We explore individual EFW scores, % Δ *EFW*, and CES scores for each indicator of energy insecurity in Table 4.9. It is notable that there doesn't appear to be any pattern in these data. EFW scores and short-term changes in neoliberalism (% Δ *EFW*) do not appear to be related to concerns about energy dependency, energy affordability, or clean energy. Moreover, short-term changes in neoliberalism scores tend to be rather small, and only

TABLE 4.9 Cross-National Differences in Energy Insecurity and Economic Freedom in 2022

Country	*Energy Dependency*	*Energy Affordability*	*Clean Energy*	*EFW Score*	*% Δ EFW*
South Africa	44.00	33.00	33.00	6.65	.76
Norway	42.00	28.00	25.00	7.58	–4.41
Sweden	41.00	27.00	21.00	7.61	–3.67
Great Britain	38.00	41.00	25.00	7.88	–4.25
Italy	36.00	32.00	31.00	7.22	–3.99
Poland	36.00	35.00	31.00	6.85	–6.29
Hungary	35.00	30.00	30.00	7.12	–4.81
Turkey	35.00	28.00	33.00	5.57	–16.24
France	34.00	33.00	23.00	7.49	–2.47
New Zealand	34.00	33.00	36.00	8.39	–4.44
Belgium	33.00	43.00	17.00	7.42	–2.50
United State	33.00	25.00	26.00	8.09	–4.03
Argentina	33.00	23.00	38.00	4.55	–20.04
Malaysia	32.00	17.00	25.00	7.56	.40
Australia	31.00	37.00	23.00	7.98	–3.51
Canada	31.00	28.00	22.00	7.99	–2.32
Netherlands	30.00	33.00	20.00	7.74	–2.52
Chile	30.00	25.00	35.00	7.45	–7.57
Mexico	29.00	23.00	31.00	6.94	–1.70
Germany	28.00	34.00	23.00	7.80	–2.74
Brazil	28.00	11.00	26.00	6.56	–1.94
Spain	27.00	32.00	26.00	7.54	–2.58
Saudi Arabia	25.00	21.00	22.00	7.03	6.68
China	24.00	24.00	25.00	6.14	–.16
Columbia	24.00	26.00	33.00	6.54	–1.36
Peru	22.00	22.00	31.00	7.41	–3.52
Japan	10.00	10.00	40.00	7.90	–1.74
South Korea	16.0	11.00	29.00	7.52	–2.79

Source: Energy Insecurity data come from the Ipsos the *Context Energy Survey* (CES). Data on economic freedom come from the Fraser Institute (fraserinstitute.org).

one country's EFW score (i.e., Argentina) changes by more than 20%. Moreover, EFW scores tend to be relatively high in all countries. Only Turkey has a score that is less than 6 on that index.

One weakness of the data in Table 4.9 is that there is a limited number of countries, and only one year of energy security data exist. Therefore, these data miss significant changes in neoliberalization that have occurred over the last 50 years, and data that do exist are largely associated with declines in neoliberalization that occurred during the COVID-19 pandemic. Despite

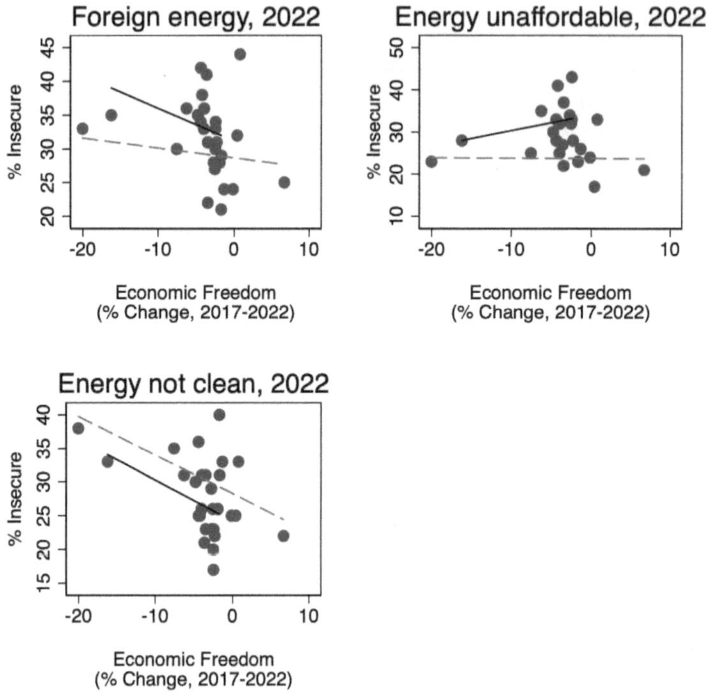

FIGURE 4.3 Energy Insecurity as a Function of Short-Term Neoliberalism (EFW% Δ) in the Global North and Global South, 2022

these weaknesses, we present scatterplots for the relationship between % Δ *EFW* and energy insecurity scores for energy dependency, energy affordability, and clean energy in Figure 4.3. Those scatterplots include the regression lines for the Global North and the Global South, given the different experiences these countries face with respect to energy insecurity. In each graph, the solid line represents the relationship in the Global North, and the dashed line represents the relationship in the Global South.

The results in Figure 4.3 are mixed. Short-term decreases in neoliberalization correspond with slightly greater levels of energy insecurity in Global North and Global South when it comes to concerns about reliance on foreign energy. The greater the drop in the % Δ *EFW* score, the greater the percentage of the population that believes there is too much reliance on foreign energy sources. In simple terms, a 1-point increase in neoliberalization (i.e., % Δ *EFW)* between 2017 and 2022 was associated with an 0.48% decrease in energy security in 2022 in the Global South and a 0.15% decrease in energy security in the Global North. Figure 4.3 also plots out the association between neoliberalization and affordable energy. There is a tendency for short-term decreases in neoliberalization to correspond with slightly lower levels of concerns about energy affordability in the Global North. That is, a 1-point decrease in neoliberalization (i.e., % Δ *EFW*) was associated with a 0.38% decrease in perceptions that energy is not affordable in 2022. There is no correlation between short-term changes in neoliberalization and affordability in the Global South. Finally, when it comes to clean energy, we find that movement away from neoliberalization is associated with greater levels of concern about the lack of clean energy in both the Global North and the Global South. The 2022 clean energy scatterplot suggests that among Global North countries, a 1-point increase in neoliberalization between 2017 and 2022 corresponds to a 0.61% increase in the mean average concern about clean energy. In short, reductions in neoliberalism are associated with higher percentages of the population who are concerned about clean energy. This finding contradicts the neoliberalism-insecurity hypothesis in the case of energy. The association between neoliberalization and concern about clean energy is also contradictory to expectations in the Global South. That is, a 1-point decrease in neoliberalization between 2017 and 2022 corresponds to a 0.50% increase in average concern about clean energy. Again, this finding contradicts the expected association between neoliberalism and concern for clean energy.

Overall, the scatterplots shown in Figure 4.3 provide mixed findings at the national level of analyses. These mixed results stand out as unique, given that most countries in Table 4.3 have decreasing EFW scores between 2017 and 2022. In particular, those countries that turn away from neoliberalism (i.e., those that have the greatest drop in % Δ *EFW*) are most concerned, on average, about clean energy and dependence on foreign energy. These findings, while interesting, suggest there is a need for alternative methods (and better data from more countries) to examine the potential relationship between neoliberalism and energy insecurity, such as those that we undertake in Chapter 7.

Conclusion

Energy security is critical to humankind and provides people with access to energy services needed for healthy living, including those needed to meet other household needs. The energy needed to drive those household services that provide energy security is, however, largely provided by dirty energy sources, for example, fossil fuels such as oil, gas, and coal. Nevertheless, even when using these dirty energy sources, energy insecurity exists and is unevenly distributed across and within countries around the world. As the world draws closer to peak oil, it is unlikely that oil and gas consumption will decrease, even as renewable energy sources continue to develop. As this chapter makes clear, energy insecurity occurs when households or countries don't have access to affordable, reliable, clean, and/or sufficient energy to meet the needs of people in a way that supports a healthy lifestyle. In short, energy is essential for sustainable human development and well-being.

While several conceptualizations of energy insecurity exist, in later chapters, we employ the concept of insecurity that was adopted by the BEIS questionnaire (Table 4.4), as it includes measurements of worry about the ability to pay energy insecurity. This approach is not only consistent with the Food and Agriculture Organization definition of food insecurity, examined in Chapter 3, but also emphasizes both the emotional and potential physical impact that energy security can have on people (i.e., by cutting back energy use needed to maintain comfortable/safe living environments). As noted, energy security is something that takes place across the globe in countries in both the Global North and Global South. While energy consumption in the Global South is increasingly catching up to that of the Global North, significant inequalities still exist in the distribution of energy, both between and within countries. These inequalities are built on the neoliberal, corporate, and governmental influences on energy development, where countries of the Global North were able to exploit economically weaker countries of the South. This overall neglect for human security in the case of local populations who reside in the Global South will only intensify conflict and resentment between energy-rich countries in the Global South and more wealthy consumer countries in the Global North.

To examine the association between neoliberalism and insecurity, we used existing, though limited, data that measure neoliberalism and energy insecurity at a national level. Energy insecurity was measured using the Ipsos CES, and neoliberalism by using EFW scores. While that analysis was limited, the association between these scores allows us to examine how the process of neoliberalization is related to energy. While we emphasize the lack of time-series data as significant, we find that concern about affordable energy tends to be highest in countries that didn't experience a significant neoliberal downturn.

Despite the linkages we have drawn between neoliberalism and energy insecurity in this chapter, the situation and the structural inequalities that have traditionally existed are being challenged by citizens and governments around the globe. Many countries have begun to control their own energy destiny to transition from non-renewable to renewable energy sources. Nevertheless, all countries across the globe are influenced by global financial institutions and neoliberal polices that incentivize the development of fossil fuels energy over renewable energy. As a result, energy security can only be understood and addressed as a function of the global political economy, which is dominated by powerful corporate actors that derive their profits from fossil fuels. Our final form of insecurity, job insecurity, is also partly a function of the global political economy – a topic to which we now turn our attention to.

References

Alves, Ana Cristina. 2008. *China and Gabon: A growing resource partnership*. The South African Institute of International Affairs (SAIIA), Braamfontein. Accessed at https://www.saiia.org.za/wp-content/uploads/2008/04/chap_rep_04_alves_200805.pdf.

Ambrose, Aimee, William Baker, Graeme Sherriff, and Joseph Chambers. 2021. "Cold Comfort: Covid-19, Lockdown and the Coping Strategies of Fuel Poor Households." *Energy Reports* 7: 5589–5596. https://doi.org/10.1016/j.egyr.2021.08.175.

Ambrose, Jillian. 2024. "UK 'Risks Repeat of Surging Energy Bills' Amid Continued Reliance on Gas." *The Guardian*. October 15, 2024. Accessed at https://www.theguardian.com/environment/2024/oct/15/uk-risks-repeat-of-surging-energy-bills-amid-continued-reliance-on-gas.

André-Paul, Sam, Belsham-Harris, Alex, Brooke Bullard, Tom, Emmanuel, Olu, Howarth, Lauren, and Will Johnstone. 2024. "Fixing the Foundations: The Need for Better Targeted Support for Energy Consumers." National Association of Citizens Advice Bureau. August 21, 2024. Accessed at https://assets.ctfassets.net/mfz4nbgura3g/9Cul6LpsPU2A5I01fWkmB/03f13ed14a2d91130459d6951ef6ffae/Final_version_-_Fixing_the_foundations_-_August_2024_v3.pdf.

Ang, Beng Wah, Wei Lim Choong, and Tsan Sheng Ng. 2015. "Energy Security: Definitions, Dimensions and Indexes." *Renewable and Sustainable Energy Reviews* 42: 1077–1093. https://doi.org/10.1016/j.rser.2014.10.064.

Bardi, Ugo. 2019. "Peak Oil, 20 years Later: Failed Prediction or Useful Insight?." *Energy Research & Social Science* 48: 257–261. https://doi.org/10.1016/j.erss.2018.09.022.

Bardi, Ugo. 2009. "Peak oil: The Four Stages of a New Idea." *Energy* 34(3): 323–326. https://doi.org/10.1016/j.energy.2008.08.015.

Barnes, Douglas F., Shahidur R. Khandker, and Hussain A. Samad. 2010. "Energy Access, Efficiency, and Poverty: How Many are Energy Poor in Bangladesh?" Policy Research Working Paper 5332. The World Bank.

Boateng, Godfred O., Mobolanle R. Balogun, Festus O. Dada, and Frederick A. Armah. 2020. "Household Energy Insecurity: Dimensions and Consequences for Women, Infants and Children in Low-and Middle-Income Countries." *Social Science & Medicine* 258: 113068. https://doi.org/10.1016/j.socscimed.2020.113068.

Bonds, Eric. 2013. "Assessing the Oil Motive after the US War in Iraq." *Peace Review* 25(2): 291–298. https://doi.org/10.1080/10402659.2013.785769.

Bordoff, Jason and Meghan L. O'Sullivan. 2023. "The Age of Energy Insecurity: How the Fight for Resources is Upending Geopolitics." *Foreign Affairs* 102: 104.

Bouchama, Abderrezak, Mohammed Dehbi, Gamal Mohamed, Franziska Matthies, Mohamed Shoukri, and Bettina Menne. 2007. "Prognostic Factors in Heat Wave–Related Deaths: A Meta-Analysis." *Archives of Internal Medicine* 167(20): 2170–2176. https://doi:10.1001/archinte.167.20.ira70009.

Bourdieu, Pierre. 1984. *Distinction: A Social Critique of the Judgement of Taste*. Cambridge, MA: Harvard University Press.

Bout, Marie. 2022. "Fossil Fuels are Fuelling War." *Greenpeace*, April 1, 2022. Retrieved from https://www.greenpeace.org/international/story/52988/fossil-fuels-are-fuelling-war/.

Brown, Marilyn A., Anmol Soni, Ameet D. Doshi, and Charlotte King. 2020. "The persistence of high energy burdens: A bibliometric analysis of vulnerability, poverty, and exclusion in the United States." *Energy Research & Social Science* 70: 101756. https://doi.org/10.1016/j.erss.2020.101756.

Brown, Marilyn A. and Benjamin K. Sovacool. 2007. "Developing an Energy Sustainability Index to Evaluate Energy Policy." *Interdisciplinary Science Reviews* 32(4): 335–349. https://doi.org/10.1179/030801807X211793.

Cabestan, Jean-Pierre. 2014. "Gabon-China Relations: Towards a More Cautious Partnership." *African East-Asian Affairs* 2. https://doi.org/10.7552/0-2-135.

Chandler, Adam. 2016. "Where the Poor Spend More than 10 Percent of Their Income on Energy." *The Atlantic*, June 8, 2016. Retrieved from https://www.theatlantic.com/business/archive/2016/06/energy-poverty-low-income-households/486197/.

Cherp, Aleh and Jessica Jewell. 2011. "The Three Perspectives on Energy Security: Intellectual History, Disciplinary Roots and the Potential for Integration." *Current Opinion in Environmental Sustainability* 3(4): 202–212.

Coleman-Jensen, Alisa, Matthew P. Rabbitt, Christian Gregory, and Anita Singh. 2015. *Household Food Security in the United States in 2014. ERR-194.* St. Paul, Minnesota, University of Minnesota: U.S. Department of Agriculture, Economic Research Service. Retrieved from https://www.ers.usda.gov/media/189.

Colgan, Jeff 2013. "Fueling the Fire: Pathways from Oil to War." *International Security* 38(2): 147–180. https://www.jstor.org/stable/24480933.

Conibear, Luke, Edward W. Butt, Christoph Knote, Stephen R. Arnold, and Dominick V. Spracklen. 2018 "Residential Energy Use Emissions Dominate Health Impacts from Exposure to Ambient Particulate Matter in India." *Nature Communications* 9(1): 617.

Cook, John T., Deborah A. Frank, Patrick H. Casey, Ruth Rose-Jacobs, Maureen M. Black, Mariana Chilton, Stephanie Ettinger decuba et al. 2008. "A Brief Indicator of Household Energy Security: Associations with Food Security, Child Health, and Child Development in US Infants and Toddlers." *Pediatrics* 122(4): e867–e875. https://doi.org/10.1542/peds.2008-0286.

Corman, Hope, Marah A. Curtis, Kelly Noonan, and Nancy E. Reichman. 2016. "Maternal Depression as a Risk Factor for Children's Inadequate Housing Conditions." *Social Science & Medicine* 149: 76–83. https://doi.org/10.1016/j.socscimed.2015.11.054.

De Graaff, Naná. 2012. "The Rise of Non-Western National Oil Companies: Transformation of the Neoliberal Global Energy Order?" Pp. 161–178 in *Neoliberalism in Crisis*, edited by Henk Overbeek and Bastiaan van Apeldoorn. International Political Economy Series. London: Palgrave Macmillan. https://doi.org/10.1057/9781137002471_8.

Deming, David. 2023. "M. King Hubbert and the Rise and Fall of Peak Oil Theory." *AAPG Bulletin* 107(6): 851–861. https://doi.org/10.1306/03202322131.

Demski, Christina, Wouter Poortinga, Lorraine Whitmarsh, Gisela Böhm, Stephen Fisher, Linda Steg, Resul Umit, Pekka Jokinen, and Pasi Pohjolainen. 2018. "National Context is a Key Determinant of Energy Security Concerns across Europe." *Nature Energy* 3(10): 882–888.

Department for Business, Energy and Industrial Strategy. 2023. "Public Attitudes Tracker, 2021–2022: Secure Access [data collection]." 2nd Edition. UK Data Service. SN: 9025. https://doi.org/10.5255/UKDA-SN-9025-2.

Doel, Ronald. 1989. *Interview of M. King Hubbert on 1989 January 17.* College Park, MD: Niels Bohr Library & Archives, American Institute of Physics. Retrieved from www.aip.org/history-programs/niels-bohr-library/oral-histories/5031-4.

Dixon, Jeffrey C. 2020. "Understanding Perceived Worker Insecurity in Europe, 2002–2016: Economic Freedom and Neoliberalism as Alternative Theories?" *Sociological Perspectives* 63: 5–28.

Dixon, Jeffrey C. 2022. "Where are the Neoliberals? Examining Economic Freedom, Perceived Freedom, and Free Market Values." *Comparative Sociology* 21: 142–197.

Enerdata. 2024. "Global Energy Trends, 2024." Retrieved from https://www.enerdata.net/publications/reports-presentations/world-energy-trends.html.

Foster, John Bellamy, Jonna, Jamil R. and Brett Clark. 2021. "Contagion of Capital." *The Monthly Review* 72(8). Retrieved from https://monthlyreview.org/2021/01/01/the-contagion-of-capital/.

Fry, Jane M., Lisa Farrell, and Jeromey B. Temple. 2023. "Energy Poverty and Food Insecurity: Is there an Energy or Food Trade-off Among Low-Income Australians?" *Energy Economics* 123: 106731. https://doi.org/10.1016/j.eneco.2023.106731.

Global Energy Institute. 2020a. *U.S. Energy Security Risk Index Report.* Washington D.C., U.S. Chamber of Commerce. Available at https://www.globalenergyinstitute.org/sites/default/files/2020-10/024036%20Global%20Energy%20Institute%20US%20Index_Web.pdf.

Global Energy Institute. 2020b. *International Index of Energy Security Risk: Assessing America's Global Energy Market.* Washington D.C., U.S. Chamber of Commerce. Available at https://www.uschamber.com/energy/index-of-us-energy-security-risk-assessing-americas-vulnerabilities-global-energy-market.

Guertler, Pedro and Peter Smith. 2018. *Cold Homes and Excess Winter Deaths: A Preventable Public Health Epidemic that Can No Longer be Tolerated.* England, National Energy Action. Available at https://www.precarite-energie.org/IMG/pdf/e3g-nea-cold-homes-and-excess-winter-deaths.pdf. Accessed February 15, 2025.

Guo, Yue, Yu Yang, Michael Bradshaw, Chang Wang, and Mathieu Blondeel. 2023. "Globalization and Decarbonization: Changing Strategies of Global Oil and Gas Companies." *Wiley Interdisciplinary Reviews: Climate Change* 14(6): e849. https://doi.org/10.1002/wcc.849.

Greenpeace. 2021. *The Sirens of Oil and Gas in the Age of Climate Crisis.* Rome, Greenpeace Italy. Retrieved from https://www.greenpeace.org/italy/rapporto/15346/the-sirens-of-oil-and-gas-in-the-age-of-climate-crisis/.

Gwartney, James, Robert Lawson, and Ryan Murphy. 2023. *Economic Freedom of the World 2023 Annual Report.* https://www.fraserinstitute.org/sites/default/files/economic-freedom-of-the-world-2023.pdf.

Harvey, David. 2005. *A Brief History of Neoliberalism.* Oxford and New York: Oxford University Press.

Heflin, Colleen. 2016. "Family Instability and Material Hardship: Results from the 2008 Survey of Income and Program Participation." *Journal of Family and Economic Issues* 37(3): 359–372. https://doi.org/10.1007/s10834-016-9503-6.

Hernández, Diana. 2016. "Understanding 'Energy Insecurity' and Why It Matters to Health." *Social Science and Medicine* 167: 1–10. https://doi.org/10.1016/j.socscimed.2016.08.029.

Hubbert, Marion. 1949. "Energy from Fossil Fuels." *Science* 109: 103–109.

Hubbert, Marion. 1934. "Future Ore Supply and Geophysical Prospecting." *Engineering and Mining Journal* 135(1): 18–21. Retrieved from https://www.aspo.be/app/uploads/2018/12/Hubbert_1934_FutureOreSupply_EngMinJ.pdf.

Huesemann, Michael. 2001. "Can Pollution Problems be Effectively Solved by Environmental Science and Technology? An Analysis of Critical Limitations." *Ecological Economics* 37(2): 271–287. https://doi.org/10.1016/S0921-8009(00)00283-4.

International Energy Agency. 2024. "Strategies for Affordable and Fair Clean Energy Transitions." Retrieved from https://iea.blob.core.windows.net/assets/86f2ba8c-f44b-494a-95cc-e75863cebf95/StrategiesforAffordableandFairCleanEnergyTransitions.pdf.

International Energy Agency. 2023a. "Glossary." Retrieved from https://www.iea.org/glossary.

International Energy Agency. 2023b. *SDG7: Data and Projections*. Paris: IEA. https://www.iea.org/reports/sdg7-data-and-projections, Licence: CC BY 4.0.

Ipsos. 2023. "*Context Energy Survey*, 2022." https://www.ipsos.com/sites/default/files/Ipsos%20Context%20Energy%2C%20Global%20Summary%2C%20Jan%202023.pdf.

Jahedi, Salar and Fabio Méndez. 2014. "On the Advantages and Disadvantages of Subjective Measures." *Journal of Economic Behavior & Organization* 98: 97–114. https://doi.org/10.1016/j.jebo.2013.12.016.

Jain, Garima. 2010. "Energy Security Issues at Household Level in India." *Energy Policy* 8(6): 2835–2845. https://doi.org/10.1016/j.enpol.2010.01.016.

Jorgenson, Andrew K. 2016. "Environment, Development, and Ecologically Unequal Exchange." *Sustainability* 8(3): 227. https://doi.org/10.3390/su8030227.

Kosai, Shoki and Hironobu Unesaki. 2020. "Short-term vs Long-term Reliance: Development of a Novel Approach for Diversity of Fuels for Electricity in Energy Security." *Applied Energy* 262: 114520. https://doi.org/10.1016/j.apenergy.2020.114520.

Le, Thai-Ha, Youngho Chang, Farhad Taghizadeh-Hesary, and Naoyuki Yoshino. 2019. "Energy Insecurity in Asia: A Multi-Dimensional Analysis." *Economic Modelling* 83: 84–95. https://doi.org/10.1016/j.econmod.2019.09.036.

Le, Thai-Ha and Donghyun Park. 2021. "What Drives Energy Insecurity Across the World? A Panel Data Analysis." *Energy Research & Social Science* 77: 102093. https://doi.org/10.1016/j.erss.2021.102093.https://doi.org/ 10.1016/j.erss.2021.102093.

Lefebvre, Ben 2024. "Why Harris and Trump are Debating the F-word." *Politico*. September 9, 2024. Retrieved from https://www.politico.com/news/2024/09/09/trump-harris-fracking-feud-explained-00177583.

Lewis, Jamal, Diana Hernández, and Arline T. Geronimus. 2020. "Energy Efficiency as Energy Justice: Addressing Racial Inequities through Investments in People and Places." *Energy Efficiency* 13: 419–432. https://doi.org/10.1007/s12053-019-09820-z.

Long, Michael A., Michael J. Lynch, Md Belal Hossain, and Paul B. Stretesky. 2024. "Neoliberalism, World System Position, and Biodiversity Loss: A Cross-National Examination of Threatened Species." *Sociology of Development* 10: 335–365.

Lubell, Harold. 1961. "Security of Supply and Energy Policy in Western Europe." *World Politics* 13(3): 400–422. https://doi.org/10.2307/2009482.

Mainali, Brijesh, Shonali Pachauri, Narasimha D. Rao, and Semida Silveira. 2014. "Assessing Rural Energy Sustainability in Developing Countries." *Energy for Sustainable Development* 19: 15–28. https://doi.org/10.1016/j.esd.2014.01.008.

Månsson, André. 2014. "Energy, Conflict and War: Towards a Conceptual Framework." *Energy Research & Social Science* 4: 106–116. https://doi.org/10.1016/j.erss.2014.10.004

McLean, Craig, Michael A. Long, Paul B. Stretesky, Michael J. Lynch, and Steve Hall. 2019. "Exploring the Relationship between Neoliberalism and Homicide: A Cross-National Perspective." *International Journal of Sociology* 49: 53–76

Mayer, Adam. 2022. "Fossil Fuel Dependence and Energy Insecurity." *Energy, Sustainability and Society* 12(1): 27.

Meloni, Giorgia. 2023. *President Meloni's Statement on Anniversary of the Death of Enrico Mattei [courtesy translated] 27 October 2023*. Rome, Italian Government Presidency of the Council of Ministers. Accessed at https://www.governo.it/en/articolo/president-meloni-s-statement-anniversary-death-enrico-mattei/24083.

Memmott, Trevor, Sanya Carley, Michelle Graff, and David M. Konisky. 2021. "Sociodemographic Disparities in Energy Insecurity among Low-income Households before and during the COVID-19 Pandemic." *Nature Energy* 6(2): 186–193.

Mohanty, Manoranjan. 2018. "Inequality from the Perspective of the Global South." In Mark Juergensmeyer, Saskia Sassen, Manfred B Steger and Victor Faessel. *The Oxford Handbook of Global Studies*, 211–228, New York, Oxford. Available at https://doi.org/10.1093/oxfordhb/9780190630577.013.42.

Najm, Alyaa Suhail. 2022. "The Global Markets for Crude Oil and the Extent of the Dominance of the Seven Major Companies (the seven sisters) Over Italy." *World Bulletin of Management and Law* 9: 1–11.

Narula, Kapil and B. Sudhakara Reddy. 2016. "A SES (sustainable energy security) Index For Developing Countries." *Energy* 94: 326–343. https://doi.org/10.1016/j.energy.2015.10.106.

New York Times. 1962. "Italian Oil Chief Dies in Air Crash; Mattei, Long Stormy Figure, Killed With 2 Near Milan." *New York Times*, 28 October 1962: 16. Retrieved from https://www.nytimes.com/1962/10/28/archives/italian-oil-chief-dies-in-air-crash-mattei-long-stormy-figure.html.

Odell, Peter. 2013. *Oil and World Power (Routledge Revivals)*. Abingdon, Oxon, UK: Routledge.

Painter, David S. 2012. "Oil and the American Century." *The Journal of American History* 99(1): 24–39.

Papascoma, S. and Mary Heiss, eds. 2016. *NATO in the Post-Cold War Era: Does It Have a Future?* Cham, CH: Springer, 2016.

Pearle, Richard. 1981. "MEMORANDUM FOR ASSISTANT TO THE PRESIDENT FOR NATIONAL SECURITY AFFAIRS." Declassified 22 September 2004. Ronald Reagan Presidential Library Digital Library Collections. Retrieved from https://www.reaganlibrary.gov/public/2022-03/40-750-80627194-001-041-2021.pdf.

Power, Meg. 2006. "Fuel Poverty in the USA: The Overview and the Outlook." *Energy Action 98*. Available at https://tepri.org/resource-tag/energy-burdens/.

Pradhan, Bhavin and Gabriel Chan. 2024. "Minnesota's Energy Paradox: Household Energy Insecurity in the Face of Racial and Economic Disparities." *The Electricity Journal* 37(6): 107423. https://doi.org/10.1016/j.tej.2024.107423.

Pratt, Joseph A. 2012. "Exxon and the Control of Oil." *The Journal of American History* 99(1): 145–154.

Ranjan, Ashish and Larry Hughes. 2014. "Energy Security and the Diversity of Energy Flows in an Energy System." *Energy* 73: 137–144. https://doi.org/10.1016/j.energy.2014.05.108.

Robine, Jean-Marie, Siu Lan Cheung, Sophie Le Roy, Herman Van Oyen, François Herrmann 2007. "The Excess Mortality in Summer 2003: Results of the Canicule Project." Paper presented at: the World Health Organization Meeting, Regional Office for Europe: Public Health Responses to Extreme Weather Events—euroHEAT March 22–23, 2007, Bonn, Germany. Retrieved from https://ec.europa.eu/health/ph_projects/2005/action1/docs/action1_2005_a2_15_en.pdf.

Rehfuess, Eva. 2006. *Fuel for Life: Household Energy and Health*. Geneva, World Health Organization. Retrieved from https://www.who.int/publications/i/item/9789241563161.

Saravanan, A., Venkatasubramanian, Ramaswamy. Khare, Ruchi. Surakasi, Raviteja. Boopathi, Sriram. Ray, Samrat, and Sudhakar, Maruthamuthu. 2022. "Policy Trends of Renewable Energy and Non-Renewable Energy." Research Gate. Retrieved from https://www.researchgate.net/profile/Samrat-Ray/publication/368227589_POLICY_TRENDS_OF_RENEWABLE_ENERGY_AND_NON_RENEWABLE_ENERGY/links/63dd1eea62d2a24f92f5501b/POLICY-TRENDS-OF-RENEWABLE-ENERGY-AND-NON-RENEWABLE-ENERGY.pdf.

Schnaiberg, Allan. 1980. *The Environment, from Surplus to Scarcity*. Oxford and New York: Oxford University Press.

Siegel, Eva Laura, Kathryn Lane, Ariel Yuan, Lauren A. Smalls-Mantey, Jennifer Laird, Carolyn Olson, and Diana Hernández. 2024. "Energy Insecurity Indicators Associated with Increased odds of Respiratory, Mental Health, and Cardiovascular Conditions: Study Examines Energy Insecurity and Health Conditions." *Health Affairs* 43(2): 260–268. https://doi.org/10.1377/hlthaff.2023.01052.

Simes, Miranda, Farzana Khan, and Diana Hernández. 2023. "Energy Insecurity and Social Determinants of Health." Pp. 2119–2137 in *Handbook of Social Sciences and Global Public Health*. Cham: Springer International Publishing.

Simmons, Matthew. 2008, June 25. "Comment: Kicking the Oil Habit." *New Scientist* 198(2662): 22.

Snell, Carolyn, Hannah Lambie-Mumford, and Harriet Thomson. (2018). "Is there Evidence of Households Making a Heat or Eat Trade off in the UK?" *Journal of Poverty and Social Justice* 26(2): 225–243.

Snyder, Lynne Page and Christopher A. Baker. 2010. "Affordable Home Energy and Health: Making the Connections." *AARP Public Policy Institute* 1: 5–36. Retrieved from https://neada.org/wp-content/uploads/2013/02/aarp_neada_report_affordable_home_energy_and_health_june_2010.pdf.

Sovacool, Benjamin. 2011. "Evaluating Energy Security in the Asia Pacific: Towards a More Comprehensive Approach." *Energy Policy* 39(11): 7472–7479. https://doi.org/10.1016/j.enpol.2010.10.008.

Sovacool, Benjamin and Michael Dworkin. 2014. *Global Energy Justice: Principles, Problems, and Practices*. Cambridge University Press: Cambridge.

Sovacool, Benjamin and Ishani Mukherjee. 2011. "Conceptualizing and Measuring Energy Security: A Synthesized Approach." *Energy* 36(8): 5343–5355. https://doi.org/10.1016/j.energy.2011.06.043.

Steele, Amanda Harker and John C. Bergstrom. 2021. "Brr! It's Cold in Here" Measures of Household Energy Insecurity for the United States." *Energy Research & Social Science* 72: 101863. https://doi.org/10.1016/j.erss.2020.101863.

Steffen, Will, Katherine Richardson, Johan Rockström, Sarah E. Cornell, Ingo Fetzer, Elena M. Bennett, Reinette Biggs et al. 2015. "Planetary Boundaries: Guiding

Human Development on a Changing Planet." *Science* 347(6223): 1259855. https://doi/org/10.1126/science.1259855.

Stretesky, Paul B. and Michael J. Lynch. 2009. "A Cross-national Study of the Association between Per Capita Carbon Dioxide Emissions and Exports to the United States." *Social Science Research* 38(1): 239–250. https://doi.org/10.1016/j.ssresearch.2008.08.004.

Tank Terminals 2024. "EIA Sees U.S. Setting New Oil Production Records in 2025." *Tank Terminals.com*, October 1, 2024. https://tankterminals.com/news/eia-sees-u-s-setting-new-oil-production-record-in-2025/.

Topham, Gwyn. 2024. "Half of Britons Plan to Ration Energy Use this Winder as 10% Bill Rise Looms." *The Guardian*, September 30, 2024. Retrieved from https://www.theguardian.com/money/2024/sep/30/half-of-britons-plan-to-ration-energy-use-this-winter-as-10-bill-rise-looms.

Tracy, Melissa, Margaret E. Kruk, Christine Harper, and Sandro Galea. 2010. "Neo-Liberal Economic Practices and Population Health: A Cross-National Analysis, 1980–2004." *Health Economics, Policy and Law* 5: 171–199.

Trifonov, Ivan, Dmitry Trukhan, Yury Koshlich, Valeriy Prasolov, and Beata Ślusarczyk. 2021. "Influence of the Share of Renewable Energy Sources on the Level of Energy Security in EECCA Countries." *Energies* 14(4): 903.

United Nations. 2024. "Sustainable Development Goals: Ensure Access to Affordable, Reliable, Sustainable and Modern Energy." Retrieved from https://www.un.org/sustainabledevelopment/energy/.

United States Energy Information Administration. 2024. "Short-Term Energy Outlook." 8 October, 2024. Retrieved from https://www.eia.gov/outlooks/steo/report/global_oil.php.

Veblen, Thorstein. 2001 [1899]. *The Theory of the Leisure Class*. New York: Modern Library.

Venditti, Bruno. 2023. "Visualizing the Top Energy Priorities of Major Countries." Retrieved from https://www.visualcapitalist.com/visualizing-the-top-energy-priorities-of-major-countries/.

Wilkinson, Paul, Kirk R. Smith, Michael Joffe, and Andrew Haines. 2007. "A Global Perspective on Energy: Health Effects and Injustices." *The Lancet* 370(9591): 965–978.

Williams, Paul A. 2006. Projections for the Geopolitical Economy of Oil after War in Iraq. Futures, 38(9): 1074–1088. https://doi.org/10.1016/s0140-6736(07)61252-5.

Whistleblower Lawyer Team. 2017. *Sinopec under Investigation over Bribery in Nigeria*. Constantine Cannon, August 31, 2017. Retrieved from https://constantinecannon.com/whistleblower/whistleblower-insider-blog/sinopec-investigation-bribery-nigeria/.

White, Lawrence J. 1976. "The Seven Sisters: The Great Oil Companies and the World They Shaped." *Political Science Quarterly* 8: 364–366.

Wilson Center Digital Archives. 2022. "Enrico Mattei, 'On the Decolonization of States and of the Economy'." Speech on 10 June, 1960. Record ID 291045. Retrieved from https://digitalarchive.wilsoncenter.org/document/enrico-mattei-decolonization-states-and-economy.

World Health Organization. 2006. *Fuel for Life: Household Energy and Health*. Retrieved from https://iris.who.int/bitstream/handle/10665/43421/9241563168_eng.pdf.

5

THE POLITICAL ECONOMY OF WORK AND JOB INSECURITY

The global rise of nonstandard and precarious forms of employment over the last 50 years has created a workplace environment in which job insecurity is such a common experience that workers simply take it for granted. According to a report from the United Nations, the recent rise in forms of nonstandard work, such as part-time, casual contracts (i.e., zero hours or on-call), and contract work, has created labor market flexibility on the one hand, and contributed to rising inequality in wages and working conditions on the other hand (United Nations 2021:2).

In this chapter, we turn our focus to job insecurity and how it has co-evolved with neoliberalism in countries across the globe. Our focus on job insecurity is like that of food security and energy insecurity, as it highlights the absence of an important aspect of life. However, the following discussion of job insecurity deviates slightly from our previous discussions of food and energy for two important reasons. First, as we have previously suggested, even while people worry about food and energy, these forms of insecurity are largely driven by objective economic conditions (e.g., one may not be able to afford to buy enough food or heat and cool one's home). However, job insecurity is a phenomenon with subjective and objective elements. Specifically, it is a subjective experience rooted in objective conditions in the workplace and local labor market. Thus, these forms of insecurity are different from the indicators of food and energy insecurity, as we make clear in this chapter. Second, unlike food and energy insecurity, Bourdieu (1998) had much to say about job insecurity. As a result, we purposefully direct more of our attention to Bourdieu's theoretical conception of job insecurity by highlighting several forms of job insecurity associated with his field-theoretic perspective.

DOI: 10.4324/9781003326892-5

We begin by building on our general definition of insecurity, from Chapter 1, as the inability to successfully predict a stable and secure future. Consistent with this general definition of insecurity, we define job insecurity as the inability of workers to anticipate stable employment in the near future. In his writing on neoliberalism and insecurity, Bourdieu (1998) noted that uncertainty about the future of one's employment situation makes:

> the whole future uncertain, it prevents all rational anticipation and, in particular, the basic belief and hope in the future that one needs in order to rebel, especially collectively, against present conditions, even the most intolerable.
>
> *(82)*

Uncertainty and its paralyzing effect on the most vulnerable workers is an integral part of the global neoliberal capitalist field. Insecurity is politically mediated and manipulated by employers operating within neoliberal political environments to strengthen their bargaining position vis-à-vis workers.

According to our definition, job insecurity has an obvious "subjective" dimension because it is rooted in workers' expectations. However, those expectations are embedded in the economic realities of the workplace and the broader local labor market (e.g., see Klandermans, Hesselink, and Van Vuuren 2010:558), which also gives it an "objective" dimension. The hyper-focus on subjective vs. objective measures of job insecurity in the literature overlooks their interconnectedness and fails to see that they are two sides of the same coin (Butler 2022; Merleau-Ponty 1968). Our use of the Bourdieusian concept of a neoliberal capitalist field allows us to bypass this traditional objective/subjective dualism, which is invoked in most studies of job insecurity. Bourdieu (1984, 1990, 2020) challenged the objective/subjective dualism through his theory of practice, which explains social action as the result of a struggle between actors endowed with different stocks of capital (internalized in the form of a habitus) taking place within a relatively autonomous social space governed by its own set of rules (i.e., nomos), assumptions, and unstated beliefs. (i.e., doxa). The habitus is a set of dispositions and schemes of perception arising from the internalization of field structures, which becomes embodied and operates primarily in a practical state below the level of consciousness. The habitus is thus the embodiment of past social structures, which challenges the claims that (1) social phenomenon can easily be classified as objective (i.e., external to the individual) or subjective (i.e., within the individual), and (2) factors can easily be labeled as structural or agentic. He summarized this position succinctly in *The Logic of Practice*:

> Overriding the spurious opposition between the forces inscribed in an earlier state of the system, outside the body, and the internal forces

> arising instantaneously as motivations springing from free will, the internal dispositions – the internalization of externality – enable the external forces to exert themselves, but in accordance with the specific logic of the organisms in which they are incorporated.
>
> *(Bourdieu 1990:54–55)*

The social space within which an action takes place is a "space of objective probabilities" (Bourdieu 2020:123). Through the internalization of social structures within the space, individuals anticipate potential outcomes of their actions and adjust their expectations in accordance with objective probabilities. Social structures thus live a double life. They exist simultaneously in fields and in the habitus of individuals within those fields. Thus, we cannot think of the probability of job loss as something that exists exclusively within jobs ("objectively") or within the minds of workers ("subjectively"). It exists in both forms simultaneously.

We incorporate the structure of objective probabilities within the field of labor by using our concept of security capital, which we introduced in Chapter 1. Security capital (along with economic capital) structures the social space in which workers compete with one another, and it is also embedded in the cognitive categories of workers in the form of their work habitus or set of work-related dispositions. It is this "double genesis" (Wacquant 2024:12) in dispositions and social structures that gives workers a sense of their own security, even if it is only a practical one, which surfaces as expectations of job loss and the mental and physical health consequences that come with this potential threat (Barling and Kelloway 1996; Burgard, Brand, and House 2009; Ferrie et al. 1998; Fullerton et al. 2020a; Lam, Fan, and Moen 2014; Rugulies et al. 2008).

Previous Studies of Job Insecurity

As with much exploratory research in new subdisciplines, early research on job insecurity looked to related areas of scholarship for direction on conceptualization, measurement, and research design. Jacobson (1991a) details how early job insecurity research developed out of research on job loss. Job insecurity was often conceptualized as stage one in the job-loss process. However, the focus on these studies was ultimately on job loss, measured as whether a respondent was still employed at the organization, was made redundant, or was let go in some manner. This variable is viewed as an objective indicator of an objective state of reality. The respondent is employed at the organization on a given day or not.

The phenomenon of job insecurity in its contemporary context and its study is relatively new. Job insecurity became a regular concern for workers of countries in the Global North shortly after the turn to neoliberal economic policies in the late 1970s and early 1980s (Harvey 2005). Subsequently, research on job insecurity began to spring up in the early to mid-1980s, primarily in organizational psychology, as a feeling or a perception. Thus, unlike research on job loss, this new research on job insecurity was more subjective. The perception of job insecurity, or likelihood of being fired in its simplest operationalization, varies from worker to worker based on a host of other variables (e.g., aspects of position in the family space, such as race, class, and gender), and therefore these subjective perceptions vary among respondents in a study. Jacobson (1991a:39) highlighted the differences between job insecurity and loss research when he noted, "[a]bove all, the distinction between job insecurity and job loss is a distinction between a purely subjective experience and an objective reality...."

Early job insecurity research included attempts at clarifying both the conceptualization of job insecurity as a research object (Greenhalgh and Rosenblatt 1984; Jacobson 1991a, 1991b) and empirical studies of job insecurity (e.g., Hartley, Dan Jacobson, and Van Vuuren 1991; van Vuuren and Klandermans 1994). These early empirical studies often employed samples of workers from one or more organizations that were currently undergoing restructuring or downsizing (Greenhalgh and Rosenblatt 1984; van Vuuren and Klandermans 1994). In one of the earliest and most influential studies of job insecurity, Greenhalgh and Rosenblatt (1984), conceptualized job insecurity as a subjective threat rooted in objective threat within the organization that operates through multiple channels. The degree of job insecurity is a combination of the severity of the threat and one's powerlessness to counteract it (Greenhalgh and Rosenblatt 1984:440). While the transition from job loss to job insecurity research began to reify the objective/subjective dualism in job insecurity research, these early job insecurity studies that focused on workers who were currently employed in organizations undergoing change continued to solidify this dualism, while also blurring the lines between the two. By focusing solely on workers who were employed in an organization that was undergoing change, their subjective perceptions of job insecurity were based partly on an external state within the organization – that is, change. However, more recent research on organizational change suggests that the role of worker agency is often overlooked. Supposedly external, structural changes in the workplace are contingent upon workers and their responses to managerial attempts at restructuring (Vallas 2006).

More recent scholarship on job insecurity conducted by economists and sociologists, in addition to psychologists, often employed national or international random samples of workers or individuals. While the majority of this recent sociological and psychological scholarship on job insecurity has focused on subjective indicators of job insecurity (e.g., Erlinghagen 2008;

Fullerton et al. 2020a; Fullerton and Wallace 2007; Jiang and Lavaysse 2018; Klandermans et al. 2010), some economists and labor relations scholars have suggested that "job stability," often measured by employee tenure (e.g., Auer 2006; Auer and Cazes 2003; Diebold, Neumark, and Polsky 1997; Farber 2008), is actually an objective indicator of job insecurity (see also Kalleberg 2018). While one can certainly argue whether the length of time working for an employer is truly an objective indicator of job insecurity, that is beside the point. Recent job insecurity research, whether in sociology, psychology or economics, continues to be conceptualized, as it always has, as either an objective characteristic of a job or a subjective characteristic of an individual. Research on the subjective expectation of job insecurity has shown that it is associated with working in precarious types of employment, such as temporary work (Klandermans, Hesselink, and van Vuuren 2010) and is predictive of actual job loss in the future (Stephens 2004). Thus, job insecurity is a subjective experience firmly grounded in objective conditions. It is real both in its foundations and in its consequences for workers, such as physical and mental health problems (e.g., see Ferrie et al. 1998; Fullerton et al. 2020a; Rugulies et al. 2008).

Despite early research on the conceptualization of job insecurity (Ashford, Lee, and Bobko 1989; Greenhalgh and Rosenblatt 1984), studies on job insecurity typically place more emphasis on the type of insecurity than on the underlying theory. The three main types of job insecurity are cognitive job insecurity, labor market insecurity, and affective job insecurity (see Anderson and Pontusson 2007; Fullerton, Dixon, and McCollum 2020b). Cognitive job insecurity refers to the perceived likelihood of job loss and is perhaps the most studied type of job insecurity. However, cognitive job insecurity alone is inadequate to fully capture our conceptualization of job insecurity as the inability to anticipate a stable employment relationship in the future. It also requires labor market insecurity, which is the perceived likelihood of being able to find a comparable job in the labor market (Anderson and Pontusson 2007:215). Workers able to find comparable jobs in the labor market in the face of potential job loss have more power to counteract the threat and maintain overall "employment security" (Chung and van Oorschot 2011; Dixon, Fullerton, and Robertson 2013) by changing employers. Finally, scholars have also studied workers' emotional responses to the threat of job loss. This is captured by the concept of affective job insecurity, which is the extent to which workers worry about the threat of job loss (Borg and Elizur 1992; Jiang and Lavaysse 2018; Sverke and Hellgren 2002). Affective job insecurity is closely related to the previous two forms of insecurity (Anderson and Pontusson 2007), but recent research shows that it is a distinct dimension that is more closely related to worker outcomes, such as organizational commitment, turnover intention, and health (Jiang and Lavaysse 2018).

Job Insecurity in the Global North

Over the past 25 years, there have been a number of studies of cross-national differences in job insecurity. Most of the focus has been on European countries and other rich capitalist countries in the Global North, such as the US and Japan. One of the most consistent findings across studies is that workers are more likely to perceive their jobs as insecure in countries with higher unemployment rates (Anderson and Pontusson 2007; Dixon et al. 2013; Erlinghagen 2008, Chung and van Oorschot 2011; Fullerton, Robertson, and Dixon 2011; Green, Felstead, and Burchell 2000; Green 2006, 2009; Kalleberg 2018). Job insecurity is also higher in countries with lower rates of union density (Dixon et al. 2013; Fullerton et al. 2011) or collective bargaining coverage (Inanc and Kalleberg 2022; Kalleberg 2018), in less generous welfare states with lower spending levels for unemployment benefits in particular (Anderson and Pontusson 2007; Dixon et al. 2013; Fullerton et al. 2011; Inanc and Kalleberg 2022; Kalleberg 2018), and in post-Socialist countries relative to other European countries (Dixon et al. 2013; Fullerton et al. 2011).

On balance, previous research on cross-national differences in job insecurity highlights the importance of economic conditions and the institutional context. The varieties of capitalism perspective (Hall and Soskice 2001) suggests that firms tend to coordinate their activities through either deregulated liberal market economies or highly regulated coordinated market economies. Thus, the evidence suggests that job insecurity is greater in liberal market economies where neoliberalism has a greater hold. Insecurity may also be greater in these countries due to the weakened bargaining position of workers, which supports Korpi's (2006) power resources perspective and the role of class conflict (Wright 2000).

Job Insecurity in the Global South

We know far more about the causes and consequences of job insecurity in the US and Europe than in any other region of the world. One could point to the geographic limitations of existing cross-national social science data sets, such as the European Social Survey, the World Values Survey, and the International Social Survey Program (ISSP) as an explanation. However, this does not explain *why* social surveys tend to focus on Europe and North America. Postcolonialism, however, does offer an explanation. Dominant forms of social science and, in particular, sociology are rooted in the concept of empire, which Go (2016) defines as a "transnational political formation by which a state exerts power and influence over weaker societies" (2). The influence of empire means that social science tends to be metrocentric (i.e., universalizing patterns observed in the metropole and ignoring social life in current and former colonies) and therefore focuses data collection efforts on rich capitalist countries of the Global North (Connell 2007; Go 2016; Steinmetz 2023). This metrocentric ideology downplays the importance of perspectives outside of the metropole (e.g., in former colonies located in the Global South) and universalizes the empirical patterns observed in the Global North. For example, all 11 countries included in the ISSP's first Work Orientations module in 1989 (ISSP Research Group 1991) are in the Global North. This limits our understanding of work and job insecurity, specifically due to the structural conditions in former colonies that make job insecurity more likely; moreover, the transferability of the mechanisms operating in the North to previously unstudied Southern contexts is, at best, questionable. In the analysis we present at the end of this chapter, job insecurity is more prevalent in countries within the Global South in the later waves of the Work Orientations module incorporating a larger and more diverse sample of countries (e.g., see ISSP Research Group 2017). Recent studies of job insecurity in countries such as Brazil, Nigeria, India, and South Africa provide additional evidence that more research on insecurity in understudied contexts outside of Europe and North America is needed to understand how national institutional environments shape the causes and consequences of insecurity (e.g., Fakier and Ehmke 2014; Llosa et al. 2023; Probst and Ekore 2010; van Wyk and Pienaar 2008). More diverse cross-national samples will also allow scholars to understand the ways neoliberalism shapes job insecurity, given the uneven geographic spread of neoliberalism across the globe (Fourcade-Gourinchas and Babb 2002).[1]

The Spread of Neoliberalism and Its Consequences for Job Insecurity

The global spread of neoliberalism in the 1980s and 1990s took place within an economic landscape of increasing global competition, deindustrialization, declining union density, and a restructuring of work, emphasizing more flexible forms of employment, including nonstandard (Carré et al. 2000; Kalleberg 2000, 2011) and contingent employment (Belous 1989). These shifts reflect a change in the balance of power from workers to employers (Harvey 2005; Kalleberg 2018; Wilson 2018) and signaled a fundamental transformation in the social contract at work, calling into question the idea of lifetime job security (Rubin 1996). The standard employment relationship was built on the idea of a stable, full-time job, with an expectation of long-term job security that takes place at the employer's place of business. Nonstandard workers are employed in positions that deviate from the standard employment relationship in one or more of these ways. The most common type of nonstandard work, part-time work, is particularly problematic for workers that are employed in these positions involuntarily (i.e., they would prefer full-time work). Involuntary part-time work tends to be lower quality, and this type of part-time work has been driving recent trends in the growth of part-time work (Pedulla 2020). Nonstandard workers often find themselves in precarious employment relationships, offering little, if any, guarantees of long-term employment. Thus, job insecurity is an everyday fact of life. The shift of power from workers to employers, and the spread of neoliberal ideology emphasizing the benefits of competition and the promotion of an entrepreneurial view of all workers (not just the self-employed), help explain the global spread of nonstandard forms of employment and the ubiquitousness of job insecurity in the contemporary workplace.

Neoliberalism's roots are in the economic crises of the 1970s, including oil shocks and stagflation (see Chapter 2), and its emergence as the new political and economic orthodoxy in the 1990s (with the "Washington Consensus") led to an increase in the relative income of elites and dramatic shifts in government social spending, reflecting a new market orientation and an emphasis on social responsibility (Harvey 2005; Wilson 2018). Recent trends in income and wealth inequality reflecting increasing levels of inequality, particularly in the top 1% (Piketty 2014), support the claim that neoliberalism is a political project that serves the interests of economic elites and has contributed to growing inequality on a global scale (Chancel et al. 2022).

Despite the global reach of neoliberalism, it has developed unevenly over time and across space (Fourcade-Gourinchas and Babb 2002). There is no single path to neoliberal capitalism, and the global neoliberal capitalist field, which we introduced in Chapter 1, is a meta-field comprising variations within different national spaces with different trajectories. The space of neoliberal capitalism operating within the US is distinctive in terms of not only the degree to which neoliberalism is embedded within economic, political, and social institutions but also in the role of the penal system in its historical development. The US has one of the highest levels of "economic freedom,"[2] which is the euphemism for neoliberalism promoted by organizations such as the Fraser Institute, but there are several countries with slightly higher levels of economic freedom relative to the US. The US ranks 7th in the world based on the most recent data (Gwartney, Lawson, and Murphy 2023). Hong Kong, Singapore, Switzerland, New Zealand, Denmark, and Australia outrank the US as of 2022. However, the US also ranks 6th in the world in the rate of incarceration. The incarceration rate in the US is three to eight times greater than in a handful of countries with higher levels of economic freedom (Fair and Walmsley 2024). This suggests that the criminalization of poverty and the use of the "iron fist" of the penal system to regulate the low-wage labor market and manage the social insecurity created by deindustrialization, declining union density, and welfare state retrenchment (Western 2006; Wacquant 2009) may be just one of many variants of neoliberal capitalism. The penal system is clearly less integral to the low-wage labor market in a country such as Denmark, which combines one of the highest economic freedom scores in the world with an extremely low incarceration rate (69 per 100,000, compared to 531 per 100,000 in the US [see Fair and Walmsley 2024]). Although the penal system is critical to understanding the development of the US neoliberal capitalist space, the size of the prison population is not correlated with the degree of economic freedom in a country. For example, in 2015 (the year of the most recent Work Orientations ISSP module), the correlation between the size of the prison population and the Fraser economic freedom score was 0.02, which indicates that they are statistically unrelated. This finding speaks to the power of neoliberal ideology. It has managed to take root in a vast array of countries with different institutional environments, political and economic histories, systems of stratification, and cultures. More cross-national work is needed to uncover how the carceral culture of neoliberalism and politically induced precarity in the US compares to other countries that continue to rely on the traditional welfare state, which Bourdieu (1998) referred to as the "left hand of the state," rather than the punitive "right hand of the state" (Wacquant 2009), characterizing the regulation of poverty and social insecurity in the US.

Neoliberalism and the Symbolic Violence of the Entrepreneurial Self

In Chapter 1, we briefly considered the symbolic violence wielded by the neoliberal State to set the boundaries of the workforce, which systematically excludes one of the most precarious groups (i.e., the incarcerated). The State has the symbolic power to arbitrarily set the limits of the national neoliberal capitalist space. However, the symbolic violence of neoliberalism affects work in a much more fundamental way than drawing its boundaries. Scholars typically describe neoliberalism as a "set of social, cultural, and political-economic forces that puts competition at the center of social life" (Wilson 2018:2). At the most fundamental level, neoliberalism puts forward a theory of the self that is based on an extreme form of *homo economicus* (see Chapter 6), turning all workers into utility-maximizing entrepreneurs focused on competition, self-reliance, and personal gain. Success and failure are interpreted in individualistic terms, which justify the deregulation of labor markets and cuts in social spending to support the unemployed. This view of the self is at odds with the social nature of the self and its emergence through interactions with others (Butler 2004; White 1992). The neoliberal image of the ideal worker is one that is primarily interested in social connections to increase one's stock of social and symbolic capital and enhance one's future labor market prospects. Viewing others first and foremost as competitors (or sources of insider information in the labor market) and blaming oneself for experiences with unemployment or missed opportunities for career advancement reinforce the hyper-individualism at the core of neoliberalism (Wilson 2018:3).

The neoliberal State wields its symbolic power through the implicit acceptance of the "entrepreneurial self" (Bröckling 2016) among workers and the individualizing of economic failures rooted in long-term structural changes in the global economy, labor market deregulation, and welfare state retrenchment. Misrecognition of the structural roots of economic success and failure in favor of individualistic explanations gives symbolic power its efficacy (Bourdieu 2000, 2023), because the spread of the neoliberal view of the self in recent years is not interpreted as an exercise of State or corporate power. It is simply an acceptance of the "way things are." The power to define this reality is the very definition of symbolic power. To wield this power is to engage in symbolic violence, and the State has a monopoly over it (Bourdieu 2014:4). However, this is not to say that the symbolic violence of the entrepreneurial self is merely symbolic. The acceptance of this view of the self is simultaneously embedded in individuals as mental schemes ("symbolic") and in positions within the neoliberal capitalist space ("material"), meaning it shapes how workers view themselves (and others) while also influencing their economic rewards and labor market prospects.

In the next section, we examine the empirical relationship between job insecurity and neoliberalism and how it has changed over time. We conceptualize the global neoliberal capitalist field as a meta-field composed of national spaces of neoliberal capitalism operating within different national contexts at a given point in time. In Chapter 7, we empirically examine this social space within the US in 2024, utilizing MCA (Le Roux and Rouanet 2010) on a representative sample of US residents.

Example: Neoliberalism and Job Insecurity, 1989–2015

Data and Method

In this section, we illustrate the experiences of workers with different forms of job insecurity during the period of consolidation of neoliberalism under advanced capitalism.[3] The individual-level data for this example come from the first four editions of the ISSP's Work Orientations module, which were fielded in 1989, 1997, 2005, and 2015. The ISSP data include a collection of probability-based, nation-wide samples from a group of member nations (for more details on sampling, see ISSP Research Group 1991, 1999, 2013, 2017). The sample is somewhat limited in 1989, with 11 countries all from the Global North, including: Austria, Great Britain, Hungary, Ireland, Israel, Italy, Netherlands, Northern Ireland, Norway, US, and West Germany. The ISSP samples are more diverse in later years, with eight countries from the Global South included in the fourth edition of the module in 2015. Regardless, our ability to generalize from this data source to the experiences of countries classified as the Global South is still somewhat limited but vastly improved compared to the data available to comparative scholars of job insecurity in the 1980s and 1990s. The earliest cross-national studies of job insecurity tended to focus on a relatively small number of European countries (e.g., Näswall and De Witte 2003), a larger group of European countries (e.g., Erlinghagen 2008; Dixon et al. 2013; Fullerton et al. 2011; Fullerton et al. 2020a), or a group of OECD countries (e.g., Anderson and Pontusson 2007; for an exception, see Green 2009).

We focus on the three main types of employment insecurity found in the literature: cognitive job insecurity, labor market insecurity, and affective job insecurity (see Anderson and Pontusson 2007). *Cognitive job insecurity* is the perceived likelihood of job loss in the near future. The ISSP measure that most closely captures this concept is based on responses to the following statement: "my job is secure" (1 = strongly agree, 2 = agree, 3 = neither agree nor disagree, 4 = disagree, and 5 = strongly disagree).[4] Workers who strongly disagree with this statement have the highest level of cognitive job insecurity. One's future job stability is also a function of the ease with which one could find a new job in the labor market. Therefore, we also consider *labor market insecurity*, which is the perceived difficulty in finding a (comparable) job if one was to look for work. The question from the ISSP surveys is worded as follows: "How difficult or easy do you think it would be for you to find a job at least as good as your current one?" (1 = very easy, 2 = fairly easy, 3 = neither easy nor difficult, 4 = fairly difficult, and 5 = very difficult).[5] Finally, the cost of job insecurity is higher if the perception of job loss leads to anxiety and stress over the threat of unemployment. Therefore, we also examine *affective job insecurity*, which is the extent to which one worries about the threat of job loss. The ISSP measure, which was not included in the 1989 survey, is based on the following question: "to what extent, if at all, do you worry about the possibility of losing your job?" (1 = a great deal, 2 = to some extent, 3 = a little, 4 = not at all).

To simplify the analysis and place the focus on the experience of insecurity (rather than levels of insecurity), we combine the two most insecure categories for each of the three employment insecurity variables to create three separate binary measures of cognitive job insecurity, labor market insecurity, and affective job insecurity (1 = insecure, 0 = secure). We then aggregate these measures to the country level to examine how the proportion of workers experiencing one or more forms of job insecurity in a country relates to neoliberalism. We present descriptive statistics for these three macro-level measures in Table 5.1. The proportion of workers in a country experiencing cognitive job insecurity, on average, increased from 0.13 in 1989 to 0.21 in 1997, and then decreased somewhat to 0.19 in 2005 and 0.15 in 2015. We see a similar increase for the proportion of workers experiencing labor

TABLE 5.1 Descriptives for Macro-Level Measures of Job Insecurity and Economic Freedom

	1989		1997		2005		2015	
	Mean	*SD*	*Mean*	*SD*	*Mean*	*SD*	*Mean*	*SD*
Job Insecurity								
Cognitive job insecurity	0.13	0.05	0.21	0.07	0.19	0.05	0.15	0.06
Labor market insecurity	0.43	0.11	0.56	0.16	0.52	0.11	0.54	0.09
Affective job insecurity			0.28	0.15	0.30	0.19	0.37	0.22
Economic Freedom								
Fraser Economic Freedom Index								
Current score	7.34	1.16	7.19	1.26	7.72	0.64	7.55	1.02
Five-year % change	8.06	8.03	8.58	11.62	2.12	6.42	1.48	4.83

Source: Individual-level data come from the 1989, 1997, 2005, and 2015 waves of the ISSP. Macro-level data on economic freedom comes from the Fraser Institute (fraserinstitute.org).

market insecurity, from 1989 to 1997 (from 0.43 to 0.56), and then a leveling off of this proportion (0.52 to 0.54). However, it is important to keep in mind that the number of countries in the ISSP sample increased from 11 to 26, with a more diverse sample in 1997. Given the changes from year to year in the composition of the samples (and question wording in some cases), we present separate analyses for each year.

Recall, the indicator of neoliberalism we utilize in this book, the Economic Freedom of the World (EFW) index, comes from the Fraser Institute, which is described as a measure of "economic freedom" constructed from 44 variables covering five areas of economic life (size of government, legal system and property rights, sound money, trade, and regulation) (see Gwartney, Lawson, and Murphy. 2023).[6] Each country receives a score on a scale from 0 to 10. The data for the EFW index derive from multiple sources, including the IMF, World Bank, World Economic Forum, and the United Nations (see Gwartney, Lawson, and Murphy 2023). Previous studies have used the EFW index as an indicator of neoliberalism (e.g., Dixon 2020, 2022; Long et al. 2024; McLean et al. 2019; Tracy et al. 2010;). Many of the countries we examine in this analysis had already reached high levels of neoliberalization by 1989, yet others, including post-Socialist countries in Europe and Eurasia, went through rapid periods of neoliberalization during the 1990s in response to external political and economic forces, such as regional integration (e.g., entry into the EU) (Appel and Orenstein 2016). There is no single path to neoliberal hegemony, and the path that a particular country takes is dependent upon its national institutional conditions (Fourcade-Gourinchas and Babb 2002) and has a lasting effect on the security of workers navigating that transition.

Following Dixon (2020), we focus on both the current level of neoliberalism in a country (i.e., the EFW index value for the current year) and the five-year change (%) in the EFW index, which we interpret as an indicator of short-term neoliberalization (i.e., a rapid increase in the level of neoliberalism associated with changing norms regarding the security of employment relations). We expect countries with higher levels of neoliberalism will have larger proportions of workers experiencing all three forms of job insecurity. However, there is reason to expect a stronger relationship with the short-term rate of neoliberalization. Dixon (2020) finds that job insecurity is significantly lower in European countries with higher current levels of neoliberalism, but countries experiencing a higher rate of neoliberalization over the past five years have significantly higher job insecurity. Post-Socialist countries in Europe began undergoing a process of rapid neoliberalization, which may help explain the higher levels of European job insecurity there (Dixon, Fullerton, and Robertson 2013; Fullerton et al. 2011).

Bourdieu's (1988, 1996, 2000) work on the "Don Quixote" or "hysteresis" effect offers us a theoretical explanation for the insecurity-inducing

TABLE 5.2 Cross-National Differences in Job Insecurity and Economic Freedom in 1989

Country	*% of Workers Experiencing*		*Economic Freedom Index (EFI)*	
	Cognitive Job Insecurity	*Labor Market Insecurity*	*EFI Score*	*EFI % Δ*
Austria	0.06	0.42	7.56	5.15
Great Britain	0.17	0.33	8.32	0.97
Hungary	0.09	0.49	5.33	18.18
Ireland	0.18	0.56	7.14	3.18
Israel	0.20	0.40	5.42	21.80
Italy	0.14	0.63	7.04	18.12
Netherlands	0.10	0.34	8.00	2.96
Norway	0.17	0.46	7.69	6.51
US	0.11	0.26	8.70	2.11
West Germany	0.05	0.36	8.20	1.61

Source: Individual-level data come from the 1989, 1997, 2005, and 2015 waves of the ISSP. Macro-level data on economic freedom come from the Fraser Institute (fraserinstitute.org). Due to data availability, the EFI score is from 1990, and the EFI % change score is from 1985 to 1990.

effects of rapid neoliberalization. During periods of stability, a worker's habitus is attuned to the field structures to the extent that everyday experiences in the workplace make sense, and many things, such as the expectation of long-term employment for many workers, may be taken for granted. However, during periods of rapid social, economic, and political change, field structures change faster than changes in workers' dispositions (i.e., habitus), which produces a mismatch between the work habitus and the structures within the economic and labor fields. The tendency for the habitus to remain rooted in structures no longer present in the field is the "hysteresis effect" (Strand and Lizardo 2017). The worker's habitus is now confronted with an unfamiliar field, which produces internal conflict and suffering, with the potential to create a divided or "cleft" habitus (Bourdieu 2004, 2008). Due to the potential for disruption in the work habitus caused by structural changes in political, economic, and labor fields – changes that devalue social support for workers while promoting an individualistic culture of personal responsibility and entrepreneurial selves – we expect that the short-term growth in neoliberalization will be more closely related to job insecurity than the current level of neoliberalism.

In Tables 5.2–5.5, we present the descriptive results for job insecurity and neoliberalism based on the Work Orientations modules of the ISSP in 1989, 1997, 2005, and 2015, respectively. In 1989, a period of rapid neoliberalization for several countries in the sample, including Hungary, Israel, and Italy (see Table 5.2), we find descriptive support for the expectation of greater

TABLE 5.3 Cross-National Differences in Job Insecurity and Economic Freedom in 1997

Country	*% of Workers Experiencing*			*Economic Freedom Index (EFI)*	
	Cognitive Job Insecurity	*Labor Market Insecurity*	*Affective Job Insecurity*	*EFI Score*	*EFI % Δ*
Bangladesh	0.21	0.73	0.16	5.08	23.90
Bulgaria	0.38	0.72	0.59	4.97	7.11
Canada	0.21	0.42	0.16	8.14	-2.63
Cyprus	0.22	0.47	0.17	7.01	13.61
Denmark	0.13	0.40	0.12	7.97	0.25
France	0.31	0.60	0.27	7.39	0.14
Germany	0.19	0.64	0.39	7.97	–2.80
Great Britain	0.26	0.52	0.29	8.43	1.32
Hungary	0.24	0.68	0.19	6.60	23.83
Israel	0.20	0.50	0.26	6.36	17.34
Italy	0.13	0.74	0.27	7.27	3.27
Japan	0.17	0.83	0.14	7.66	-6.70
New Zealand	0.19	0.48	0.18	8.91	8.92
Norway	0.11	0.28	0.11	7.98	3.77
Philippines	0.15	0.43	0.61	6.90	16.36
Poland	0.22	0.53	0.30	5.81	30.86
Portugal	0.29	0.79	0.46	7.38	11.65
Russia	0.29	0.69	0.54	4.43	32.24
Sweden	0.17	0.54	0.22	7.55	0.67
Switzerland	0.16	0.50	0.24	8.42	–3.33
US	0.14	0.27	0.17	8.74	0.46

Source: Individual-level data come from the 1989, 1997, 2005, and 2015 waves of the ISSP. Macro-level data on economic freedom come from the Fraser Institute (fraserinstitute.org). Due to data availability, the EFI score is from 1995, and the EFI % change score is from 1990 to 1995.

job insecurity in these countries. Israel has the highest level of cognitive job insecurity in the relatively small ISSP sample in 1989. Approximately one in five workers in Israel felt that their jobs were insecure. Israel also had the highest five-year growth rate in neoliberalism. The EFW index in Israel grew nearly a full point (from 4.45 to 5.42 on a 0–10 scale) between 1985 and 1990.[7] However, Ireland had a similar level of cognitive job insecurity and even greater labor market insecurity, but its neoliberal trajectory was very different. By 1985, Ireland had a substantially higher level of neoliberalism (6.92 vs. 4.45) and experienced a more modest 3% growth in neoliberalism

TABLE 5.4 Cross-National Differences in Job Insecurity and Economic Freedom in 2005

Country	*% of Workers Experiencing*			*Economic Freedom Index (EFI)*	
	Cognitive Job Insecurity	*Labor Market Insecurity*	*Affective Job Insecurity*	*EFI Score*	*EFI % Δ*
Australia	0.18	0.49	0.19	8.24	-1.55
Belgium	0.13	0.58	0.09	7.64	-2.80
Bulgaria	0.29	0.76	0.65	7.11	26.06
Canada	0.17	0.47	0.17	8.39	-0.24
Cyprus	0.16	0.31	0.21	7.77	13.60
Czech Republic	0.19	0.63	0.38	7.58	5.87
Denmark	0.13	0.37	0.11	8.18	-1.56
Dominican Republic	0.24	0.32	0.54	6.54	-0.76
Finland	0.21	0.53	0.11	8.18	-1.45
France	0.27	0.51	0.24	7.70	0.39
Germany	0.16	0.75	0.36	8.07	-1.34
Great Britain	0.11	0.43	0.21	8.41	-2.77
Hungary	0.18	0.63	0.22	7.34	4.41
Ireland	0.15	0.45	0.10	8.32	1.09
Israel	0.22	0.52	0.26	7.46	7.80
Japan	0.21	0.64	0.23	8.07	0.00
Latvia	0.33	0.51	0.58	7.82	3.58
Mexico	0.19	0.45	0.73	6.94	4.20
Netherlands	0.12	0.50	0.16	7.96	-2.09
New Zealand	0.16	0.46	0.14	8.65	-2.15
Norway	0.15	0.47	0.16	7.98	-0.13
Philippines	0.21	0.58	0.72	6.96	0.43
Portugal	0.23	0.59	0.36	7.46	-4.11
Russia	0.17	0.65	0.50	5.78	15.60
Slovenia	0.11	0.54	0.43	7.12	5.33
South Africa	0.27	0.51	0.46	6.99	0.29
South Korea	0.27	0.60	0.27	7.60	6.89
Spain	0.18	0.35	0.45	7.94	-0.50
Sweden	0.12	0.53	0.16	7.94	-2.10
Switzerland	0.18	0.61	0.21	8.53	-4.37
Taiwan	0.21	0.50	0.12	7.72	2.93
US	0.16	0.38	0.19	8.59	-2.83

Source: Individual-level data come from the 1989, 1997, 2005, and 2015 waves of the ISSP. Macro-level data on economic freedom come from the Fraser Institute (fraserinstitute.org). The EFI score is from 2005, and the EFI % change score is from 2000 to 2005.

TABLE 5.5 Cross-national Differences in Job Insecurity and Economic Freedom in 2015

Country	*% of Workers Experiencing*			*Economic Freedom Index (EFI)*	
	Cognitive Job Insecurity	*Labor Market Insecurity*	*Affective Job Insecurity*	*EFI Score*	*EFI % Δ*
Australia	0.20	0.60	0.27	8.27	0.24
Austria	0.09	0.49	0.17	7.96	0.76
Belgium	0.15	0.59	0.22	7.74	1.04
Chile	0.18	0.50	0.63	8.10	–0.86
China	0.19	0.57	0.23	6.13	4.07
Croatia	0.14	0.48	0.38	7.32	7.33
Czech Republic	0.12	0.56	0.49	7.94	2.32
Denmark	0.15	0.46	0.19	8.17	1.74
Estonia	0.07	0.54	0.40	8.23	1.23
Finland	0.20	0.67	0.11	8.03	-1.23
France	0.26	0.56	0.27	7.80	-0.13
Georgia	0.14	0.64	0.72	8.03	8.81
Germany	0.08	0.54	0.18	8.14	1.50
Great Britain	0.13	0.51	0.27	8.31	2.09
Hungary	0.11	0.47	0.20	7.42	-1.20
Iceland	0.07	0.44	0.13	7.54	8.18
India	0.18	0.26	0.71	6.43	4.55
Israel	0.09	0.41	0.26	7.62	1.20
Japan	0.23	0.66	0.27	7.90	0.64
Latvia	0.20	0.55	0.55	8.12	4.64
Lithuania	0.13	0.52	0.50	8.03	5.94
Mexico	0.16	0.40	0.74	7.16	3.17
New Zealand	0.15	0.62	0.22	8.75	2.58
Norway	0.10	0.54	0.16	7.54	-3.33
Philippines	0.11	0.63	0.73	7.39	3.65
Poland	0.34	0.72	0.32	7.45	7.04
Russia	0.12	0.55	0.55	6.32	3.95
Slovak Republic	0.24	0.51	0.36	7.60	-1.81
Slovenia	0.09	0.61	0.37	7.40	3.50
South Africa	0.21	0.49	0.54	6.82	-0.87
Spain	0.21	0.70	0.68	7.81	0.90
Suriname	0.14	0.61	0.27	6.33	-0.31
Sweden	0.08	0.47	0.12	8.06	1.13
Switzerland	0.07	0.51	0.20	8.53	0.00
Taiwan	0.21	0.63	0.09	7.92	2.06
US	0.10	0.40	0.16	8.40	1.82
Venezuela	0.13	0.62	0.91	2.77	-21.75

Source: Individual-level data come from the 1989, 1997, 2005, and 2015 waves of the ISSP. Macro-level data on economic freedom come from the Fraser Institute (fraserinstitute.org). The EFI score is from 2015, and the EFI % change score is from 2010 to 2015.

between 1985 and 1990. Countries with the lowest levels of both types of job insecurity tended to have some of the highest current levels of neoliberalism and lowest short-term rates of neoliberalization. However, we do not have enough information to make strong claims about neoliberalism and job insecurity in 1989 due to the small sample size.[8]

In 1997, the ISSP expanded the number of countries in the sample dramatically (from 11 to 26) and included countries spanning multiple continents. Although representation from the Global South is still very limited (two countries out of 26), the sample is more diverse relative to the 1989 sample. The descriptive results in Table 5.3 are based on a subset of 21 countries, which combines some countries in the original ISSP data and drops some cases due to missing data.[9] The average short-term rate of neoliberalization was 8.58% in 1997. There were four countries with rates above 20%, and two were above 30%, which exceeds the pace of neoliberalization observed in any of the countries in 1989. The high levels of all three forms of job insecurity in Russia is expected, given its rapid pace of neoliberalization in the 1990s. Russia's EFW score increased by over one point (from 3.35 to 4.43) between 1990 and 1995. Approximately three out of every ten Russian workers described their jobs as insecure. However, even more staggering is the finding that seven out of ten Russian workers felt it would be difficult to find an "acceptable" job in the current labor market if they had to look for work, and just over half of them worried about the threat of job loss. "Shock therapy" (Harvey 2005) clearly had a devastating impact on Russian workers and their future employment prospects. We see a very similar neoliberalization trajectory in Poland, but the levels of job insecurity were somewhat lower. Hungary and Bangladesh also saw sharp increases in neoliberalization in the early 1990s. Although cognitive and affective job insecurity were relatively lower in these countries, they also had among the highest levels of labor market insecurity in the sample. Thus, the descriptive results reveal a tendency for countries experiencing rapid neoliberalization in the first half of the 1990s to have extremely high levels of labor market insecurity.

In 2005, the ISSP sample included 32 countries and a slightly larger group of countries from the Global South (Dominican Republic, Mexico, Philippines, Taiwan, and South Africa). The average pace of neoliberalization slowed down considerably between 1997 and 2005. The average short-term neoliberalization rate in 2005 was 2.12%. Additionally, several of the countries in the sample experienced slight declines in neoliberalism between 2000 and 2005, which is indicated by negative values of the change scores. However, few countries were still experiencing substantial increases in neoliberalization in the early 2000s. For example, Bulgaria experienced an increase of almost 1.5 points in its EFW score between 2000 and 2005 (from 5.64 to 7.11). All three forms of job insecurity were also extremely high in 2005. Approximately three out of ten Bulgarian workers described their jobs as insecure, three quarters of them thought it would be difficult to find a "comparable" job in the labor market, and two-thirds of them worried about the threat of job loss. Russia also continued to experience increasing neoliberalization during the early 2000s and maintained high levels of labor market and affective job insecurity. However, other countries, such as Cyprus, experienced increasing neoliberalization without corresponding high levels of job insecurity.

In 2015, the ISSP data included 37 countries (eight from the Global South), and rates of short-term neoliberalization had stabilized in many of them. However, several countries continued experiencing modest increases in rates of short-term neoliberalization, including countries from the Global South such as the Philippines. Neoliberalization increased by 3.65 percentage points (from 7.13 to 7.39) in the Philippines. Although cognitive job insecurity was low in this country, most workers in the Philippines experienced labor market and affective job insecurity in 2015 (63% and 73%, respectively). Poland is another country that continued experiencing growth in neoliberalization in the early 2000s, combined with high levels of cognitive job insecurity and labor market insecurity. There is one outlier in the 2015 sample, however. Venezuela experienced a rapid decrease in neoliberalization in the early 2000s, and has the highest level of affective job insecurity, with 91% of Venezuelan workers worried about the potential threat of job loss.[10] However, the overall link we have observed between job insecurity and the short-term growth in neoliberalization continued in 2015.

To examine the link between neoliberalization and job insecurity in a more systematic fashion, we present scatterplots for the relationship between the five-year change score (i.e., "neoliberalization") and the proportion of workers experiencing each type of insecurity separately for each outcome and year. We group the scatterplots by the type of insecurity and include the regression lines summarizing the relationship for Global North countries and Global South countries (beginning in 2005) separately, given their different neoliberal paths (Connell and Dados 2014). In Figure 5.1, we present the graphs for cognitive job insecurity. In all four years, there was a modest, positive relationship between the short-term neoliberalization and the proportion of workers experiencing cognitive job insecurity. In each graph, the solid line represents the relationship in the Global North, and the dashed line represents the relationship in the Global South.[11] The relationship between neoliberalization and cognitive job insecurity was strongest in 2005. For the 27 Global North countries in the ISSP sample, a ten-percentage point increase in neoliberalization between 2000 and 2005 was associated with an increase of 0.03 in the proportion of workers experiencing cognitive job insecurity. However, the five countries from the Global South (Dominican Republic, Mexico, Philippines, South Africa, and Taiwan) had significantly higher levels of cognitive job insecurity, on average, and an increase in neoliberalization

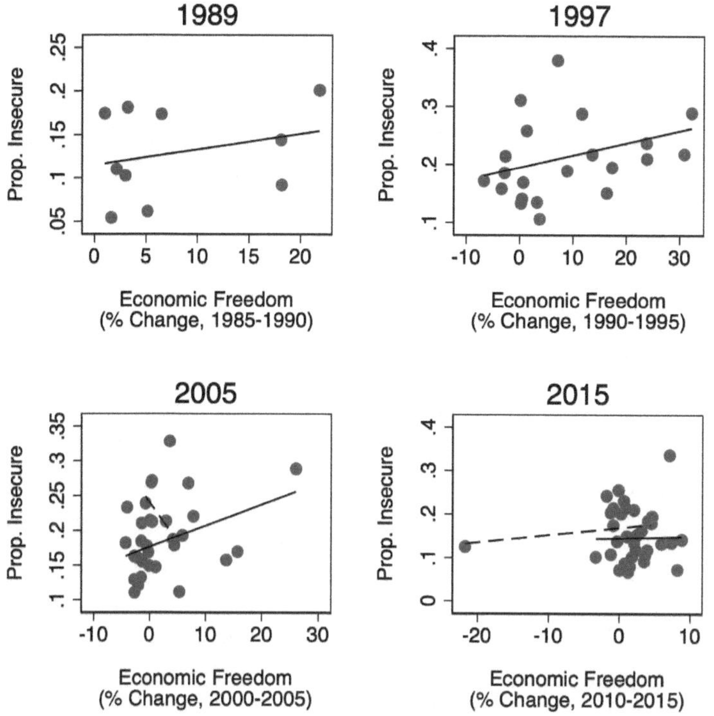

FIGURE 5.1 The Relationship between Neoliberalism and the Proportion of Workers Experiencing Cognitive Job Insecurity in the Global North and Global South, 1989–2015

was negatively associated with cognitive job insecurity in this region.[12] In 2015, short-term neoliberalization rates leveled off in many countries, and as a result, there was no association with the experience of cognitive job insecurity. Overall, the results in Figure 5.1 indicate that there was a tendency for short-term increases in neoliberalization to correspond with slightly greater levels of cognitive job insecurity in the Global North.[13]

Figure 5.2 presents graphs of the relationship between neoliberalization and (cognitive) labor market insecurity. We see similar patterns for both types of cognitive insecurity. The proportions of workers anticipating a difficult job search process were somewhat larger in countries experiencing more rapid short-term neoliberalization, and this relationship was strongest in 2005. In the Global North countries, a ten percentage point increase in neoliberalization from 2000 to 2005 was associated with an increase of .05 in the proportion of workers experiencing labor market insecurity, which is marginally significant (p =.092). For the five countries in the Global South, the relationship was also positive but non-significant, partly due to the small sample size. Apart from a few outliers such as Cyprus, which had a relatively

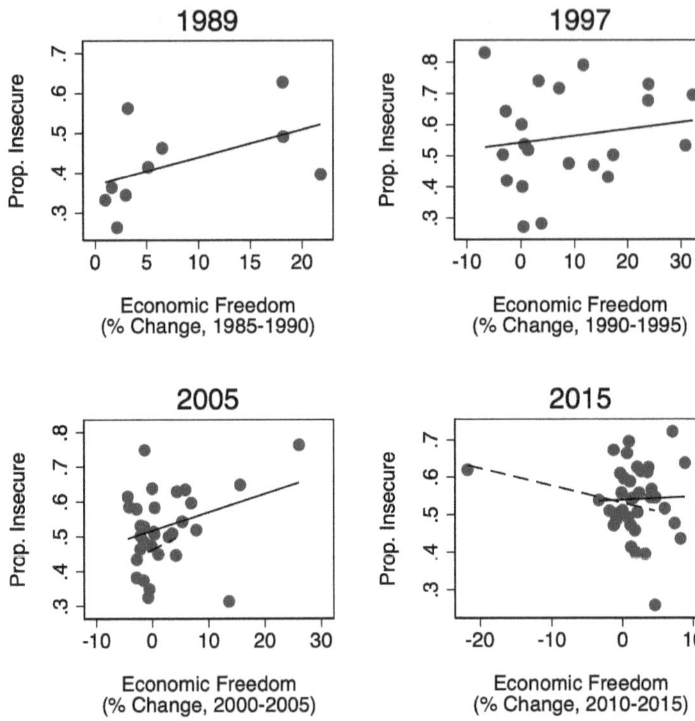

FIGURE 5.2 The Relationship between Neoliberalism and the Proportion of Workers Experiencing Labor Market Insecurity in the Global North and Global South, 1989–2015

low proportion of insecurity (0.31) and a high rate of neoliberalization (13.6%), countries in both the Global North and South that experienced more rapid rates of neoliberalization also had higher proportions of workers experiencing labor market insecurity in 2005. We also see a similar pattern in 2015, with the leveling off of neoliberalization rates corresponding with a weakening of the relationship with labor market insecurity. On balance, the results in the graphs indicate that neoliberalization was associated with modest increases in labor market insecurity.[14]

In Figure 5.3, we present the final set of graphs for affective job insecurity, which was only available in the ISSP data beginning in 1997. Once again, we observed a modest, positive relationship between neoliberalization and insecurity in the Global North countries in 1997. However, the relationship was considerably stronger for this type of insecurity in 2005 compared to the two measures of cognitive insecurity. The effect size was approximately 3.5 times greater for affective insecurity than for the two measures of cognitive insecurity. A ten percentage point increase in neoliberalization from 2000 to 2005 was associated with an increase of 0.14 in the proportion of

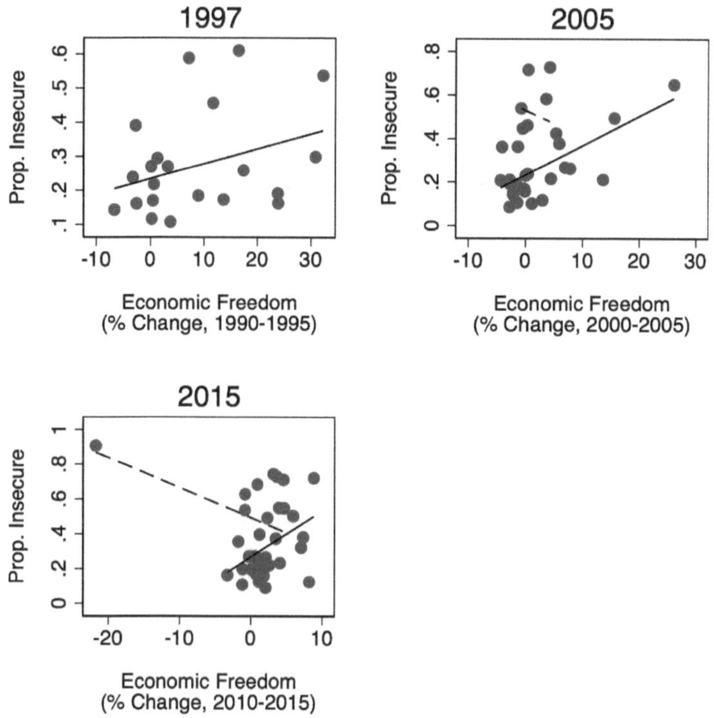

FIGURE 5.3 The Relationship between Neoliberalism and the Proportion of Workers Experiencing Affective Job Insecurity in the Global North and Global South, 1997–2015

workers experiencing affective job insecurity in the Global North. As the dashed line indicates in the 2005 graph, the relationship was negative (but non-significant) for the countries in the Global South. We do not have enough information to generalize beyond our small sample of five countries from the Global South in 2005 (and eight countries in 2015), but these results do provide support for the importance of future studies of insecurity in the Global South to verify these preliminary findings.[15] Finally, unlike in the models of cognitive insecurity, neoliberalization was positively associated with affective job insecurity in 2015, despite the declining rates of neoliberalization in most countries in the sample. Overall, the results suggest that neoliberalization was associated with greater levels of affective job insecurity in the Global North. Workers were more likely to worry about the potential threat of job loss in Northern countries experiencing more rapid rates of neoliberalization.

There are three key findings from the analysis of the ISSP data that have important implications for our understanding of the links between neoliberalism and job insecurity. First, it is the short-term process of neoliberalization, rather than the current level of neoliberalism, that is associated with heightened insecurity, which supports previous research (Dixon 2020).[16] Countries, such as the US, which have had extremely high levels of neoliberalism for decades and relative stable levels since the 1990s, tend to have lower levels of job insecurity than countries with lower levels of neoliberalism. It is the countries currently experiencing rapid neoliberalization (e.g., Bulgaria in the early 2000s) that tend to have greater levels of insecurity.

Second, given that it is the process of neoliberalization rather than the current level that translates into greater insecurity, studies of neoliberalism need to pay attention to the time period in addition to the geographic parameters of the study. Cross-national studies typically involve a relatively small number of countries from a single year or span of a few years. The temporal and geographic limits of the study will play an important role in shaping the findings regarding neoliberalism's consequences for job insecurity. During periods of relative stability (e.g., the early 2010s) and in relatively homogenous samples from a single region (e.g., Western Europe), studies may show no relationship between neoliberalism and job insecurity.

Finally, the results from our analyses suggest that neoliberalization is more closely linked to affective job insecurity than cognitive job insecurity or labor market insecurity. Affective job insecurity was the only form of insecurity that exhibited a positive association with short-term neoliberalization, even in the most recent period (2010–2015), with slower growth in neoliberalist practices. Why is neoliberalization more closely connected to the extent to which workers worry about job loss than the perceived likelihood of job loss? We explore this idea further in the next section.

Neoliberalization and Affective Job Insecurity: The Anxiety of the Entrepreneurial Self

A recent meta-analysis supports the view that cognitive and affective job insecurity are two distinct dimensions and finds that affective job insecurity is most closely related to worker outcomes (Jiang and Lavaysse 2018). A generalized sense of anxiety, among the employed and unemployed alike, is a central feature of social life in the neoliberal era. Bourdieu (1998:82) described this sense of unease as:

> The destructuring of existence, which is deprived among other things of its temporal structures, and the ensuing deterioration of the whole relationship to the world, time and space...the awareness of it never goes away: it is present at every moment in everyone's mind...it pervades both the conscious and the unconscious mind.

Worrying about the threat of job loss is part of the stress response to workers' experiences of insecurity within the global neoliberal capitalist field, which is a conscious manifestation of an insecure position within the field that is internalized within the work habitus over time.

However, during periods of rapid change in the field (e.g., the rapid neoliberalization experienced by many post-Socialist countries in the 1990s and early 2000s), the work habitus can become temporarily untethered to the current social structures in the field. This "hysteresis effect" (Bourdieu 1988, 1996), or mismatch between the structures present in the social space of the workplace and the personal space of the worker (i.e., the habitus), produces internal tension and misfirings as the world no longer seems to make sense, and acting on the basis of habit alone becomes problematic when the rules of the game are changing and new forms of capital valued in the neoliberal workplace (i.e., security capital) are emerging. A new entrepreneurial self (Bröckling 2016) is required to successfully navigate the global neoliberal capitalist field. Worrying about job loss is particularly prevalent in countries experiencing rapid changes in the national neoliberal capitalist space. This manifestation of the internal conflict caused by structural changes within the space can have negative consequences for their health (e.g., Burgard, Brand, and House 2009; Fullerton and Anderson 2013) and family well-being (Mauno, Cheng, and Lim 2017).

Neoliberalism creates an environment rife with uncertainty and anxiety. Butler (2015:14) notes that:

> neoliberal rationality demands self-sufficiency as a moral ideal at the same time that neoliberal forms of power work to destroy that very possibility at an economic level, establishing every member of the population as potentially or actually precarious, even using the ever-present threat of precarity to justify its heightened regulation of public space and its deregulation of market expansion.

Through the deregulation of labor markets and retrenchment of the welfare state, neoliberalism creates a situation in which the image of the ideal worker as an entrepreneur is increasingly difficult to maintain. In countries that rely on the penal system to regulate the most insecure regions of the neoliberal capitalist space, such as the US, failure to maintain the entrepreneurial self is criminalized. For example, "carceral work mandates," such as the threat of incarceration in the context of child support enforcement (Zatz 2020), make it clear how failure to secure employment has now become a criminal violation rather than a mere moral failure. Wacquant (2009:29) refers to this as the "penalization of precariousness." We explore the links between the penal system and the US neoliberal capitalist space in more detail in Chapter 7.

The entrepreneurial self is an inherently precarious construction because it downplays the social nature of autonomy in its fetishization of the individual.

The "paradox of autonomy," whereby individuality and a sense of self are inherently dependent upon the larger social fabric of relationships, norms, and institutions (Butler 2004:101), is overlooked entirely, which simultaneously fails to capture the social nature of individuals and blames the negative consequences of the neoliberalism-insecurity nexus on the most vulnerable segments of the population forced to confront it daily. This fetishism of the individual also serves as a justification for the withdrawal of the State from the regulation of labor markets and the provision of social services (Wacquant 2009). The misrecognition of the structural roots of inequality has always been a central part of symbolic power and the reproduction of inequality (Bourdieu 2000). It is the workplace culture promoting entrepreneurial selves and personal responsibility that performs this symbolic function under neoliberal capitalism, which has material consequences for workers and their families.

Conclusion

In this chapter, we explored the global spread of the neoliberal capitalist field as a meta-field connecting neoliberal spaces operating within different national contexts with their own political, economic, and social histories, shaping the development of neoliberal capitalism over time. Using data from four cross-sections of the ISSP Work Orientations models from 1989 to 2015, we examined how the process of neoliberalization is related to three different forms of job insecurity (cognitive job insecurity, labor market insecurity, and affective job insecurity), and how this relationship has changed over time in the Global North and, to a more limited extent, in the Global South. Job insecurity is highest in countries experiencing rapid short-term neoliberalization, and it is the emotional response to the threat of job loss that is the most responsive to the rapid growth of neoliberalism in a country.

The empirical example in this chapter reveals an important connection between neoliberalism and job insecurity, primarily in the Global North. However, this analysis is not designed to test a field-theoretic model, which we outlined in Chapter 1. The global neoliberal capitalist field is a meta-field comprising national spaces of neoliberal capitalism operating within different countries at different points in time. To illustrate the field-theoretic approach proposed in Chapter 1, we will map the space of neoliberal capitalism in the US for two reasons. First, the US has had one of the highest rates of neoliberalism over the past 40–50 years, which has made the US the "historical crucible and the planetary spearhead" of the neoliberal revolution (Wacquant 2009:xv). Second, the US also currently has one of the highest rates of incarceration in the world, which means that mapping the US space of neoliberal capitalism will also reveal how the penal system shapes insecurity.

We present an MCA of the US neoliberal capitalist space in Chapter 7. In the next chapter, however, we turn our attention to the micro-level impacts of neoliberalism on insecurity.

Notes

1 Green (2009) was among the first to include a diverse group of countries in his cross-national study of employment insecurity.
2 The Fraser economic freedom index is constructed from 44 variables spanning five major areas, including size of government, legal system and security of property rights, sound money, freedom to trade internationally, and regulation (for more details, see the Appendix to the 2022 Economic Freedom of the World Report: https://www.fraserinstitute.org/sites/default/files/uploaded/2022/economic-freedom-of-the-world-2022-appendix.pdf).
3 We are referring to labor market insecurity as a type of job insecurity, as we define it in this chapter, which is the lack of an expectation for stable employment in the future. We can think of labor market insecurity as the difficulty in finding a new job, and thus the expectation of continuing job instability in the future.
4 For more details regarding ISSP survey items, see ISSP Research Group (1991, 1999, 2007, 2017).
5 The question wording for this measure changed over time. In 1989, the question refers to an "acceptable" job rather than one that is "as good as your current one."
6 A similar measure of "economic freedom" is available from the Heritage foundation, but we do not include it in our analyses, given that it is not available for all the years included in our analyses.
7 We use 1990 data for the current value, and the change from 1985 to 1990 for the five-year change score, given that the EFW scores are only available every five years prior to 2000. For the 1997 ISSP data, we use EFW scores from 1995 for the current value, and the change from 1990 to 1995 for the five-year change score.
8 We only include 10 of the 11 countries from the 1989 ISSP sample due to lack of data on neoliberalism in Northern Ireland.
9 To match the list of countries in the ISSP and Fraser data sets, we combine East and West Germany into "Germany." Additionally, we drop Spain from the analysis because there were only three valid cases remaining after dropping missing cases, we drop the "Arab" sample due to lack of EFW data, and we drop the Czech Republic and Slovenia due to lack of EFW data prior to 1995 (producing missing data on the change score).
10 The decline in Venezuela's level of economic freedom is no doubt due to the deterioration of democratic institutions and relative absence of accountability in recent political regimes in this Socialist state (Maya 2018).
11 The ISSP sample did not include any countries from the Global South in 1989, and only two countries in 1997. Therefore, we only include a regression line for the Global South in 2005 and 2015. The Global South samples are extremely small in the latter two years. Therefore, we present the regression line as a summary of the relationship for these cases, but we are cautious in generalizing these results.
12 The regression slopes fail to reach statistical significance in both regions in 2005.
13 We also examined the relationship between the current level of neoliberalism and cognitive job insecurity and found that the relationship was negative in all four years in the Global North. However, the regression slope in the North only reached statistical significance in 1997. This finding supports previous research on neoliberalism and job insecurity in Europe (Dixon 2020).

14 The current level of neoliberalism is negatively related to labor market insecurity in 1989, 1997, and 2005, but the regression slopes only reach statistical significance in the Global North in 1997 and 2005.
15 The regression slope for neoliberalization is statistically significant in the Global North in 2005 and 2015, but non-significant in 1997. The current value of neoliberalism continues to have a negative relationship with insecurity, but is only significant in 1997 and 2005. The current level and change in neoliberalization are negative and non-significant in 2005 and 2015 in the Global South.
16 Although the current level of neoliberalism is negatively related to insecurity in several of the models, it more often than not fails to reach statistical significance.

References

Anderson, Christopher J. and Jonas Pontusson. 2007. "Workers, Worries, and Welfare States: Social Protection and Job Insecurity in 15 OECD Countries." *European Journal of Political Research* 46: 211–235.
Appel, Hilary and Mitchell A. Orenstein. 2016. "Why did Neoliberalism Triumph and Endure in the Post-Communist World?" *Comparative Politics* 48: 313–331.
Ashford, Susan J., Cynthia Lee, and Philip Bobko. 1989. "Content, Causes, and Consequences of Job Insecurity: A Theory-Based Measure and Substantive Test." *Academy of Management Journal* 32: 803–829.
Auer, Peter. 2006. "Protected Mobility for Employment and Decent Work: Labour Market Security in a Globalized World." *Journal of Industrial Relations* 48: 21–40.
Auer, Peter and Sandrine Cazes. 2003. "The Resilience of the Long-Term Employment Relationship: Evidence from the Industrialized Countries." *International Labor Review* 139: 379–408.
Barling, Julian and E. Kevin Kelloway. 1996. "Job Insecurity and Health: The Moderating Role of Workplace Control." *Stress Medicine* 12: 253–259.
Belous, Richard S. 1989. *The Contingent Economy: The Growth of Temporary, Part-Time, and Subcontracted Workforce*. Washington, DC: National Planning Association.
Borg, Ingwer and Dov Elizur. 1992. "Job Insecurity: Correlates, Moderators and Measurement." *International Journal of Manpower* 13: 13–26.
Bourdieu, Pierre. 2020. *Habitus and Field: General Sociology, Volume 2*. Cambridge: Polity Press.
Bourdieu, Pierre. 2008. *Sketch for a Self-Analysis*. Chicago, IL: University of Chicago Press.
Bourdieu, Pierre. 2004. *Science of Science and Reflexivity*. Chicago, IL: University of Chicago Press.
Bourdieu, Pierre. 2000. *Pascalian Meditations*. Stanford, CA: Stanford University Press.
Bourdieu, Pierre. 1998. *Acts of Resistance: Against the Tyranny of the Market*. New York: The New Press.
Bourdieu, Pierre. 1996. *The State Nobility*. Stanford, CA: Stanford University Press.
Bourdieu, Pierre. 1990. *The Logic of Practice*. Stanford, CA: Stanford University Press.
Bourdieu, Pierre. 1988. *Homo Academicus*. Stanford, CA: Stanford University Press.
Bourdieu, Pierre. 1984. *Distinction: A Social Critique of the Judgement of Taste*. Cambridge, MA: Harvard University Press.

Bourdieu, Pierre. 2014. *On the State: Lectures at the College de France, 1989–1992.* Cambridge, UK: Polity Press.
Bröckling, Ulrich. 2016. *The Entrepreneurial Self: Fabricating a New Type of Subject.* Thousand Oaks, CA: Sage.
Burgard, Sarah A., Jennie E. Brand, and James S. House. 2009. "Perceived Job Insecurity and Worker Health in the United States." *Social Science & Medicine* 69: 777–785.
Butler, Judith. 2022. *What World Is This? A Pandemic Phenomenology.* New York: Columbia University Press.
Butler, Judith. 2015. *Notes toward a Performative Theory of Assembly.* Cambridge, MA: Harvard University Press.
Butler, Judith. 2004. *Undoing Gender.* New York: Routledge.
Carré, Françoise, Marianne A. Ferber, Lonnie Golden, and Stephen A. Herzenberg (eds.). 2000. *Nonstandard Work: The Nature and Challenges of Changing Employment Arrangements.* Ithaca, NY: Cornell University Press.
Chancel, Lucas, Thomas Piketty, Emmanuel Saez, and Gabriel Zucman. 2022. *World Inequality Report 2022.* https://wir2022.wid.world/www-site/uploads/2021/12/WorldInequalityReport2022_Full_Report.pdf.
Chung, Heejung and Wim van Oorschot. 2011. "Institutions Versus Market Forces: Explaining the Employment Insecurity of European Individuals During (the Beginning of) the Financial Crisis." *Journal of European Social Policy* 21: 287–301.
Connell, Raewyn. 2007. *Southern Theory.* Cambridge: Polity Press.
Connell, Raewyn and Nour Dados. 2014. "Where in the World Does Neoliberalism Come From? The Market Agenda in Southern Perspective." *Theory and Society* 43: 117–138.
Diebold, Francis X., David Neumark, and Daniel Polsky. 1997. "Job Stability in the United States." *Journal of Labor Economics* 15: 206–233.
Dixon, Jeffrey C. 2022. "Where are the Neoliberals? Examining Economic Freedom, Perceived Freedom, and Free Market Values." *Comparative Sociology* 21: 142–197.
Dixon, Jeffrey C. 2020. "Understanding Perceived Worker Insecurity in Europe, 2002–2016: Economic Freedom and Neoliberalism as Alternative Theories?" *Sociological Perspectives* 63: 5–28.
Dixon, Jeffrey C., Andrew S. Fullerton, and Dwanna L. Robertson. 2013. "Cross-National Differences in Workers' Perceived Job, Labour Market, and Employment Insecurity in Europe: Empirical Tests and Theoretical Extensions." *European Sociological Review* 29: 1053–1067.
Erlinghagen, Marcel. 2008. "Self-Perceived Job Insecurity and Social Context: A Multi-Level Analysis of 17 European Countries." *European Sociological Review* 24: 183–197.
Fair, Helen and Roy Walmsley. 2024. *World Prison Population List, Fourteenth Edition.* https://www.prisonstudies.org/sites/default/files/resources/downloads/world_prison_population_list_14th_edition.pdf.
Fakier, Khayaat and Ellen Ehmke (eds.). 2014. *Socio-Economic Insecurity in Emerging Economies: Building New Spaces.* New York: Routledge.
Farber, Henry S. 2008. "Short(er) Shrift: The Decline in Worker-Firm Attachment in the United States." Pp. 10–37 in *Laid Off, Laid Low: Political and Economic Consequences of Employment Insecurity*, edited by Katherine S. Newman. New York: Columbia University Press.

Ferrie, Jane E., Martin J. Shipley, Michael G. Marmot, Stephen Stansfeld, and George Davey Smith. 1998. "The Health Effects of Major Organisational Change and Job Insecurity." *Social Science & Medicine* 46: 243–254.

Fourcade-Gourinchas, Marion and Sarah L. Babb. 2002. "The Rebirth of the Liberal Creed: Paths to Neoliberalism in Four Countries." *American Journal of Sociology* 108: 533–579.

Fullerton, Andrew S. and Kathryn Freeman Anderson. 2013. "The Role of Job Insecurity in Explanations of Racial Health Inequalities." *Sociological Forum* 28: 308–325.

Fullerton, Andrew S., Jeffrey C. Dixon, and Destinee B. McCollum. 2020b. "The Institutionalization of Part-Time Work: Cross-National Differences in the Relationship between Part-Time Work and Perceived Insecurity." *Social Science Research* 87: 1–20.

Fullerton, Andrew S., Destinee B. McCollum, Jeffrey C. Dixon, and Kathryn Freeman Anderson. 2020a. "The Insecurity Gradient in Health: How Inequality in the Distribution of Job Insecurity Matters for the Relationships between Job Insecurity and Self-Rated Health in Europe." *The Sociological Quarterly* 61: 107–127.

Fullerton, Andrew S., Dwanna L. Robertson, and Jeffrey C. Dixon. 2011. "Reexamining the Relationship between Flexibility and Insecurity: A Multilevel Study of Perceived Job Insecurity in 27 European Countries." *Research in the Sociology of Work* 22: 9–41.

Fullerton, Andrew S. and Michael Wallace. 2007. "Traversing the Flexible Turn: U.S. Workers Perceptions of Job Security, 1977–2002." *Social Science Research* 36: 201–221.

Go, Julian. 2016. *Postcolonial Thought and Social Theory*. Oxford: Oxford University Press.

Green, Francis. 2009. "Subjective Employment Insecurity around the World." *Cambridge Journal of Regions, Economy and Society* 2: 343–363.

Green, Francis. 2006. *Demanding Work: The Paradox of Job Quality in the Affluent Economy*. Princeton, NJ: Princeton University Press.

Green, Francis, Alan Felstead, and Brendan Burchell. 2000. "Job Insecurity and the Difficulty of Regaining Employment: An Empirical Study of Unemployment Expectations." *Oxford Bulletin of Economics and Statistics* 62: 855–883.

Greenhalgh, Leonard and Zehava Rosenblatt. 1984. "Job Insecurity: Toward Conceptual Clarity." *Academy of Management Review* 9: 438–448.

Gwartney, James, Robert Lawson, and Ryan Murphy. 2023. *Economic Freedom of the World 2023 Annual Report*. https://www.fraserinstitute.org/sites/default/files/economic-freedom-of-the-world-2023.pdf.

Hall, Peter A. and David Soskice (eds.). 2001. "An Introduction to Varieties of Capitalism." Pp. 1–70 in *Varieties of Capitalism: The Institutional Foundations of Comparative Advantage*. Oxford: Oxford University Press.

Harvey, David. 2005. *A Brief History of Neoliberalism*. Oxford: Oxford University Press.

Hartley, Jean F., Dan Jacobson, Bert Klandermans, and Tinka Van Vuuren. 1991. *Job Insecurity: Coping with Jobs at Risk*. Thousand Oaks, CA: Sage.

Inanc, Hande and Arne L. Kalleberg. 2022. "Institutions, Labor Market Insecurity, and Well-Being in Europe." *Social Sciences* 11: 1–25.

ISSP Research Group. 2017. *International Social Survey Programme: Work Orientations IV – ISSP 2015*. Köln: GESIS Datenarchiv. ZA6770 Datenfile Version 2.1.0, https://doi.org/10.4232/1.12848.

ISSP Research Group. 2013. *International Social Survey Programme: Work Orientations III – ISSP 2005*. Köln: GESIS Datenarchiv. ZA4350 Datenfile Version 2.0.0, https://doi.org/10.4232/1.11648.

ISSP Research Group. 1999. *International Social Survey Programme: Work Orientations II - ISSP 1997*. Köln: GESIS Datenarchiv. ZA3090 Datenfile Version 1.0.0, https://doi.org/10.4232/1.3090.

ISSP Research Group. 1991. *International Social Survey Programme: Work Orientations I – ISSP 1989*. Köln: GESIS Datenarchiv. ZA1840 Datenfile Version 1.0.0, https://doi.org/10.4232/1.1840.

Jacobson, Dan. 1991a. "The Conceptual Approach to Job Insecurity." Pp. 23–39 in *Job Insecurity: Coping with Jobs at Risk*, edited by Jean Hartley et al. London: Sage.

Jacobson, Dan. 1991b. "Toward a Theoretical Distinction between the Stress Components of the Job Insecurity and Job Loss Experiences. *Research in the Sociology of Organizations* 9: 1–9.

Jiang, Lixin and Lindsey M. Lavaysse. 2018. "Cognitive and Affective Job Insecurity: A Meta-Analysis and a Primary Study." *Journal of Management* 44: 2307–2342.

Kalleberg, Arne L. 2018. *Precarious Lives: Job Insecurity and Well-Being in Rich Democracies*. Cambridge: Polity Press.

Kalleberg, Arne L. 2011. *Good Jobs, Bad Jobs: The Rise of Polarized and Precarious Employment Systems in the United States, 1970s–2000s*. New York: Russell Sage Foundation.

Kalleberg, Arne L. 2000. "Nonstandard Employment Relations: Part-Time, Temporary and Contract Work." *Annual Review of Sociology* 26: 341–365.

Klandermans, Bert, John Klein Hesselink, and Tinka van Vuuren. 2010. "Employment Status and Job Insecurity: On the Subjective Appraisal of an Objective Status." *Economic and Industrial Democracy* 31: 557–577.

Korpi, Walter. 2006. "Power Resources and Employer-Centered Approaches in Explanations of Welfare States and Varieties of Capitalism: Protagonists, Consenters, and Antagonists." *World Politics* 58: 167–206.

Lam, Jack, Wen Fan, and Phyllis Moen. 2014. "Is Insecurity Worse for Well-Being in Turbulent Times? Mental Health in Context." *Society and Mental Health* 4: 55–73.

Le Roux, Brigitte and Henry Rouanet. 2010. *Multiple Correspondence Analysis*. Thousand Oaks, CA: Sage.

Llosa, José, Esteban Agulló-Tomás, Sara Menéndez-Espina, Camila Teixeira Heleno, and Livia de Olivera Borges. 2023. "Cross-Cultural Adaptation of the Job Insecurity Scale (JIS) in Brazil and Cross-National Analysis of Job Insecurity Effects in Brazil and Spain." *BMC Psychology* 11: 1–16.

Long, Michael A., Michael J. Lynch, Md Belal Hossain, and Paul B. Stretesky. 2024. "Neoliberalism, World System Position, and Biodiversity Loss: A Cross-National Examination of Threatened Species." *Sociology of Development* 10: 335–365.

Mauno, Saija, Ting Cheng, and Vivian Lim. 2017. "The Far-Reaching Consequences of Job Insecurity: A Review on Family-Related Outcomes." *Marriage & Family Review* 53: 717–743.

Maya, Margarita López. 2018. "Populism, 21st-Century Socialism and Corruption in Venezuela." *Thesis Eleven* 149: 67–83.

McLean, Craig, Michael A. Long, Paul B. Stretesky, Michael J. Lynch, and Steve Hall. 2019. "Exploring the Relationship between Neoliberalism and Homicide: A Cross-National Perspective." *International Journal of Sociology* 49: 53–76.

Merleau-Ponty, Maurice. 1968. *The Visible and the Invisible*. Evanston, IL: Northwestern University Press.

Näswall, Katharina and Hans De Witte. 2003. "Who Feels Insecure in Europe? Predicting Job Insecurity from Background Variables." *Economic and Industrial Democracy* 24: 189–215.

Pedulla, David S. 2020. *Making the Cut: Hiring Decisions, Bias, and the Consequences of Nonstandard, Mismatched, and Precarious Employment*. Princeton, NJ: Princeton University Press.

Piketty, Thomas. 2014. *Capital in the Twenty-First Century*. Cambridge, MA: Harvard University Press.

Probst, Tahira M. and John O. Ekore. 2010. "An Exploratory Study of the Costs of Job Insecurity in Nigeria." *International Studies of Management & Organization* 40: 92–104.

Rubin, Beth A. 1996. *Shifts in the Social Contract: Understanding Change in American Society*. Thousand Oaks, CA: Sage.

Rugulies, Renier, Birgt Aust, Hermann Burr, and Ute Bültmann. 2008. "Job Insecurity, Chances on the Labour Market and Decline in Self-Rated Health in a Representative Sample of the Danish Workforce." *Journal of Epidemiology and Community Health* 62: 245–250.

Steinmetz, George. 2023. *The Colonial Origins of Modern Social Thought: French Sociology and the Overseas Empire*. Princeton, NJ: Princeton University Press.

Stephens, Melvin, Jr. 2004. "Job Loss Expectations, Realizations, and Household Consumption Behavior." *The Review of Economics and Statistics* 86: 253–269.

Strand, Michael and Omar Lizardo. 2017. "The Hysteresis Effect: Theorizing Mismatch in Action." *Journal for the Theory of Social Behavior* 47: 164–194.

Sverke, Magnus and Johnny Hellgren. 2002. "The Nature of Job Insecurity: Understanding Employment Uncertainty on the Brink of a New Millennium." *Applied Psychology: An International Review* 51: 23–42.

Tracy, Melissa, Margaret E. Kruk, Christine Harper, and Sandro Galea. 2010. "Neo-Liberal Economic Practices and Population Health: A Cross-National Analysis, 1980–2004." *Health Economics, Policy and Law* 5: 171–199.

United Nations. 2021. "A Changing World of Work: Implications for the Social Contract." Policy Brief No. 94. https://www.un.org/development/desa/dpad/wp-content/uploads/sites/45/publication/PB_94.pdf.

Vallas, Steven Peter. 2006. "Empowerment Redux: Structure, Agency, and the Remaking of Managerial Authority." *American Journal of Sociology* 111: 1677–1717.

van Vuuren, Tinka and Bert Klandermans. 1994. "Social Explanations for Job Insecurity: Group Influences on Causal Attributions." *Social Justice Research* 7: 265–279.

Van Wyk, M. and J. Pienaar. 2008. "Towards a Research Agenda for Job Insecurity in South Africa." *South African Business Review* 12: 49–86.

Wacquant, Loïc. 2024. *Racial Domination*. Cambridge: Polity Press.

Wacquant, Loïc. 2009. *Punishing the Poor: The Neoliberal Government of Social Insecurity*. Durham, NC: Duke University Press.
Western, Bruce. 2006. *Punishment and Inequality in America*. New York: Russell Sage Foundation.
White, Harrison C. 1992. *Identity and Control: A Structural Theory of Social Action*. Princeton, NJ: Princeton University Press.
Wilson, Julie A. 2018. *Neoliberalism*. New York: Routledge.
Wright, Erik Olin. 2000. "Working-Class Power, Capitalist-Class Interests, and Class Compromise." *American Journal of Sociology* 105: 957–1002.
Zatz, Noah D. 2020. "Get to Work or Go to Jail: State Violence and the Racialized Production of Precarious Work." *Law & Social Inquiry* 45: 304–338.

6

NEOLIBERAL GOVERNMENTALITY, COMPETITION, INDIVIDUAL RESPONSIBILITY, AND INSECURITY

The previous three chapters discussed the structural political economy of food, energy, and job insecurity. In other words, we focused on the macro-level impacts of neoliberalism on those forms of insecurity. We now turn to the micro-level impacts of neoliberalism generally, and insecurity more specifically. Much of the work on neoliberalism's effects on individuals traces its origins to the latter work of French social theorist Michel Foucault, whose concepts of "biopolitics" and "governmentality" have become building blocks for the understanding of life during neoliberalism. This approach to the study of neoliberalism is often juxtaposed with the structural perspectives that we reviewed in the previous three chapters.

In the introduction to their edited volume, *The Government of Life: Foucault, Biopolitics, and Neoliberalism* (2014a), Lemm and Vatter (2014b:5) highlight the transition Foucault made in the study of neoliberalism:

> Foucault's turn to the study of government opened up a new avenue of research into the Marxist project of a "critique of political economy" and the reasons for the hegemony of political economy over a politics centered on sovereign power in late modernity. As Foucault makes clear at the end of *The Birth of Biopolitics*, one of his motivations to study government is given by the task to understand the rise of "civil society" and of the *homo economicus*, that is, of a human "type" that is the product of the constant application of economic thinking in all areas of natural and social life. This human "type" is the unique product of a modern conduct of conducts which Foucault calls liberalism. The reorientation of his analysis of power toward what has been called the "economization of society" made possible the productive reception of Foucault's work by post-Marxist thought in the 1990s.

DOI: 10.4324/9781003326892-6

There is a lot to unpack in this passage. This is a task we will embark on in this chapter. One of Foucault's key concepts is mentioned here by Lemm and Vatter – the rise of *homo economicus*. This "human type" is used by Foucault to emphasize how, under (neo)liberalism, individuals approach all aspects of life through rational calculation. Repercussions of this approach to life include making competition inherent in most aspects of life and the elevation in importance of individual responsibility, leading to a world where individuals mostly govern themselves. Government has given way to "governmentality." Where in the past, governments (or more broadly the State) were the primary mechanism which maintained social order, now individuals are consciously and unconsciously regulating themselves. The "hyperconnectivity" associated with the digital age (Brubaker 2023) and the quantification of the self-produced through digital interactions between individuals and corporations (Fourcade and Healy 2024; Zuboff 2019) have reinforced this neoliberal self-regulation and helped lock it into place.

Norms for a Changing Economy

Before we dive into Foucault's work on how individuals were remade and turned into self-governing, individualistic calculators of the *homo economicus* human type, we need to spend a little time discussing why this transformation of "individuals' souls," through the application of market principles to all aspects of life, as Margaret Thatcher famously said almost 50 years ago, became necessary with the onset of neoliberal capitalism. Dardot and Laval (2013:65) point us in the right direction:

> Neo-liberalism was based on the dual observation that capitalism had inaugurated a period of permanent revolution in the economic order, but that human beings were not spontaneously adapted to this changing market order because they had been formed in a different world.

It took time for social norms to catch up with the economic pivot to neoliberalism in the late 1970s and early 1980s. Norms of behavior were formed during the days of Keynesian-influenced economic policy, and individuals now had to reorient their behavior and values around the new neoliberal philosophy and what would increase their probabilities of success in a neoliberal world. These new norms were disseminated across the globe by advanced capitalist nations (e.g., UK, US, and Germany) and through the international financial institutions and organizations that we discussed in Chapter 2 (i.e., the IMF, World Bank, the General Agreement on Tariffs, and, later, the WTO).

Competition became the central organizing principle of the economy in neoliberalism – an idea that we have discussed, and will discuss further later in this chapter. We again can turn to Dardot and Laval (2013:65) for an elaboration on this idea:

> If the Keynesian and Fordist economic order was based on the idea that competition between capitalist enterprises and economies should be supervised by common fixed rules about exchange rates, trade policy and income distribution, the new neo-liberal norm established in the late 1980s elevated competition into the highest universal rule of government.

Once competition became integral to the success of neoliberal economic policies, it became necessary for individuals to internalize competition as a norm of behavior in the new neoliberal world. They had to become Foucault's *homo economicus*. It is easier for governments to regulate the behavior of their citizens, if the citizens essentially do it for them, rather than having to do it by unpopular laws and sometimes even force. This is the essence of what Bourdieu (1991) called "symbolic power," which we discuss at the end of the chapter. And contrary to some superficial understandings of neoliberalism, national governments have a role to play in structuring government apparatuses, so they are aligned with global capitalism, and which also need self-calculating, competitive individuals to make the system work. The desire to compete is a fundamental part of neoliberal life, and it forms the basis for the "illusio" (i.e., investment in the stakes of the game [Bourdieu 2000]) in the global neoliberal capitalist field.

The change in individual norms in neoliberal capitalism and the self-regulation of behavior is what we will explore in the first several sections of this chapter. Lemm and Vatter (2014:5) refer to *The Birth of Biopolitics* (2008), which is generally viewed as one of Foucault's primary works focused on biopolitics, governmentality, and the precursors of neoliberalism (along with *Security, Territory Population*, 2007). In the next section, we will review Foucault's argument and then discuss how subsequent scholars have advanced this literature. We then turn to how living in a neoliberal world is linked with insecurity – both generally and with the specific forms of insecurity we focus on in this book. We end the chapter with a discussion of what we refer to as the "insecure neoliberal subject," who is the competitive, self-regulated, perpetually insecure individual of neoliberal capitalism. The neoliberal subject is the embodiment of insecurity, as the structures of the neoliberal capitalist space are internalized and subsequently find expression in the practices of daily life. The same insecurity that structures the space of neoliberal capitalism thus also structures the thoughts, feelings, and actions of neoliberal subjects via the habitus.

Foucault and Neoliberalism

In his later scholarly work, French social theorist and critic Michel Foucault turned his attention to the study of eighteenth-century liberalism, the emerging neoliberalism, and how individuals were governed in societies that adopted these practices (e.g., Foucault 2007, 2008).

The philosophy of liberalism, which prioritized a *laissez faire* approach to economics and the "free market," was popular in the eighteenth century. In Foucault's (2007:48) words, "[t]he game of liberalism – not interfering, allowing free movement, letting things follow their course, *laisser faire, passer et*," was an important first step in understanding the government of individuals in the present day. Foucault then turned his attention to neoliberalism, although, because of his early death in 1984, his work was largely based on the past, his present, and theoretical discussion of the future of neoliberalism's impact on the government of individuals. The latter work of Foucault has become famous for, among other things, his discussions of biopolitics and governmentality. We briefly review these concepts in the subsequent section.

Biopolitics and Governmentality

While much of the recent discussions and work on biopolitics and governmentality in the work of late Foucault rely on his 1977–1978 and 1978–1979 lectures at the College de France, these were not the first instances that Foucault referenced these important topics. As Gros (2014:24) notes:

> In 1976, in *The Will to Knowledge*, Foucault constructs an opposition between an "anatomo-politics" understood as power over the individual's body through discipline, at work in institutions like the school, the factory, and the barracks, and a "biopolitics" understood as power over the population in its biological dimension through a regulatory politics carried out by the state.

What Foucault is suggesting is that the more traditional form of power, that of a sovereign entity (such as a nation and its government and laws), has at least partially given way to a new form of power, which he refers to as "biopolitics." Biopolitics has two targets: the individual and the population. Control over both individual people and complete societies was the ultimate goal of biopolitics (Foucault 2007:2008). In the first of his lectures (1975–1976), published as *Society Must Be Defended*, Foucault introduces the concept, "technologies of security," which are those biopolitical measures that help control populations (Foucault 2003:249). These technologies of security enable power to be maintained over people by concentrating on risk prevention and mitigation. Quantitative evaluation and monitoring, statistical analyses, and the like constitute typical technologies of security that are regularly employed to regulate the behavior of individuals in a society, primarily governed through biopolitics.

Before continuing, it is useful to note here that Foucault uses the language of "security" in his analyses of governing individuals and societies. Part of our larger argument is that (in)security is a fundamental aspect of the global neoliberal capitalist field. An important aspect of that argument is how insecurity is used as a tool of governance (i.e., regulating individuals, groups of individuals, and their behaviors) – an argument made convincingly by Isabell Lorey in *State of Insecurity: Government of the Precarious* (2015), which we will return to in greater detail later in this chapter. Recalling our broad definition of insecurity from Chapter 1 – where we suggest that insecurity is essentially the inability to accurately predict a stable and secure future – it is not difficult to make the mental leap from lacking the ability to predict the future to being susceptible to governance by technologies of security, especially when you have been socialized to be *homo economicus*. The norm of competition suggests being insecure is a measure of failure – you are losing (or, in some cases, have already lost) the competition. Individuals are taught to look within themselves to account for their failures, not toward the State and to the lack of assistance it provides to those that are insecure. Therefore, to make themselves more secure, individuals need to strive to do better in competitions, often aided (or nudged) by technologies of security.

As Muhle (2014:79) notes, the two Foucault lectures where biopower and related concepts received their most detailed treatment are *Security, Territory, Population* (1977–1978) and *The Birth of Biopolitics* (1978–1979), highlighting that, in these lectures, Foucault, "reformulates and amplifies the notion of biopower, referring to it by the name of governmentality. The introduction of this new name of power might be a reaction to a slightly too 'narrow' notion of biopolitics...." Muhle goes on to suggest that "this hypothesis is confirmed by Foucault's reformation of the biopolitical techniques under the name of 'security techniques' in his lectures on governmentality that follow the same scheme, that of biological normativity" (Muhle 2014:88). Over time, discussions of biopower morphed into discussions about governmentality.

The concept of governmentality is complex and probably not as well understood as the amount of scholarly work that employs governmentality in some way. In September 2024 (during the writing of this chapter), we did a Google Scholar search of "governmentality." The search returned "about 186,000" results. We, therefore, cannot provide a detailed review of the governmentality literature. Rather, in what follows, we define governmentality from a Foucauldian perspective, and then highlight a few of the major relevant theoretical advances on the topic that have emerged since Foucault's work on it in the late 1970s. We will then focus on how governmentality applies in our case – neoliberalism, and the relationship between neoliberalism and insecurity.

To begin, we turn to the definition of governmentality provided by Foucault in *Security, Territory, Population.*

> By this word 'governmentality' I mean three things. First, by 'governmentality' I understand the ensemble formed by institutions, procedures, analyses and reflections, calculations, and tactics that allow the exercise of this very specific, albeit very complex, power that has the population as its target, political economy as its major form of knowledge, and apparatuses of security as its essential technical instrument. Second, by 'governmentality' I understand the tendency, the line of force, that for a long time, and throughout the West, has constantly led towards the pre-eminence over all other types of power – sovereignty, discipline, and so on – of the type of power that we can call 'government' and which has led to the development of a series of specific governmental apparatuses on the one hand, [and, on the other] to the development of a series of knowledges. Finally, by 'governmentality' I think we should understand the process, or rather, the result of the process by which the state of justice of the Middle Ages became the administrative state in the fifteenth and sixteenth centuries and was gradually 'governmentalized.'
>
> *(Foucault 2007:108)*

To be sure, there are many facets to this three-pronged definition of governmentality provided by Foucault. The first prong deserves most of our attention. What Foucault is arguing is that there is a form of self-regulation – which he eventually labels "the conduct of conduct" (Foucault 2008; see also, Lemke 2002) – that is directed by individuals on themselves due to a political economy that cultivates and maintains the norm of self-regulation, by framing it as a positive (e.g., competition is natural, it brings out the best in people, and sorts individuals in a society by levels of productivity).

The political economy during the time he was giving the lectures at the Collège de France (the late 1970s) was the very beginning of the neoliberal capitalist revolution that began in the UK and the US, which then quickly spread to Western Europe and, eventually, most of the world. As we noted earlier, scholars have highlighted how neoliberalism has made competition a central norm of society – both in economics and in life. This leads to the subsequent questions on *why* and *how* neoliberal capitalism needs the logic of competition to operate effectively.

The *why* question is simple – it is easier to control people if they do it themselves, rather than having a sovereign power do it by force. Symbolic power, which is the power exerted by the State through the categories of perception inscribed in the habitus, is particularly effective because it is not recognized as a use of force. The origin in external power relations operating within the bureaucratic and economic fields is obscured by the co-presence of social structures within the habitus and fields, which gives externally derived categories their internal feeling. The categories are misrecognized as natural and politically neutral, which means the dominated are complicit in this process (Bourdieu 2000). As we have explained in this book so far, neoliberal policies have many negative consequences for middle- and working-class individuals, as well as the poor. Further, income inequality has been shown to rise after the implementation of neoliberal policies (Piketty 2014). In other words, large segments of populations under neoliberal capitalism are negatively impacted by policies put in place to help neoliberal capitalism flourish. The elites (i.e., politicians and business leaders) who argue for and implement these neoliberal policy measures are usually the ones who benefit from them. It is easy to see why these elites would rather have the rest of the population control themselves, rather than having to do it more authoritatively. To continue to profit from neoliberal capitalism, elites need to make sure that the majority of individuals are on board, even if these policies actually harm most of these same people. Individuals internalizing competitive norms and regulating themselves, a la governmentality, make the job of getting people to regularly act against their own self-interests quite a bit easier.

The question of *how* elites can get individuals to value competition and regulate their behavior in a manner that is amenable to neoliberal capitalism – whether it benefits them or not – is more complicated. However, this is what Foucault focused on in the first part of his definition. The "institutions, procedures, analyses and reflections, calculations, and tactics" bring the norms of competition, self-regulation, and individual responsibility to the fore, and "apparatuses of security" become the mechanisms which work to internalize those norms within individuals – to such a degree that these individuals do not even realize it is occurring. The norms of competition and individual responsibility are seemingly part of human nature, not constructions of the elites at the controls of global neoliberal capitalism. These apparatuses of security that are used to enforce these norms take the form of extensive monitoring, evaluation, and a general quantification of productivity in and out of the workplace. For self-regulation to develop and be internalized, there also needs to be a system of rewards and punishments that helps guide (and incentive) self-regulation. Due to all of this, scholars can conceptualize a distinctly neoliberal governmentality.

Neoliberal Governmentality

As we noted earlier, many scholars have worked on extending the theoretical framework of governmentality and/or employing the concept in empirical research. In our view, one of the most influential and important statements on neoliberalism, governmentality, and related topics (which we have already drawn on) is Pierre Dardot and Christian Laval's *The New Way of the World: On Neoliberal Society*, with the English translation published in 2014. We will expand on the work of Dardot and Laval later in the chapter; here, we borrow from them a simple statement regarding the relationship between neoliberalism and governmentality. "The very concept of governmentality – acting on the actions of individuals who are supposedly free to choose – makes it possible to redefine discipline as a technique of government peculiar to market societies" (Dardot and Laval 2013:168). The term "market societies" includes neoliberal capitalism. Discipline is necessarily different under neoliberalism. It becomes a technology of the self, done by individuals to themselves, because it has become the norm in neoliberal societies. Governmentality becomes the vehicle through which the State and other powerful elites regulate human behavior.

So, what exactly is "neoliberal governmentality?" Lorey (2015:34–35) provides a detailed answer to this question.

> What distinguishes [neo]liberal forms of governmentality is that the governability of each and every individual within a population always also becomes possible through the way in which they conduct themselves. The art of governing, according to Foucault, consists in conducting conduct. The power of governing is not just exercised repressively from above. Instead liberal governmental governing entails individuals having an acting influence on the actions of others, on the possibilities of conduct. Subjectivized in this way, this subject then recurrently participates in the (re-)production of the conditions for governmentality, because it is in this scenario that the possibilities of agency first arise...It is precisely through the way they conduct themselves, how they govern themselves, that individuals become amenable to social, political and economic steering and regulation.

Governing a population, as Lorey notes, is done through individuals regulating their own, and other individuals,' conduct. As we discussed earlier, this is accomplished through a norm of competition, which is instilled in the subjects of neoliberal societies (Dardot and Laval 2013). The norm of competition leads individuals to self-regulate and self-discipline in ways that will help them be victorious in the many competitions they must engage in daily. Individuals also contribute to the regulation and discipline of other individuals in neoliberal societies. Again, this happens primarily through individuals engaging against each other in competition. Individuals who don't play by the rules are sanctioned by others in the competition. This regulation and discipline of the self and others occurs because neoliberal elites set the rules of the game and have figured out how to instill within individuals the normative justification and values for this regulation and discipline. This, in turn, makes it easy for elites and the State to "steer" the behavior of individuals in directions beneficial to neoliberal global capitalism, regardless of whether it is good for the individuals or not. Neoliberal governmentality, then, is the primary form of governance in the current stage of advanced capitalism. This suggests that the *laissez faire* approach to the State, which the liberals of the eighteenth-century advocated for, was not compatible with neoliberalism. Rather, a reformation of the State to a facilitator of global capitalism became the norm under neoliberalism.

Neoliberalism, Governmentality, and the State

Foucault did not live to see neoliberalism mature. While his work, especially the Lectures, has been highly influential and prescient in unpacking how neoliberalism had impacted and changed human behavior, it was based on historical analysis of eighteenth-century liberalism and observations at the beginning of the neoliberal revolution. Rather, it has been left to subsequent generations of scholars to fill in aspects of the approach that Foucault never touched on and to expand his concepts of biopolitics, governmentality, security techniques, and the like.

One area where scholars have focused their work is closely examining the role of the State in a neoliberal capitalist society. Often, brief definitions of neoliberalism suggest that neoliberal economic policies are incompatible with State intervention, equating the approach with *laissez faire* economics. Adam Smith's "invisible hand" will regulate the market more efficiently than the State. Neoliberalism, however, does need the intervention of the State to facilitate integration with the global neoliberal capitalist field. Governments set the stage for neoliberalism to succeed (or at least, attempts to succeed). As we mentioned earlier, creating and maintaining competition is paramount for neoliberals. As Dardot and Laval (2013:47) note, "while neo-liberals accept the need for state intervention and reject pure government passivity, they are opposed to any action that might frustrate the operation of competition between private interests." How, then, do neoliberals ensure competition at all levels of society? The answer is that individuals living in neoliberal societies have internalized the norms of self-government, self-regulation, and individual responsibility. Competition is therefore an organizing principle of life under neoliberal capitalism, allowing neoliberal governmentality to structure how individuals behave. Successful individuals become entrepreneurs in all aspects of their lives, as competition is lauded as the route to happiness and a fruitful life (Dardot and Laval 2013, see also Bröckling 2016).

In short, these scholars have shown how neoliberalism has its roots in eighteenth-century liberalism, but important differences exist, the most glaring of which is an active role for the State in neoliberalism. The State is necessary to align societies as closely with the global marketplace as possible, thereby enabling competition and entrepreneurship at the individual and firm levels to foster economic growth through neoliberal means. Neoliberal governmentality provides the regulation of the self, which is necessary for individuals to develop the entrepreneurial mindset that neoliberal capitalism requires.

Scholars working in the Foucauldian tradition have demonstrated how neoliberalism highlights the role of "freedom" in society; however, insecurity also plays an important role in creating and maintaining neoliberal governmentality, as individuals continuously work toward a more secure existence. As Lemke (2014:65), with a little assistance from Foucault (2008:66), notes:

> Liberalism does not only produce freedoms, which are permanently endangered (by their own conditions of production) and require mechanisms of security. Danger and insecurity (the threat of unemployment, poverty, social deregulation, etc.) are not just unwanted consequences or negative side effects but essential conditions and positive elements of liberal freedom. In this sense, liberalism nurtures danger, its subjects enter into an economic calculus, weighing its advantages against its costs. Liberal government must never fix security, since the striving for security and the danger of insecurity are complementary aspects of liberal governmentality: "Everywhere you see this stimulation of the fear of danger which is, as it were, the condition, the internal psychological and cultural correlative of liberalism. There is no liberalism without a culture of danger" [quote from Foucault 2008:66]. This cultivation and stimulation of danger points to the moral dimension of liberal government. Individuals are expected to cope with social risks and insecurities, to measure and calculate them, taking precautions for themselves and their families. In this perspective it is entrepreneurial action, rational risk management, and individual responsibility that accounts for social success or failure.

The "fear of danger" that Foucault speaks of can easily be thought of as a fear of insecurity, a fear of the inability to predict a stable secure future. Individuals are expected to cope with that fear by becoming entrepreneurs and risk managers – individual solutions to what are conceptualized under neoliberal capitalism as individual problems. Lemke's passage highlights the relationship between neoliberal governmentality and insecurity, a topic to which we shall now focus our attention on.

Neoliberal Governmentality and Insecurity

We have argued that neoliberalism and insecurity are connected during advanced capitalism. Foucault discussed this in *Security, Territory, Population*, going so far as to refer to a "society of security" (Foucault 2007:11). Power has become less disciplinary and more focused on technologies of security, which have increased tremendously during neoliberalism. Recall, technologies of security refer to regular quantitative monitoring and evaluation of individuals. Society under neoliberalism has become about "risk management," often through technologies of security. By managing risk themselves, individuals become less reliant on the State and more entrepreneurial. In other words, individuals are now responsible for their own well-being, in all aspects of life, thereby taking the State off the hook. Ulrich Beck (1990) famously argued that we are living in a "risk society," and the management of risks (large and small) has become a daily activity for most people under neoliberalism. To manage risks, individuals are constantly assessing risks, which leads to a constant fear of failure and, as Lemke (2014:68) opines, "[f]ear fulfills an important moral function in neoliberal government. The constant threat of unemployment and poverty, and anxiety about the future, induce foresight and prudence." Insecurity leads to caution (even though, ironically, people are supposed to be entrepreneurs in life) and attempts to predict the future. The fear and anxiety that individuals regularly experience contribute to what Lemke (2014:68) refers to as the "neoliberal government of insecurity" and what Lorey (2015) has called the "government of the precarious." Insecurity is a vital component of neoliberal societies and the maintenance of order in neoliberal societies.

Insecurity as a General Concept

As noted in Chapter 1, and reiterated above, we view *insecurity* as a more general concept in the same vein as some other recent social critics (e.g., Lorey 2015; Taylor 2023). That is, we see value in studying the broader concept of insecurity, not just different forms of insecurity (e.g., food, energy, job), so much so that we believe it is one of the structuring capitals that delineate the global neoliberal capitalist field and locates individuals within it. We defined insecurity as the inability to successfully predict a stable and secure future. This is purposely a broad definition because there are many forms of insecurity (including those that we don't cover in this book, such as, housing insecurity, medical insecurity, and water insecurity), which we believe can be brought together under one umbrella definition for the purposes of theoretical advancement. Insecurity is here to stay and, as we argue, fundamental to the global neoliberal capitalist field. In the foreword to Lorey's book, Judith Butler states this point more eloquently than we do, as they note that, "precarity [insecurity] is not a passing or episodic condition, but a new form of regulation that distinguishes this historical time" (Butler in Lorey 2015:iiv).

The jump from insecurity as the inability to predict a stable and secure future to individuals becoming personal risk managers is not a long one. Risk management is a fundamental part of life in a neoliberal society. The concept of risk refers to the likelihood of severe, adverse effects resulting from a hazard or some other form of vulnerability (National Safety Council 2003) that is the result of both contextual and social structural factors (Kendra, Clay, and Gill 2018; Kroll-Smith 2018; Tierney 2014. Relatedly, risk perceptions are subjective evaluations of risk made by individuals (Paek and Hove 2017; Slovic 2000) – like the subjective element of job insecurity – where the actual level of risk (or insecurity) is unknown. People are assessing how vulnerable they are to the myriad risks in contemporary society. Although the objective probability of risk or insecurity is usually not known, individuals regularly act and make decisions based on their subjective perceptions – another strand of the self-regulation of individuals. Neoliberal governmentality requires that individuals constantly monitor their own risks – including the risk of insecurity. We now shift our attention to how neoliberal governmentality operates in the cases of food, energy, and job insecurity.

Food Insecurity

In Chapter 3, we reviewed the political economy of food insecurity, focusing on how the structural changes brought about by neoliberalism have impacted the level of food insecurity in countries in both the Global North and Global South. Recall from Chapter 1 the definition of food security/insecurity. *Food security* is a condition that is met "when all people, at all times, have physical, social and economic access to sufficient, safe and nutritious food that meets their dietary needs and food preferences for an active and healthy life" (FAO 2000:26). *Food insecurity* is the absence of food security.

Moving from the macro-level to micro-level impacts of food insecurity, the focus turns to individuals and households. It is important to note that research on food insecurity at the micro-level often focuses on households rather than on individuals (Long, Defeyter, and Stretesky 2021; Long et al. 2018). The household is seen as the more appropriate unit of analysis because, in most cases, all members of a household must be fed with the same budget and resources. In food-insecure households, particularly those with children, not everyone in the household gets an equal amount of food/calories. When food is limited in households with children, parents almost always make sure their children are adequately fed before eating themselves. While it is admirable for the parents to prioritize their children first, they often remain food insecure themselves, which can lead to many health and social consequences, all the while trying to be responsible parents. The reduced energy that comes from being food insecure can impact parents' abilities to look after their children. So, in short, micro-level food insecurity should be examined at both the individual and household levels for a comprehensive understanding of the issue.

The relationship between neoliberalism and food insecurity at the micro-level is, to little surprise, primarily about the effects of neoliberal governmentality on food-insecure households and their opportunities to reduce some of that insecurity through various forms of food aid. As we have described, neoliberal governmentality utilizes a norm of individual responsibility to convince individuals, including those who are food insecure, that the problems they face are the result of individual failures rather than structural conditions (many of which we reviewed in Chapter 3), which affects who has access to resources (including food) and who does not (Long et al. 2021).

Being food insecure and utilizing food aid (e.g., food banks and pantries) in a neoliberal world often comes with shame (e.g., Bernal, Frongillo, and Jaffe 2016; Peterson, Freidus, and Tereshenko 2022; Pineau et al. 2021; Purdam, Garratt, and Esmail 2016). Research (most of which has occurred in countries in the Global North) demonstrates that having difficulty feeding yourself and your family leads to stress and (real and perceived) stigma. You are branded by society as "poor," "not good enough," as well as other shameful labels. Criminologists have long examined the powerful (and long-lasting) effects of labeling (Becker [1963] 2018). Another way of looking at it is they lost the great neoliberal game of competition.

The poor label and the feelings of shame, stress, and anxiety that come with being food insecure also impact who takes advantage of food aid and who stays away. Some people who are food insecure do not take advantage of food banks, food pantries, and the like because they don't want to have to admit to others that they are not able to provide their household with enough food to eat and that they are poor (Defeyter, Stretesky, and Long 2019; Reutter et al. 2009). They are embarrassed. Neoliberal governmentality has convinced them that they should be embarrassed (Long et al. 2021). It is not just parents who feel shame about being poor, food insecure, and in need of food aid. Children sometimes decide to go hungry rather than use food aid that would identify them to their friends as poor. For example, research has shown that in the UK, many children who are eligible for free and reduced school lunches do not take advantage of them due to the shame and embarrassment they feel about being food insecure and needing aid (Addis and Murphy 2019; Chambers, Dundas, and Torsney 2016).

In sum, research has shown that neoliberal governmentality impacts how food insecure individuals and households act and whether they take advantage of programs and places that are designed to help people who are food insecure. Heads of households blame themselves for being unable to provide food for their families. As losers of the neoliberal race, they must take responsibility for their failures, compete harder, and try again, while keeping their gaze off the State, which has failed to provide them with opportunities for well-paying jobs and the basic human right to food – a right many countries agreed to uphold when they ratified the International Declaration of Human Rights, as discussed in Chapter 3. Neoliberal governmentality and its technologies of security have successfully regulated the food insecure.

Energy Insecurity

We turned our attention to the macro-level relationship between neoliberalism and energy insecurity in Chapter 4. As we move to an analysis of the micro-level impacts of neoliberalism and energy insecurity, we first revisit our definition of energy insecurity from Chapter 1 – *energy insecurity* can be defined as "an inability to adequately meet basic household energy needs" (Hernández 2016:2). Like the micro-level studies of food insecurity, the main unit of analysis for energy insecurity is the household – indeed, "household" is part of the energy insecurity definition. In most cases, individuals are a part of a household that is billed for the household's energy use, not individual users, and therefore a focus on the household is appropriate.

In the case of food-insecure households, we noted above that parents sometimes must make hard choices, such as eating less food themselves to make sure their children get enough to eat. Difficult choices are part of the lives of energy insecure individuals as well. One way that people address food insecurity is by not paying their utility bills (Defeyter, Graham, and Prince 2015), in essence, trading energy security for temporary relief from food insecurity – a decision that has come to be referred to as "heat or eat." Households often must play the game of which type of insecurity is less bad. Most of the time purchasing food to stave off hunger for another day wins out over paying energy bills – even during the very cold and very hot times of year, when a lack of heating and air conditioning can make life very uncomfortable, and life threatening in some instances. In some of our earlier research, we encountered people who were so energy insecure that they would regularly forgo hot, cooked meals because they could not afford to turn their stoves on to cook food (Long et al. 2021). Insecurity exacerbates other forms of insecurity. As we noted in Chapter 1, the intersection of insecurities is a core element of our approach to the study of insecurity.

Neoliberal governmentality works on the energy insecure in much the same way as the food insecure. This is primarily due to two reasons. First, the food insecure and energy insecure are often the same individuals and households. Second, the norms of competition and individual responsibility in the neoliberal world apply to energy insecurity just as they apply to food insecurity. Energy-insecure households have only themselves to blame for their lack of energy. They need to do better and work harder, and neoliberal capitalism will reward them – in this case – with basic energy needs. From a hierarchy of needs perspective (Maslow 1943, 1954), most would agree that food is a more basic need than energy. However, as we have noted above and in Chapter 3, there is a tremendous amount of food aid available through food banks, pantries, and other means to help alleviate food insecurity. While we have noted a number of problems with the food aid model briefly in this book, and in more detail elsewhere (Defeyter et al. 2019; Long et al.

2021; Long, Gonçalves, Stretesky, and Defeyter 2020), options do exist for those willing to use them to help reduce household food insecurity – at least temporarily. Similar options do not exist for energy insecurity. There are no meaningful "energy aid" organizations that help people with their immediate energy needs on a regular basis, if necessary. Energy-insecure households are usually left to "make do" with blankets/wearing outdoor clothes indoors during the cold months and suffering through the heat during the hot months, all the while not being sure whether you will have enough energy to cook meals for the household.

Job Insecurity

In Chapter 5, the third and final chapter that examined the macro-level effects of neoliberalism on insecurity, we reviewed the structural impacts of neoliberalism on work and job insecurity. Food and energy insecurity, as we have noted, are primarily measured and understood at the micro-level, using the household as the unit of analysis. Job insecurity, however, can be primarily conceptualized as an individual phenomenon. Returning to our definition of job insecurity from Chapter 1, *job insecurity* has two components: "cognitive job insecurity" and "affective job insecurity." "'Cognitive job insecurity' is an individual's estimate of the probability of job loss in the near future, while 'affective job insecurity' refers to worry or anxiety about losing one's job." (Anderson and Pontusson 2007:214).

While food and energy insecurity are similar in many ways, including those who are food insecure are also often energy insecure and vice versa, job insecurity is different. While there is undoubtedly some overlap between individuals who are food, energy, and job insecure, job insecurity can and does affect individuals of any social class or income level, not just the poor. High-wage earners can be job insecure, just as people who work for minimum wage. Job insecurity, then, is a strong actor in the government of the precarious. In fact, Dardot and Laval (2013:180) suggest that a flexible labor market, with perpetually insecure workers, is an essential part of neoliberal governmentality.

> Self-government of the self is not spontaneously obtained merely by the impact of a deductive managerial discourse manipulating everyone's aspirations to autonomy. The control of subjectivity only works effectively in the context of a flexible labour market where the threat of unemployment is on the horizon of every wage-earner.

Job insecurity is used as a motivator by business and firm managers to raise the productivity of workers. Produce more or you will lose your job. This leads to self-regulation and self-monitoring to increase productivity by workers, as they try to alleviate some of the job insecurity and the related physical and mental health problems that often accompany job insecurity (Burgard et al. 2009; Ferrie et al. 2005; Fullerton et al. 2020). One could argue that governing through job insecurity is one of neoliberal capitalism's greatest achievements. Workers keep themselves in line through constantly striving to be the most productive worker – self-regulation through competition; neoliberal governmentality, indeed.

Bourdieu (1998) refers to this self-regulation imposed by neoliberalism as a new "mode of domination." As with other sociosymbolic modes of domination, such as racial domination (Wacquant 2024) or masculine domination (Bourdieu 2001), the neoliberal mode of domination is composed of symbolic and material elements. The same insecurity-inducing neoliberal structures, existing in objectified form within fields, are also inscribed within the habitus. They thus shape the entrepreneurial view of the self that has become the norm, fostering the tendency to blame individuals for failures that stem from larger structural changes, including welfare state retrenchment and the deregulation of labor markets (Wacquant 2009). It is the agreement between the neoliberal habitus and its classificatory schemes (i.e., the symbolic), and the space of neoliberal capitalism and its social positions characterized by different objective probabilities of insecurity (i.e., the material), that give neoliberal ideology its magical quality. It allows it to be misrecognized as "natural" or "obvious" rather than the result of struggles for control within the bureaucratic and economic fields that favor proponents of the neoliberal project. One does not stop to question why failure in the neoliberal competition is an individual moral shortcoming because one is simply too busy competing to even recognize it as a game.

The Insecure Neoliberal Subject

It should be clear at this point that we believe insecurity (in its many forms and more generally) is an integral part of the global neoliberal capitalist field, which we outlined in Chapter 1. It is part of the process of how neoliberalism has remade individuals in its own image. We return to Dardot and Laval (2013) one last time to remind us that, "the neo-liberal moment is characterized by a homogenization of the discourse of man around the figure of the enterprise...Henceforth various techniques help to manufacture the new unitary subject, which we shall variously call the 'entrepreneurial subject' or 'the new-liberal subject,' or, more simply, the *neo-subject*" (Dardot and Laval 2013:259–260). Humans must become enterprises unto themselves, in which they are governed by an "entrepreneurial governmentality" (Dardot and Laval 2013:261) to succeed in a neoliberal world.

Central to the concept of a "neoliberal subject," who is governed by entrepreneurial governmentality, is competition. Life is a competition. Success in life follows victory in competition. While competition works out well for the winners, the losers get more insecure. Competition, therefore, leads to insecurity for some of those in the competition. It is also important to remember that this is not some kind of negative side-effect of neoliberal capitalism. Rather, this is exactly how the system is designed to work. Without the threat of losing, what would motivate individuals and households to fully embrace the neoliberal competitive way of life?

The answer for individuals is simple – make sure you win the important competitions in your life. This will reduce insecurity. Or will it? Successfully predicting the future (i.e., being "secure") is not easy, especially given how many forms of insecurity exist in the global neoliberal capitalist field, along with the number of competitions individuals must engage in daily. Insecurity is insidious. Even when someone may be objectively "secure" by a number of measures (i.e., technologies of security), the subjective aspects of insecurity are always lurking in the background. Therefore, in our case, we suggest that an "insecure neoliberal subject" is a fundamental actor within the global neoliberal capitalist field.

Bourdieu and the Insecure Neoliberal Subject

We now need to return to our theory of practice framework. This allows us to demonstrate how the theory of practice approach helps us bypass the binary of structural vs. individual level impacts of neoliberalism, insecurity, and their association.

Recall that Bourdieu used his concept of "habitus" to avoid/transcend dualism. The habitus is influenced by both structural and individual level factors, and it operates on an unconscious level. "Dispositions," to use Bourdieu's word, are behavior patterns learned by individuals – consciously or unconsciously – that "are the product of the conditions of existence" (Bourdieu 2020:132). We argue that insecurity is a fundamental part of a neoliberal habitus and shapes an individual's dispositions. We believe that this is similar to how neoliberal governmentality works to elevate the norms of competition and individual responsibility through self-regulation. The insecure neoliberal subject has a neoliberal habitus , which is the embodiment of past structures rooted in neoliberal philosophy, policy, and ideology. The neoliberal habitus encourages self-regulation and competition, just as neoliberal governmentality does.

Getting people to regulate themselves rather than regulating them by law and/or physical force – in Foucault's terminology, governmentality – is the essence of Bourdieu's concept of symbolic power, which we covered in Chapter 1 and have occasionally referenced throughout the book. To reiterate our argument, neoliberal governmentality transforms individuals into insecure neoliberal subjects through the process of symbolic power, whereby

State-sanctioned categories of perception are inscribed in the habitus and find their counterpart in the objective structures within social spaces and fields, which makes them appear natural and allows them to be taken for granted. In other words, they become common sense and influence actions at an unconscious, practical level (Bourdieu 1991, 2000). The power of neoliberalism derives from its symbolic roots. Symbolic power operates through the implicit consent of the dominated due to the seemingly natural quality of the neoliberal worldview it instills within neoliberal subjects and the invisibility of the exercise of power required to turn a political ideology into seemingly "free" choices of individuals. A mode of domination completely dependent on the use of physical force would be far less effective.

Homo economicus is objectified and institutionalized in social space, in addition to being internalized within the neoliberal habitus. As we mentioned earlier, it is the fact that the habitus and the structures residing within social space are both structured by neoliberalism that allows people to take it for granted and misrecognize it. This "double life" of the social (embodied within individuals and objectified within fields) is at the heart of Bourdieu's theory of practice and is critical to understanding why the entrepreneurial view of the self holds so much power over individuals struggling to secure a stable future.

Conclusion

This chapter concludes our four-chapter section on (1) the macro-level relationship between neoliberalism and insecurity, with particular emphasis on food, energy, and job insecurity, and (2) the micro-level association between neoliberalism and insecurity. Taken together, these four chapters were meant to do a few things: first, provide an overview of the issues of food, energy, and job insecurity at the macro- and micro-levels of analysis; second, demonstrate how neoliberalism and insecurity are associated at both the individual and structural levels; third, highlight how a perspective that transcends macro-micro dichotomy in the study of neoliberalism and insecurity – both separately and together – would be a useful addition to the literature.

As we noted in Chapter 1, we use an approach based on Bourdieu's theory of practice (Bourdieu 1977, 1984, 1990) to simultaneously understand (and bridge) the individual and structural impacts of neoliberalism on insecurity. We posited the existence of a global neoliberal capitalist field, where individuals are located in that field through a combination of their economic and security capitals. In the following chapter, we put this theory into practice. We designed a survey to better understand insecurity in the space of US neoliberal capitalism, and then administered that survey to a representative sample of US residents. Following Bourdieu (1984) and other scholars in his tradition, we conduct a multiple correspondence analysis on the data to get a glimpse of the structure of that space.

References

Addis, Samia and Simon Murphy. 2019. "Free School Meals: Socio-Ecological Influences on School Level Take Up of Entitlement." *British Journal of School Nursing* 13(8): https://doi.org/10.12968/bjsn.2018.13.8.394.

Anderson, Christopher J. and Jonas Pontusson. 2007. "Workers, Worries and Welfare States: Social Protection and Job Insecurity in 15 OECD Countries." *European Journal of Political Research* 46(2): 211–235. https://doi.org/10.1111/j.1475-6765.2007.00692.x.

Beck, Ulrich. 1990. *World Risk Society*. Cambridge: Polity Press.

Becker, Howard S. [1963] 2018. *Outsiders: Studies in the Sociology of Deviance*. New York: Free Press.

Bernal, Jennifer, Edward A. Frongillo, and Klaus Jaffe. 2016. "Food Insecurity of Children and Shame of Others Knowing They Are without Food." *Journal of Hunger & Environmental Nutrition* 11(2): 180–194.

Bourdieu, Pierre. 2020. *Habitus and Field: General Sociology, Volume 2. Lectures at the Collège de France, 1982–1983*. Cambridge: Polity Press.

Bourdieu, Pierre. 2001. *Masculine Domination*. Stanford, CA: Stanford University Press.

Bourdieu, Pierre. 2000. *Pascalian Meditations*. Stanford, CA: Stanford University Press.

Bourdieu, Pierre. 1991. *Language & Symbolic Power*. Cambridge, MA: Harvard University Press.

Bourdieu, Pierre. 1990. *The Logic of Practice*. Stanford, CA: Stanford University Press.

Bourdieu, Pierre. 1984. *Distinction: A Social Critique of the Judgement of Taste*. Cambridge, MA: Harvard University Press.

Bourdieu, Pierre. 1977. *Outline of a Theory of Practice*. Cambridge: Cambridge University Press.

Bröckling, Ulrich. 2016. *The Entrepreneurial Self: Fabricating a New Type of Subject*. Thousand Oaks, CA: Sage.

Brubaker, Rogers. 2023. *Hyperconnectivity and Its Discontents*. Cambridge: Polity Press.

Burgard, Sarah A., Jennie E. Brand, and James S. House. 2009. "Perceived Job Insecurity and Worker Health in the United States." *Social Science and Medicine* 69: 777–785.

Chambers, Stephanie, Ruth Dundas, and Ben Torsney. 2016. "School and Local Authority Characteristics Associated with Take-up of Free School Meals in Scottish Secondary Schools, 2014." *Contemporary Social Science* 11(1): 52–63.

Dardot, Pierre and Christian Laval. 2013. *The New Way of the World*. London and New York: Verso.

Defeyter, Margaret Anne, Pamela Louise Graham, and Kate Prince. 2015. "A Qualitative Evaluation of Holiday Breakfast Clubs in the UK: Views of Adult Attendees, Children, and Staff." *Frontiers in Public Health* 3: 199. https://doi.org/10.3389/fpubh.2015.00199.

Defeyter, Margaret Anne, Paul B. Stretesky, and Michael A. Long. 2019. "Holiday Hunger: The Government Must Remove the Inequalities in Children's Access to Holiday Clubs." *The BMJ Opinion*. Available at: https://blogs.bmj.com/bmj/2019/10/23/holiday-hunger-the-government-must-remove-the-inequalities-in-childrens-access-to-holiday-clubs/.

Ferrie, Jane E., Martin J. Shipley, Katherine Newman, Stephen A. Stansfeld, and Michael Marmot. 2005. "Self-Reported Job Insecurity and Health in the Whitehall

II Study: Potential Explanations of the Relationship." *Social Science & Medicine* 60: 1593–1602.

Food and Agriculture Organisation of the United Nations (FAO). 2000. *The State of Food Security and Nutrition in the World*. Rome, Italy: FAO (accessed January 26, 2024). https://www.fao.org/publications/home/fao-flagship-publications/the-state-of-food-security-and-nutrition-in-the-world/en.

Foucault, Michel. 2008. *The Birth of Biopolitics: Lectures at the Collège de France, 1978–1979*. New York: Palgrave Macmillan.

Foucault, Michel. 2007. *Security, Territory Population: Lectures at the Collège de France, 1977–1978*. New York: Palgrave Macmillan.

Foucault, Michel. 2003. *Society Must Be Defended: Lectures at the Collège de France, 1975–1976*. New York: Palgrave Macmillan.

Fourcade, Marion and Kieran Healy. 2024. *The Ordinal Society*. Cambridge, MA: Harvard University Press.

Fullerton, Andrew S., Destinee B. McCollum, Jeffrey C. Dixon, and Kathryn Freeman Anderson. 2020. "The Insecurity Gradient in Health: How Inequality in the Distribution of Job Insecurity Matters for the Relationship between Job Insecurity and Self-Rated Health in Europe." *The Sociological Quarterly* 61: 107–127.

Gros, Frédéric. 2014. "The Fourth Age of Security." Pp. 7–28 in *The Government of Life: Foucault, Biopolitics, and Neoliberalism*, edited by Vanessa Lemm and Miguel Vatter. New York: Fordham University Press.

Hernández, Diana. 2016. "Understanding 'Energy Insecurity' and Why It Matters to Health." *Social Science & Medicine* 167: 1–10. https://doi.org/10.1016/j.socscimed.2016.08.029.

Kendra, James M., Lauren Clay, and Kimberly Gill. 2018. "Resilience and Disasters." Pp. 87–107 in *The Handbook of Disaster Research*, edited by Havidan Rodriguez, William Donner, and Joseph E. Trainor. New York: Springer.

Kroll-Smith, Steve. 2018. *Recovering Inequality*. Austin: University of Texas Press.

Lemke, Thomas. 2014. "The Risks of Security: Liberalism, Biopolitics, and Fear." Pp. 59–76 in *The Government of Life: Foucault, Biopolitics, and Neoliberalism*, edited by Vanessa Lemm and Miguel Vatter. New York: Fordham University Press.

Lemke, Thomas. 2002. "Foucault, Governmentality, and Critique." *Rethinking Marxism: A Journal of Economics, Culture & Society* 14: 49–64. https://doi.org/10.1080/089356902101242288.

Lemm, Vanessa and Miguel Vatter (eds.). 2014. *The Government of Life: Foucault, Biopolitics, and Neoliberalism*. New York: Fordham University Press.

Lemm, Vanessa and Miguel Vatter. 2014. "Introduction." Pp. 1–16 in *The Government of Life: Foucault, Biopolitics, and Neoliberalism*, edited by Vanessa Lemm and Miguel Vatter. New York: Fordham University Press.

Long, Michael A., Lara Gonçalves, Paul B. Stretesky and Margaret Anne Defeyter. 2020. "Food Insecurity in Advanced Capitalist Nations: A Review." *Sustainability* 12 (9): 3654.

Long, Michael, Margaret Anne Defeyter, and Paul B. Stretesky. 2021. *Holiday Hunger in the UK: Local Responses to Childhood Food Insecurity*. New York: Routledge.

Long, Michael A., Paul B. Stretesky, Pamela Louise Graham, Katie Jane Palmer, Eileen Steinbock, and Margaret Anne Defeyter. 2018. "The Impact of Holiday Clubs on Household Food Insecurity – A Pilot Study." *Health & Social Care in the Community* 26(2): e261–e269.

Lorey, Isabell. 2015. *State of Insecurity: Government of the Precarious.* New York: Verso.

Maslow, Abraham. H. 1954. *Motivation and Personality.* New York: Harper and Row.

Maslow, Abraham H. 1943. "A Theory of Human Motivation." *Psychological Review* 50(4): 370–396. https://doi.org/10.1037/h0054346.

Muhle, Maria. 2014. "A Genealogy of Biopolitics: The Notion of Life in Canguilhem and Foucault." Pp. 77–97 in *The Government of Life: Foucault, Biopolitics, and Neoliberalism*, edited by Vanessa Lemm and Miguel Vatter. New York: Fordham University Press.

National Safety Council. 2003. *Risk Perception: Theories, Strategies, and Next Steps.* Ithaca, NY: Campbell Institute. Available at: https://www.thecampbellinstitute.org/wp-content/uploads/2017/05/Campbell-Institute-Risk-Perception-WP.pdf.

Paek, Hye-Jin and Thomas Hove. 2017. "Risk Perceptions and Risk Characteristics." *Oxford Research Encyclopedias* (accessed September 9, 2021). https://bit.ly/3hnJeJM.

Peterson, Nicole, Andrea Freidus, and Dmitry Tereshenko. 2022. "Why College Students Don't Access Resources for Food Insecurity: Stigma and Perceptions of Need." *Annals of Anthropological Practice* 46(2): 140–154. https://doi.org/10.1111/napa.12190.

Piketty, Thomas. 2014. *Capital in the Twenty-First Century.* Cambridge, MA: Harvard University Press.

Pineau, Chloe, Patricia L. Williams, Jennifer Brady, Madeleine Waddington, and Lesley Frank. 2021. "Exploring Experiences of Food Insecurity, Stigma, Social Exclusion, and Shame among Women in High-Income Countries: A Narrative Review." *Canadian Food Studies* 8(3). https://doi.org/10.15353/cfs-rcea.v8i3.473.

Purdam, Kingsley, Elisabeth A. Garratt, and Aneez Esmail. 2016. "Hungry? Food Insecurity, Social Stigma and Embarrassment in the UK." *Sociology* 50(6): 1072–1088. https://doi.org/10.1177/0038038515594092.

Reutter, Linda I., Miriam J. Stewart, Gerry Veenstra, Rhonda Love, Dennis Raphael, and Edward Makwarimba. 2009. "Who Do They Think We Are, Anyway?: Perceptions of and Responses to Poverty and Stigma." *Qualitative Health Research* 19(3): 297–311. https://doi.org/10.1177/1049732308330246.

Slovic, Paul. 2000. *The Perception of Risk.* 1st ed. New York: Earthscan Publications.

Taylor, Astra. 2023. *The Age of Insecurity: Coming Together as Things Fall Apart.* Toronto, CA: House of Anansi Press.

Tierney, Kathleen. 2014. *The Social Roots of Risk.* Stanford, CA: Stanford University Press.

Wacquant, Loïc. 2009. *Punishing the Poor: The Neoliberal Government of Social Insecurity.* Durham, NC: Duke University Press.

Wacquant, Loïc. 2024. *Racial Domination.* Cambridge: Polity Press.

Zuboff, Shoshana. 2019. *The Age of Surveillance Capitalism: The Fight for a Human Future.* New York: PublicAffairs.

7

THE SPACE OF US NEOLIBERAL CAPITALISM

The previous six chapters have set the stage for our empirical analysis of the space of US neoliberal capitalism, which we undertake in this chapter. Before we jump into the methods and results of this study, we recap *what* we have covered in Chapters 1–6. In addition, we remind the readers *why* we covered what we have up to this point. It is easy to get "lost in the trees" of discussions of individual types of insecurity or the many effects of neoliberalism on the world and individuals. Here, we want to refocus on the metaphorical "forest" by reviewing the overall argument and rationale for crafting the first six chapters the way we did. This discussion will lead into our empirical analysis of the space of US neoliberal capitalism.

We began Chapter 1 by noting that two complex, multifaceted concepts – "neoliberalism" and "insecurity" – and their interrelation are the focus of this book. We suggested that the story starts a bit before the neoliberal revolution of the late 1970s and early 1980s, tracing the genesis of the ideas that became neoliberalism in the post-WWII period. This is the period we defined as "advanced capitalism." Recognizing the limitations and difficulties of defining neoliberalism, we noted that, in general, neoliberalism can be thought of at two levels of analysis. First, it is a structural political economic perspective that elevates entrepreneurialism, protection of private property rights, free markets, and trade, arguing that they lead to economic development and growth for all (Harvey 2005). Second, neoliberalism remakes cultural norms in a way that prioritizes individual competition (Dardot and Laval 2014) and creates Foucault's (2008) *homo economicus*. We then turned our attention to the concept of insecurity: food insecurity, energy insecurity, and job insecurity. We then argued that the broader concept of "insecurity" should also be studied for theoretical advancement. Building from the

DOI: 10.4324/9781003326892-7

scholarship of others (Lorey 2015; Taylor 2023), we defined insecurity as *the inability to successfully predict a stable and secure future.*

At this juncture, with our main concepts established and defined, we decided upon a theoretical and empirical approach based on Bourdieu's (1977, 1984, 1990) "theory of practice." We chose this approach to help bridge the dualism of structural vs. individual explications of neoliberalism and its effects that dominate the literature. We briefly outlined the theory of practice, with separate sections on the three main components of the theory of practice: field, habitus, and capital. This brought us to how a theory of practice framework could be used to help understand the global neoliberal capitalist field. We posited the existence of a global neoliberal capitalist field, which is structured by the amount and composition of economic capital and security capital. Individuals operating in the neoliberal capitalist field would then have a neoliberal habitus that orients their dispositions and actions.

We then turned our attention to the history of neoliberalism (Chapter 2), the structural political economic relationships between neoliberalism and food insecurity (Chapter 3), energy insecurity (Chapter 4), job insecurity (Chapter 5), and, the micro-level effects of neoliberalism on individuals/households generally and on the three types of insecurity that were covered in the previous three chapters (Chapter 6). Chapters 3–6 were designed to do a few things. First, to clearly connect food, energy, and job insecurity to neoliberalism, both at the macro- and micro-levels. Second, detailing the structural and individual impacts of neoliberalism on insecurity highlights the need for a perspective that can incorporate both types of impacts and, in some ways, transcends the dualism of structural vs. individual-level understandings of neoliberalism. Finally, to continue to make our case for studying "insecurity" not only in specific forms (e.g., food, energy, job, housing, medical, water) as they are frequently studied, but also as a more general concept that is part of structuring life in the global neoliberal capitalist field. All of this sets the stage for our theory of practice-based investigation of the relationship between neoliberalism and insecurity.

The current chapter provides an empirical examination of the *space of US neoliberal capitalism.* Throughout the first six chapters of this book, we have often referred to the *global neoliberal capitalist field*; however, our empirical example is of the *space of US neoliberal capitalism.* We chose this route, primarily for convenience of data collection. The global neoliberal capitalist field is a meta-field connecting national social spaces across the globe. Within countries, such as the US, we refer to the *space* of neoliberal capitalism rather than the *field* to reflect the often-overlooked difference between a field and a social space, using Bourdieu's terminology. A field is a particular type of social space "arising when a domain of action becomes sufficiently demarcated, autonomized, and monopolized" (Wacquant 2019:17). This applies to domains such as art (Bourdieu 1996) and politics/bureaucracy (Bourdieu

2014). We refer to the global field of neoliberal capitalism, which is a meta-field connecting national neoliberal capitalist spaces.[1] In a particular country, such as the US, the space of neoliberal capitalism lacks the barriers to entry and self-governing features of formal fields. The national neoliberal capitalist space is a multidimensional space combining the spaces of different forms of insecurity (e.g., food, energy, and labor). The space of US neoliberal capitalism is nested within the larger global neoliberal capitalist field. As a result, there will be substantial homologies between the US space and the global neoliberal capitalist field, including the structuring capitals (economic and security) and the location of the dominant and dominated poles.

In much of his empirical work, Bourdieu eschewed linear modeling in favor of geometric data analysis techniques, in particular correspondence analysis (CA) and multiple correspondence analysis (MCA) (Hjellbrekke 2019; Le Roux and Rouanet 2010). The utilization of CA and MCA allowed Bourdieu to locate actors within a multidimensional space[2] (i.e., in Bourdieu's terminology, a "social space" or "field") based on the composition of the structuring capitals of that social space (e.g., Bourdieu 1984). In other words, CA and MCA allow us to engage in a theory of practice-based empirical analysis. We have gathered survey data from individuals in the US on economic and security capital; in what follows, we use MCA to locate individuals in the space of US neoliberal capitalism.

Methodology

The Survey

To better understand the space of US neoliberal capitalism and its structuring capitals (economic and security), we designed and administered a survey to a representative sample of US residents. The full survey can be found in Appendix B. The survey has sections of questions on the following: the respondent's family situation growing up, the respondent's employment situation, level of job (in)security, energy use and bills, energy (in)security, food (in)security, financial literacy, adaptations to insecurity, contact with the criminal justice system, and sociodemographics. The full survey was then entered into the Qualtrics XM platform to create an online version, which could be made available to respondents virtually. The survey was administered in early June 2024.

Data Collection and the Sample

The survey and related materials were approved by the Oklahoma State University (OSU) Institutional Review Board (IRB) in the late Spring of 2024. After IRB approval, we administered the survey online through the

Prolific platform (https://www.prolific.com/). Prolific is an online service that provides research participants for studies. It has been widely used in social scientific studies to recruit participants. The inclusion criteria were simple: the participants should be 18 years or older, and the sample must be representative of the broader US population. The final sample size was n = 1,013. We now turn to a discussion of the variables that we employed in our forthcoming analysis.

Sample for MCA

We restricted the sample in a few ways before dropping missing cases in order to conduct the MCA. First, we dropped two respondents who failed the attention test question included on the questionnaire to maintain high-quality responses to the survey questions.[3] Second, we included several job-related measures of economic and security capital. Therefore, we dropped 365 respondents who were either unemployed (93) or not in the labor force (272). Finally, we dropped an additional 98 respondents with missing data on one or more variables included in the analysis. The final sample size for the MCA is 548.

Active Variables

There are two types of variables in MCA: active variables, which contribute to the construction of the clouds of individuals and categories, and supplementary variables, which do not contribute to the construction but allow researchers to analyze the structure of the data by placing these categories within the existing cloud of categories (Le Roux and Rouanet 2010:9). The two forms of capital structuring the space of US neoliberal capitalism are economic and security capital. In MCA, the number of categories in a variable determines its influence in the model. Therefore, following the advice of Le Roux and Rounet 2010 (p.38), we avoid the inclusion of variables with a disproportionate number of categories. In some cases, this required recoding variables with a large number of categories (e.g., income).

We include eight indicators of economic capital in the model, which are direct or indirect measures of economic resources. The first measure, *Full-Time Employment* (1 = full-time, 0 = part-time), is based on self-reports and included as an indirect indicator of employed-based economic resources, given its association with wages and fringe benefits. The second measure, *Family Income*, is a 14-category ordinal variable recoded into approximately the bottom, middle, and top third of the distribution (low, medium, and high income). The next four measures are binary indicators of financial accounts or investments: individual retirement account (*IRA*), *Stocks* (or mutual funds), an interest-earning *Checking Account,* and a *Savings Account. Health*

Insurance is included as a measure of economic capital, given that it is a fringe benefit associated with "good" jobs (Kalleberg, Reskin, and Hudson 2000). Finally, *Home Owner* is an indicator that one owns, rather than rents, one's house or apartment.

We include ten measures of security capital in the analysis. These are information-based resources, providing a sense of confidence in the future in the realms of jobs and finances, food, and energy. This information is a form of neoliberal cultural capital that is both embodied within individuals (finding expression in knowledge, preferences, and financial decision) and objectified in fields. The first measure is an indicator of financial literacy, which is basic financial knowledge that individuals need to successfully navigate the space of US neoliberal capitalism. It is based on three standard questions tapping aspects of *Financial Literacy*, including savings interest, inflation, and the difference between risks associated with individual stocks and mutual funds (see Stolper and Walter 2017 and Appendix B) (1 = answered all three basic questions correctly, 0 = else).[4] *Financial Advisor* is a binary indicator of whether or not one has met with a financial advisor to discuss investment or retirement goals in the past 12 months (1 = yes, 0 = no). We also include three employment-related variables promoting confidence in a stable future. *Self-Employment* is a measure of owning one's own business (1) rather than working for an employer (0). Self-employed workers have a fundamentally different relation to job insecurity, given that they have control over their own business, although that is not a guarantee of future stability. *Job Tenure* is a measure of the length of time one has been working for one's current employer (1 = low [< one year], 2 = medium [one to five years], 3 = high [> five years). This measure is commonly used as a proxy for "objective" job insecurity, but it is at best an indirect indicator of future job stability. The third employment measure, *Labor Union*, indicates membership in a labor union (1 = yes, 0 = no).

The measures of security capital we have introduced so far are traditional, job- and financial-based indicators. The second set of measures are not derived from jobs or financial institutions. We include one measure related to food security capital, *Garden/Animals*. This measure is based on questions regarding whether the respondent has a home garden for growing their own food (e.g., a vegetable garden) or animals at home used to make food products (e.g., goats or chickens). We combined these two measures into a single binary indicator of whether someone has at least one of the two alternative sources of food security (1 = garden or animals [or both], 0 = neither) given that only 4% of respondents had animals used for food, and categories with < 5% of cases should be pooled with other categories in MCA due to their disproportionate influence on the analysis (Le Roux and Rounet 2010:39). We also include two measures of energy security capital. *Generator* and *Alternative Energy* are binary indicators of the possession of a back-up electricity generator and alternative energy sources (e.g., solar panels), respectively. Finally, we include two additional indirect indicators of stability (or the lack of it) rooted in two different institutions: education and the penal system. Education is typically included as a measure of cultural capital (e.g., Bourdieu 1984), and given its importance in the labor market, it serves as an indirect measure of confidence in the future, reflecting the knowledge and advantages associated with educational credentials. Therefore, we include *Degree* in the analysis (1 = high school degree or less, 2 = some college, 3 = college degree or more). Finally, given the "mark" of a criminal record (Pager 2007), we include *Criminal Record* (1 = yes, 0 = no), which indicates whether one has ever been convicted of a crime other than a minor traffic offense. A criminal record serves as a negative resource promoting lack of confidence in a stable future, given the challenges it poses for job seekers.

Supplementary Variables

The supplementary variables we include in the cloud of categories consist of traditional measures of food, energy, and job insecurity, as well as several sociodemographic measures. *Food Insecurity* is measured using a combination of six indicators that assess how individuals may have been unable to meet basic needs, both in terms of the quantity and quality of food they consumed over the past 12 months. For the three-category measures, often true and sometimes true are combined, and the six indicators are combined into a summary scale, which is then recoded into a four-category measure consistent with the standard measure of food insecurity used in the literature.[5] Although we refer to the measure as food insecurity, we use the standard category labels from the literature (1 = food security, 2 = marginal food security, 3 = low food security, and 4 = very low food security). We include two measures of energy insecurity commonly used in the literature. *Energy Insecurity* is a count of the number of ways (from 0 to 6) that one has cut back on fuel use at home over the past 12 months because of the cost (see Question 27 in the survey in the Appendix).[6] Due to the small number of people who cut back on fuel use in all six ways (2.74%), we combined categories 5 and 6. *Affective Energy Insecurity* is the extent to which one worries about paying for energy bills (1 = not at all worried [low], 2 = not very worried [med.], 3 = fairly worried [high], and 4 = very worried [very high]). *Job Insecurity* is an additive index of one measure of cognitive job insecurity (perceived likelihood of job loss in the next 12 months) and one measure of affective job insecurity (extent of worrying about the threat of job loss). We collapsed the categories for the highest levels of insecurity due to the small number of cases in those categories. The resulting measure contains four levels of job insecurity, combining the cognitive and affective elements (1 = very low, 2 = low, 3 = medium, and 4 = high).[7]

We also include a few sociodemographic measures as supplementary variables in the analyses. They are placed in the figures generated by MCA, but do not contribute to the construction of the axes (Le Roux and Rouanet 2010). *Age* is grouped into four intervals (1 = 19–34, 2 = 35–45, 3 = 46–59, and 4 = 60–82). *Gender* is a measure of gender identification with three categories (1 = male, 2 = female, and 3 = non-binary). *Race/Ethnicity* is a measure of racial/ethnic identification with four categories (1 = white, 2 = African American, 3 = Latinx, and 4 = other races or multiple races). Finally, we also include binary measures of *Marital Status* (1 = Married, 0 = Not Married) and *Father's Education* (1 = College or More, 0 = Some College or Less). There are other supplementary variables we could have included, but we are limiting our focus to these measures for ease of presentation and to present an illustration of the neoliberal capitalist space rather than offer the most comprehensive possible treatment of the model. We present the frequency distributions for each variable in Table 7.1.

Method

We examine the space of US neoliberal capitalism using MCA, which is a geometric data analysis technique that is fundamentally different from the standard regression approach utilized in extant studies of insecurity. Rather than designating variables as independent or dependent variables, MCA takes a more inductive approach that begins with a table of individuals cross-classified by variables structuring the space (Rouanet, Ackermann, and Roux 2000; Le Roux et al. 2008; Le Roux and Rouanet 2010). Clouds of variable categories and individuals are constructed based on the variables included in the model through the construction of principal axes (each with its own variance) and the placement of the individuals and categories in the constructed space. In the MCA, we present in this chapter, we model a two-dimensional space, and we rely on our interpretation of the placement of categories and individuals within the space to interpret the axes. As geometric techniques, CA and MCA are ideally suited to relational inquiries, which is why Bourdieu used these techniques to study various fields and social spaces (see Bourdieu 1984, 1988, 1996, 2005).

The sample utilized in the analysis is restricted in two important ways. First, to consider job insecurity along with food and energy insecurity, we limit the sample to respondents that are currently employed, given that job insecurity is operationalized as the expectation of future job loss and is therefore only asked of those currently employed. Second, we briefly discussed the power of the State to exert symbolic violence in the form of the classification of individuals as criminal (vs. non-criminal) and the confinement of those convicted of certain crimes (see Chapter 1). The members of the incarcerated population in the US typically entered the prison system with a high risk of

TABLE 7.1 Variables Included in a Multiple Correspondence Analysis (MCA) of the Space of US Neoliberal Capitalism

Active Variables	
Economic Capital	*Percent*
Full-Time Employment	
Full-time	73.36
Part-time	26.64
Family Income	
Low income	21.90
Med. income	46.17
High income	31.93
IRA	
Has IRA	67.34
No IRA	32.66
Stocks	
Stocks	52.55
No stocks	47.45
Checking	
Interest-earning checking account	57.85
No checking account	42.15
Savings	
Savings account	81.20
No savings account	18.80
Health Insurance	
Health insurance	89.60
No health insurance	10.40
Home Owner	
Owns home/apartment	62.96
Rents home/apartment	37.04
Security Capital	
Job (and Financial) Security Measures	
Financial Literacy	
Financially literate	66.42
Not financially literate	33.58
Financial Advisor	
Has financial advisor	19.89
No financial advisor	80.11
Self-Employment	
Self-employed	19.71
Wage/salary worker	80.29

(*Continued*)

TABLE 7.1 (Continued)

Active Variables	
Economic Capital	*Percent*
Job Tenure	
Low (< one year)	10.58
Medium (one to five years)	41.79
High (> five years)	47.63
Labor Union	
Union member	7.12
Not union member	92.88
Food/Energy Security Measures	
Garden/Animals	
Has home garden or animals	29.56
No garden or animals	70.44
Generator	
Has backup generator	20.80
No backup generator	79.20
Alternative Energy	
Has alternative energy source	10.77
No alternative energy source	89.23
Degree	
High school or less	9.85
Some college	22.99
College degree or more	67.15
Criminal Record	
Criminal record	9.85
No criminal record	90.15
Supplementary Variables	
Traditional Measures of Food, Energy, and Job Insecurity	
Food Insecurity	
Food security	64.05
Marginal food security	9.31
Low food security	12.96
Very low food security	13.69
Energy Insecurity (Ways of Cutting Back on Fuel Use)	
None [very low]	33.58
One [low]	11.50
Two [low to medium]	16.61
Three [medium to high]	14.60
Four [high]	12.59
Five or six [very high]	11.13

(Continued)

TABLE 7.1 (Continued)

Active Variables	
Economic Capital	*Percent*
Affective Energy Insecurity	
Not at all worried [low]	38.87
Not very worried [medium]	36.50
Fairly worried [high}	17.88
Very worried (very high]	6.75
Job Insecurity (Cognitive + Affective)	
Very low job insecurity	35.22
Low job insecurity	21.35
Med. job insecurity	24.82
High job insecurity	18.61
Other Supplementary Variables	
Age	
19–34	26.28
35–45	23.18
46–59	31.75
60–82	18.80
Gender	
Male	52.19
Female	45.62
Non-binary	2.19
Race/Ethnicity	
White	62.41
African American	13.50
Latinx	9.49
Other or multiple races	14.60
Marital Status	
Married	45.80
Not married	54.20
Father's Education	
Some college or less	58.58
College or more	41.42

Source: N = 548. The first categories for age and father's education also include a few cases with missing values (5 and 13, respectively).

several forms of insecurity (Wacquant 2009), but due to their incarcerated status, they were ineligible to participate in this study. Thus, another effect of the neoliberal prison-industrial complex is to render a portion of the insecurity generated through policies promoting labor market deregulation and welfare state retrenchment invisible.[8] To make at least a small portion of this insecurity visible, we measure previous criminal convictions (as an indicator of negative security capital) and include it to map the scarring effect of incarceration onto the visible portion of the US neoliberal capitalist space.

A Note on Bourdieu's Social Space, Measures of Capital, and Interpretation of Axes

Perhaps the most well-known aspect of Bourdieu's (1984) landmark study, *Distinction*, which examines the social bases of taste and the culture of class position, is the overlaying of the social space (or "space of social positions") and the "space of life-styles" (p.128–129). Bourdieu uses these superimposed figures to illustrate the connections between class conditions and cultural consumption. The two axes are interpreted as the volume of capital (1st dimension on the *Y*-axis) and the composition of capital (2nd dimension on the *X*-axis). The composition varies from the dominated pole on the left – characterized by a high level of cultural capital and a low level of economic capital – to the dominant pole on the right – characterized by a high level of economic capital and a low level of cultural capital. There is also a third dimension, indicated in the graph, with arrows in certain positions, which is one's social trajectory.

It would certainly simplify matters to treat the structure of every type of social space as a function of the volume and composition of capitals operating in the space, but it is important to keep in mind that the social space figure from *Distinction* is actually a conceptual diagram (informed by empirical analyses) rather than a plane diagram from a CA (Bourdieu 1984:126). The plane diagrams from CAs that Bourdieu does include are for the subspaces of the dominant class (Bourdieu 1984:262) and the petite bourgeoisie (Bourdieu 1984:340). In these empirical figures, the 1st and 2nd axes correspond to the 2nd and 3rd axes from the theoretical model of the social space: the composition of capital and social trajectory. In the figures, we illustrate the space of US neoliberal capitalism; the contents of the graphs and interpretations of the axes are empirically derived. Therefore, they do not line up neatly with Bourdieu's conceptual mapping of the social space as a function of the volume and composition of two key forms of capital. Finally, due to the lack of direct measures of capital (especially economic capital), Bourdieu chose to operationalize class fractions using occupational groups (see Bourdieu 1984, Appendix 3) and structure the axes using lifestyle variables as the active variables, and measures of social position and background, such as income and father's occupation, as the supplementary variables (Bourdieu 1984:261). In our analyses, we directly measure economic and security capital, and use insecurity measures as well as sociodemographic variables to provide additional structure and confirm our interpretations of the axes.

There are important similarities between Bourdieu's social space and our space of neoliberal capitalism worth noting. First, the neoliberal capitalist space is also structured by economic and cultural capital, given that security capital is a special type of cultural capital (see Chapter 1). Second, as the volume of both types of capital is the first dimension structuring the neoliberal capitalist space in the US, it accounts for most of the inertia in the model. Lastly, although we do not find economic and security poles in the space, the composition of capitals is once again relevant. We provide more details about the construction of this space in the next section.

Results: MCA of the Space of US Neoliberal Capitalism

We ran an MCA using Stata 18.5, with the measures of economic and security capital (see Table 7.1) included as active variables and the traditional insecurity measures and additional sociodemographic measures included as supplementary variables. The active variables contribute to the construction of the clouds, and the supplementary variables are then added to the cloud of categories to provide additional context and structure (Le Roux and Rouanet 2010:9).

The first two axes combined account for 81.22% of the variance of the cloud, and the contributions of the additional axes decline substantially after the second axis. Therefore, we limit our focus to axes 1 and 2. We present the cloud of categories for the first two axes (i.e., plane 1–2) in Figure 7.1. Based on the modified rates (Benzécri 1992:412; Le Roux and Rouanet 2010:39), the first (horizontal) axis makes up 72.17% of the total variance of the cloud of categories. For reasons that we explore later, we interpret the first axis as *the overall volume of economic and security capital (combined)*. Categories reflecting a low level of capital volume are located on the left side of the graph (e.g., low income and no IRA), and categories reflecting a high level of capital volume are located on the right side (e.g., financial advisor and union member). The second (vertical) axis accounts for an additional 9.04% of the variance of the cloud. We interpret the second axis as the *composition of security capital*. Thus, security capital structures both dimensions in this space, whereas economic capital only contributes to the first dimension. Although there are some exceptions, the categories generally indicate that the forms of security capital derived from jobs are concentrated in the top half of the graph, and those derived from the areas of food and energy are concentrated in the bottom half of the graph.

It is somewhat difficult to interpret this graph due to the large number of active and supplementary categories (or "modalities") present. There are 38 active categories and 33 supplementary categories. Therefore, we present separate graphs for different groups of variables in Figures 7.2a–7.2d. Each graph is based on the same MCA presented in Figure 7.1. We focus

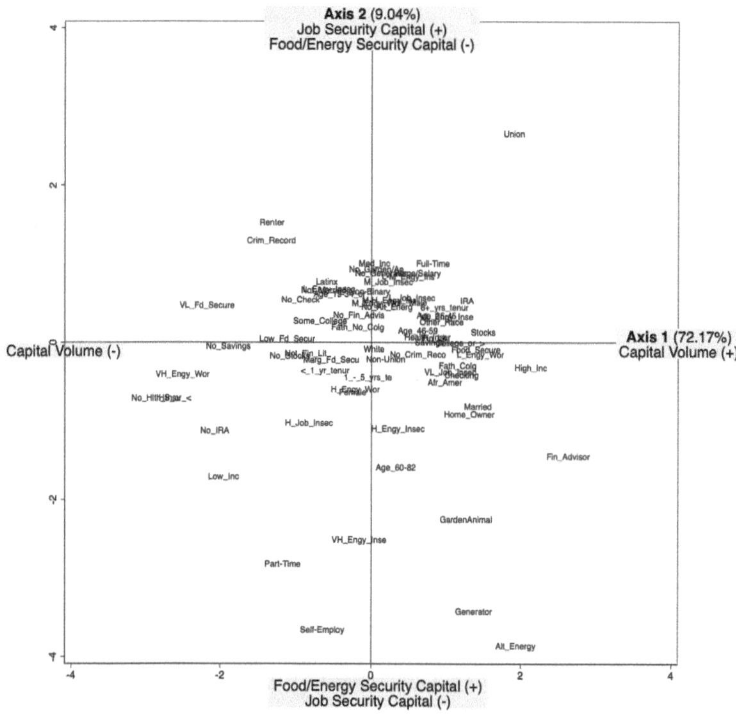

FIGURE 7.1 The Space of US Neoliberal Capitalism: Active and Supplementary Variables

on the clouds of categories in these figures (for the cloud of individuals, see Figure 7.3).

In Figure 7.2a, we focus on the measures of economic capital. Eight of the 17 categories reflect a high level of economic capital. All eight of these economic categories are on the right side of the space, and the eight categories reflecting low economic capital are on the left side (with medium income in the middle of the space). Based on distance, the economic categories that contribute most to the volume dimension are high income on the positive side, and low income, no health insurance, and no IRA on the negative side. Thus, economic capital plays an important role in the structuring of the space of US neoliberal capitalism, given that axis 1 accounts for 72% of the variance. It is also clear from this graph that economic capital does not provide a simple interpretation of axis 2. There are job-related categories at both ends of the axis, but no clear pattern that would lead us to interpret this axis in economic terms.

In Figure 7.2b, we highlight the measures of security capital. In this graph, we see that nine of the ten categories reflecting high security capital are located on the right side of the graph, which supports the interpretation of axis 1 as

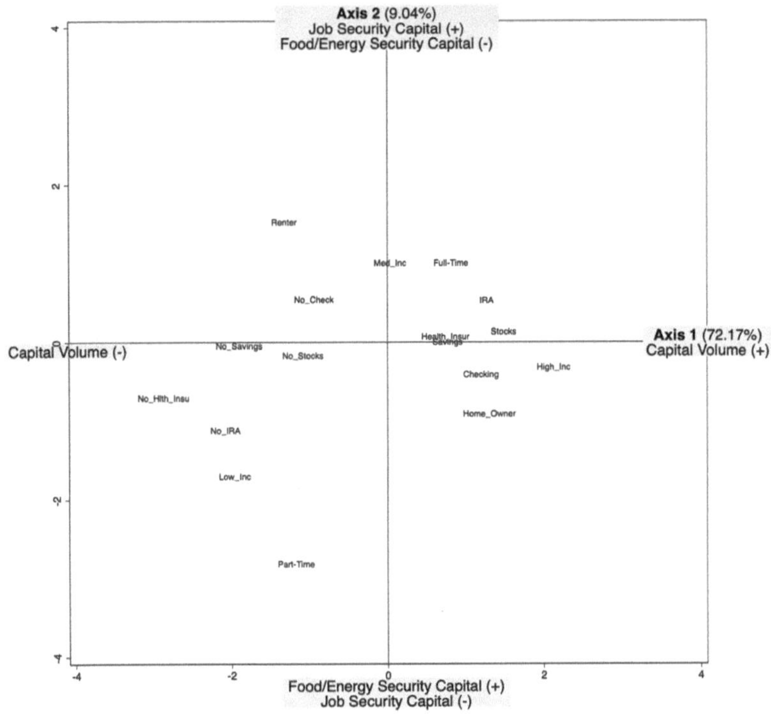

FIGURE 7.2A The Space of US Neoliberal Capitalism: Only Displaying Economic Capital Variables

the volume of capital. The one form of security capital that we expected to map onto the positive end of this space, self-employment, is on the negative side. However, it is still close to the center of the space on the first dimension, whereas it is at the lower end (and thus contributes more to) the second dimension. Thus, the security capital of self-employed individuals is rooted in non-employment-related resources, and it matters more for the composition of security capital than the overall volume of capital. Several categories reflecting low security capital are located on the negative side of the first dimension, such as the lowest level of job tenure, criminal record, and no health insurance. However, several of these categories are also located in the middle of the space, which indicates they do not contribute much to the first dimension (e.g., non-union and no financial advisor). Based on distance, the security capital categories that most distinguish a high volume of capital are union member and financial advisor, and the categories that most distinguish a low volume of capital are a low level of education and a criminal record.

There is more variation in the distances between categories on the second dimension in the graph, indicating a greater contribution of the security capital measures to the second dimension (composition of security capital).

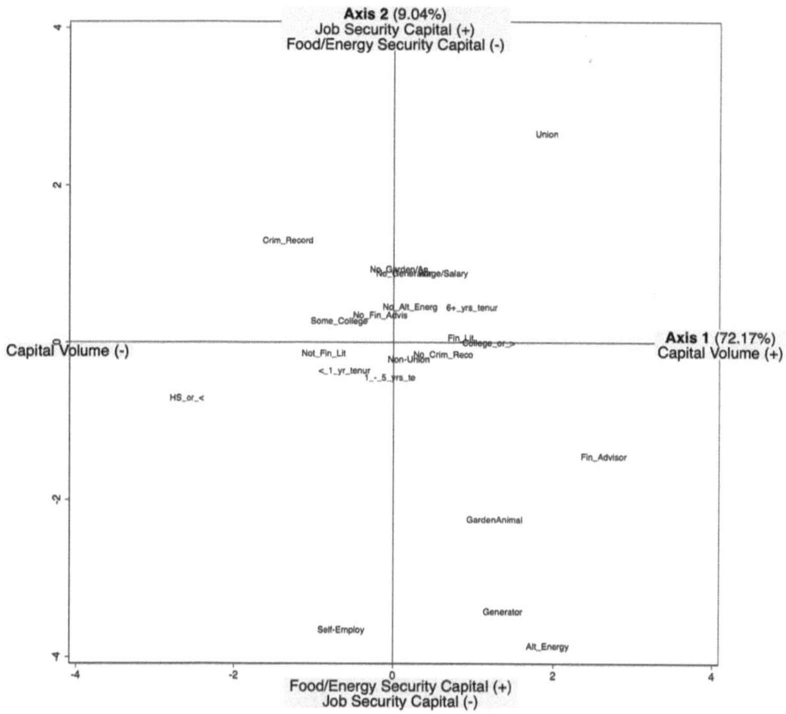

FIGURE 7.2B The Space of US Neoliberal Capitalism: Only Displaying Security Capital Variables

Categories reflecting high levels of food and energy security capital are concentrated at the bottom of the graph. In this region of the space, security is achieved through the possession of resources producing food and energy, such as home gardens and animals, generators, and alternative energy sources (such as solar panels). At the other end (i.e., at the top of the graph) of the space, job-related security measures, such as union membership and high job tenure, are concentrated. The main exception to this pattern is financial advisor, which is not a measure of food or energy insecurity. However, it is not necessarily tied to one's job either (although it may be in some cases). Based on distance, the categories that contribute most to security capital concentrated in food and energy are alternative energy and generator, and the categories contributing to a concentration in job security capital are union membership and a criminal record. We consider a criminal record as a form of negative job security capital, given the stigma associated with incarceration and extreme difficulties the formerly incarcerated face in the labor market after leaving prison (Western 2006, 2018). It is clear in this graph that a criminal record is associated with a relatively insecure position in the US neoliberal capitalist space.

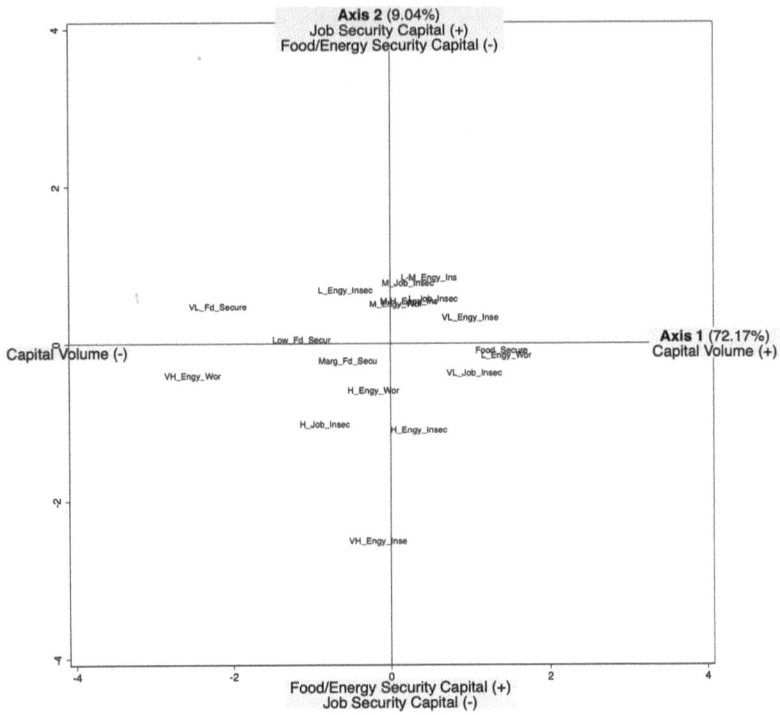

FIGURE 7.2C The Space of US Neoliberal Capitalism: Only Displaying Supplementary Variables (Insecurity Measures)

In the next Figure 7.2c, we display the traditional measures of food, energy, and job insecurity, which are treated as supplementary variables in the model. They do not contribute to the construction of the cloud, but are mapped onto the space to confirm the interpretation of the axes and provide additional structure. We intentionally chose to structure the space using measures of economic and security capital. Positions in the neoliberal capitalist space reflect different probabilities of experiencing insecurity in one's daily life. Food, energy, and job insecurity are perceptions of an uncertain future and actions taken in the present to prepare for that uncertainty. Bourdieu defined a field as a "space of objective probabilities" (Bourdieu 2020:123). Therefore, positions in social space are an indication of one's probability of engaging in a specific practice or holding a certain viewpoint (Rouanet et al. 2000:11). What each of these traditional measures of insecurity reflects is not solely an objective or subjective indicator of insecurity but rather a relation to the future that results from the internalization of one's objective position within the space of neoliberal capitalism. It is simultaneously objective due to the internalization of external social structures associated with position in space, and subjective due to the ability of the neoliberal capitalist habitus to improvise, adapt to new situations, and occasionally misfire when the conditions generating the habitus no longer exist, due to social mobility or changes in the structure of the social space over time.

If one's position in the neoliberal capitalist space reflects the probability of experiencing one or more forms of insecurity, then measures of food, energy, and job insecurity should map onto this space in expected ways. That is exactly what we see in Figure 7.2c. The lowest levels of food insecurity, cognitive energy insecurity, affective energy insecurity, and job insecurity are all located on the positive side, indicating a high volume of capital. At the other extreme are the highest levels of food insecurity (i.e., "very low food security") and affective energy insecurity. The highest levels of affective energy insecurity and job insecurity are also located on the left (negative) side of the space, indicating a low volume of capital, but they are noticeably closer to the center of the space. If the volume of capital approximates the probability of an insecure relation to the future in terms of food, energy, and work, then what the location of these categories suggests is that food and (affective) energy insecurity are the most visible manifestations of this relation. Extreme levels of deprivation in terms of the resources needed to confidently navigate the neoliberal capitalist space are internalized and likely to produce practices aimed at the conservation of resources in much the same way that Bourdieu (1984) described the petite bourgeoisie making themselves small to realize the goal of upward mobility. As with the rising petite bourgeoisie, the uncertainty of the outcome and the slope of the trajectory (Bourdieu 1984:331) define the relation to the world of individuals experiencing extremely high levels of insecurity. However, this is a far more uncertain future, and the measures taken to conserve resources reflect a complete lack of distance from necessity (e.g., not eating enough food or heating one's home in the winter because one cannot afford it).

The insecurity categories do not vary in distance as much across the second dimension (composition of security capital). A high level of cognitive energy insecurity is not associated with a particularly low level of capital volume, but it is associated with a high concentration of security capital in food and energy. The security capital, which individuals experiencing energy insecurity do have, is concentrated in food and energy (rather than in jobs). Low levels of energy insecurity tend to be associated with a stock of security capital concentrated in jobs, which is reasonable given that job security capital (e.g., union membership and job tenure) provides access to the economic resources required to make restrictions in daily energy consumption less urgent.

Finally, in Figure 7.2d, we focus on the remaining supplementary variables, which include age, gender, race, marital status, and father's education. The categories reflecting the highest levels of capital volume are being married and father with a college degree. Unexpectedly, African American and other race are also located toward the positive end of the space, along the

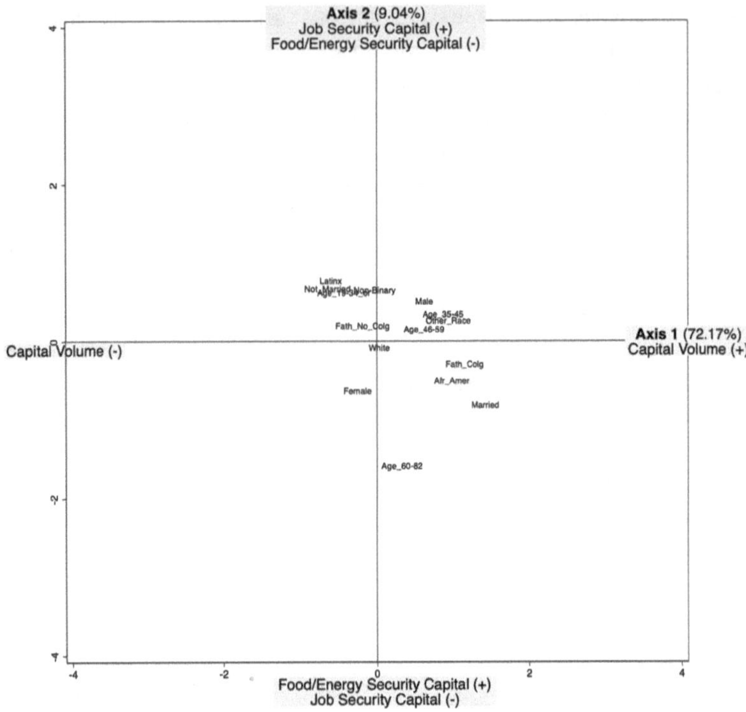

FIGURE 7.2D The Space of US Neoliberal Capitalism: Only Displaying Supplementary Variables (Sociodemographic Measures)

first dimension. At the other extreme (low volume), we see individuals who are not married, as well as those identifying as Latinx and the youngest group (19–34).

In terms of the second dimension, the oldest respondents (60–82) tend to have the highest concentration of security capital in energy and food. This is likely due to the association between age and home ownership and the tendency of workers at that age to have a weaker attachment to the labor force and thus less security capital invested in jobs. Older workers may be more likely to be employed part-time, which is a modality also located in this region of the space (see Figure 7.2a). Female and married categories are also located in the region of space exhibiting a concentration in energy and food security capital. At the other end of the space, we see that identifying as Latinx, a non-female gender, or not being married are all associated with a concentration of security capital in jobs. We should also note that, compared to the previous graphs, the modalities are more concentrated at the center of the space. The biggest difference appears to be between married and non-married individuals in terms of their volume of capital, as well as the differences in the concentration of capital among the young and old individuals. Patterns regarding age and father's education suggest that the second dimension is also partially a function of one's social trajectory, which is also the second dimension in the spaces of the dominant and middle classes (see Bourdieu 1984, Ch. 5–6).

Thus far, we have focused on the cloud of categories. In Figure 7.3, we present the cloud of individuals in the graph located in the top left corner. In the remaining graphs in Figure 7.3, we present separate clouds of individuals for subgroups defined by different combinations of food, energy, and job insecurity, which is a simplified version of the technique Bourdieu (1984) employed to highlight differences between class fractions among the dominant and middle classes (see Figures 11 and 12 on p.262, and 15 and 16 on p.341).[9] We included the traditional insecurity measures as supplementary variables in the MCA, but it would also be helpful to know where individuals experiencing different combinations of these types of insecurity are located in the US neoliberal capitalist space. For example, the most insecure individuals in the sample (i.e., those experiencing all three forms of insecurity) should be concentrated on the left side of the space, whereas the most secure individuals (i.e., those not experiencing any of these types of insecurity) should be concentrated on the right side of the space.

The left side of the space is the dominated region of the US neoliberal capitalist space where the probability of insecurity is highest, and the right side of the space is the dominant region where the probability of insecurity is lowest. We can further distinguish between dominant and dominated poles within the dominant side of the space, as Bourdieu distinguished between dominant (economic) and dominated (cultural) poles within the space of the dominant class (see Bourdieu 1984, Ch. 5). Given the cult of individualism, declining power of labor unions, and change in the capital-labor accord eliminating promises of lifetime employment, the dominant pole within the secure region of the US neoliberal capitalist space is in the bottom right corner, which is the area of the space with positions consisting of a high volume of both types of capital and a concentration of security capital in food and energy rather than jobs. Jobs remain a critical source of income, but do not provide the type of long-term security that they did before the economic crises of the 1970s and rise of neoliberalism. Therefore, we would expect the most secure individuals to be concentrated close to the food/energy pole within the right side of the neoliberal capitalist space.

Measures of insecurity are typically analyzed separately, but the unique combinations are important to explore, partly because they may map onto different positions within the neoliberal capitalist space. To simplify the process, we first created binary (high vs. low insecurity) measures of job, food, and energy insecurity, and then created a variable with categories representing each of the possible combinations of insecurity.[10] This insecurity subgroup variable consists of the following eight categories: 1 = Low Insecurity

TABLE 7.2 The Distribution of Combinations of Food, Energy, and Job Insecurity in the US

	Percent
1 = low insecurity (all three)	30.47
2 = high job insecurity only	14.78
3 = high food insecurity only	7.12
4 = high energy insecurity only	11.31
5 = high job and food insecurity	9.31
6 = high job and energy insecurity	7.48
7 = high food and energy insecurity	7.66
8 = high insecurity (all three)	11.86

Source: N = 548.

(All Three), 2 = High Job Insecurity Only, 3 = High Food Insecurity Only, 4 = High Energy Insecurity Only, 5 = High Job and Food Insecurity, 6 = High Job and Energy Insecurity, 7 = High Food and Energy Insecurity, and 8 = High Insecurity (All Three).

We present the distribution of the eight combinations of insecurity in Table 7.2. The results are revealing and support our argument that insecurity is a defining feature of the US neoliberal capitalist space. Approximately 30% of respondents do not experience any of the three forms of insecurity, which indicates that 70% of respondents experience one or more forms of insecurity. A vast majority of individuals in the sample experienced at least one type of uncertainty regarding their future. Approximately 12% of respondents experience all three forms of insecurity, which represents the most vulnerable group in the US neoliberal capitalist space. Finally, the different combinations of insecurity also show that individuals experiencing food insecurity are likely to experience it in combination with other forms of insecurity. Only 7% of individuals experience food insecurity alone (compared to 15% for job insecurity, and 11% for energy insecurity).

In Figure 7.3, we present nine graphs for the cloud of individuals: a graph for the full sample (see the graph in the top left corner), and a separate graph for each of the different insecurity subgroups from Table 7.2. In the full sample, individuals are spread throughout every quadrant in the space of US neoliberal capitalism. However, there are distinct patterns of clustering that vary across insecurity subgroups. The low insecurity group (not experiencing any of the three types) tends to cluster on the positive (secure) side of the space, and it is split fairly evenly between the dominant and dominated sides of this region of the space.

The three graphs for groups experiencing only one type of insecurity reveal important differences between food insecurity and the remaining two types of insecurity. The group experiencing only food insecurity is more concentrated

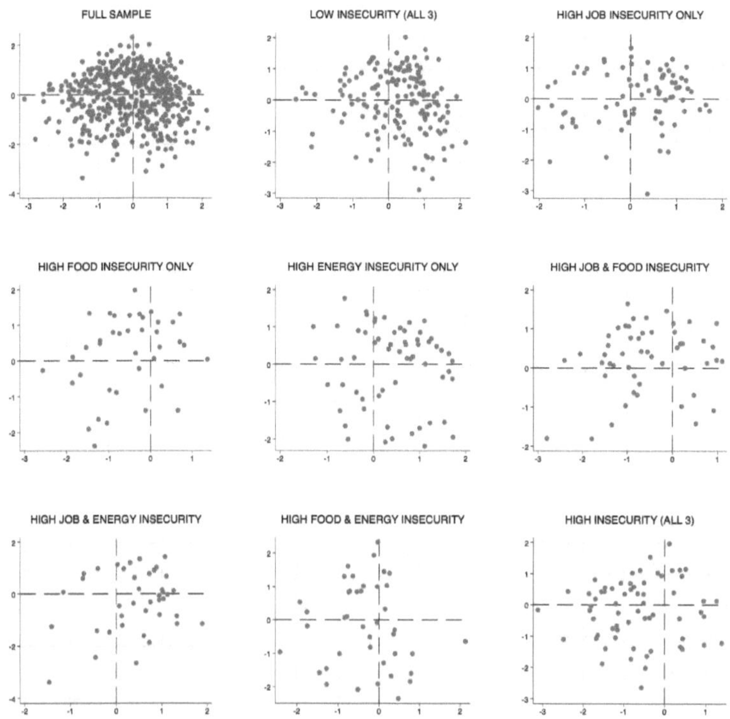

FIGURE 7.3 The Space of Individuals for Different Combinations of Food, Energy, and Job Insecurity

in the upper left region of the space (i.e., the dominated portion of the space of insecurity) than the groups only experiencing energy or job insecurity. The latter two groups are concentrated in the top right (i.e., the dominated portion of the space of security). This suggests that food insecurity alone is a decent indicator of an insecure position in the neoliberal capitalist space, whereas energy and job insecurity alone are not. There are certainly job or energy insecure individuals located in the insecure regions of the space, but the sub-cloud of these individuals is more highly concentrated on the right (secure) side of the space.

When food insecurity is combined with one or both of the other types of insecurity, we once again see a concentration of individuals in the dominated section of the insecure region in the top left corner of the graph. Individuals experiencing all three forms of insecurity are most highly concentrated in the left (insecure) area of the space, and they are evenly divided between the dominated and dominant sections of this sub-space. On balance, the graphs in Figure 7.3 support our claim that insecurity plays an important role in structuring the US space of neoliberal capitalism, and they also reveal important differences between the three types of insecurity and their combinations.

Discussion and Conclusion

The MCA results presented in this chapter show how economic and security capital structure the space of US neoliberal capitalism, which represents one national space nested within the larger global neoliberal capitalist field. As in Bourdieu's (1984:128–129) model of the social space (or space of class relations), the space is structured by the volume and composition of two types of capital: economic and cultural. In a lecture at the Collége de France in May of 1984, Bourdieu (2021:243) presented a generalized interpretation of cultural capital as a type of information capital, which "enables us to see how the incorporated, objectified information that defines cultural capital as information that is both structured and structuring." Security capital, as a form of cultural capital, is, in many ways, a type of information capital. It is the embodiment, objectification, and institutionalization of the neoliberal creed or cult of individualism that seek out individualistic solutions to collective problems (e.g., investing in home food and energy production as a means of dealing with declining labor market prospects due to labor market deregulation and welfare state retrenchment). Knowledge of the financial system and investment in different strategies of establishing a secure footing in the areas of food, energy, and employment are all structured in the sense that they are the internalization of neoliberal economic structures and also structuring in the sense that they shape one's daily practices in the home, on the job, and in one's outlook on the world.

The US space of neoliberal capitalism is perhaps distinctive and thus likely to exhibit somewhat different structural properties than other neoliberal capitalist spaces across the globe in at least two respects. First, the US is one of the birthplaces of neoliberal ideology, and thus the mature form of it shaping the social space in 2024 is likely to be different from countries that experienced different neoliberal trajectories (e.g., post-Socialist countries and countries from the Global South). Second, the US continues to have one of the highest incarceration rates in the world. Using the economic freedom index, the US ranks 7th in the world in terms of the level of neoliberalism (Gwartney, Lawson, and Murphy 2023). Several countries with similar levels of neoliberalism to the US still have significantly lower rates of incarceration. As we mentioned in Chapter 5, the incarceration rate is three to eight times higher in the US than in the handful of countries with higher levels of neoliberalism (Fair and Walmsley 2024). This suggests that the penal system plays a more important role in the US neoliberal capitalist space than it does in other parts of the world. Scholars need to investigate this issue further and rethink the "universal" quality of findings from studies of a labor market that continues to be shaped by the criminalization of poverty and the use of the "iron fist" of the penal system (Wacquant 2009; Western 2006). The ways the space of neoliberal capitalism are structured in national contexts with weaker or nonexistent carceral logics in place remain a question for future research.

Although the effects of the use of the penal system in the US to regulate low-wage labor are largely invisible due to the incarceration of the most vulnerable segments of the population (who are at a high risk of insecurity), we were able to show the scarring effect of incarceration with the "criminal record" category (see Figure 7.2b). It is unfortunately no surprise that this category is located in the most insecure region of the US neoliberal capitalist space (i.e., the upper-left quadrant). Formerly incarcerated individuals continue to face (often multiple) forms of insecurity on a daily basis, as they navigate a space that individualizes social problems and attributes failure in the labor market to individual morality and work ethic while ignoring the structural roots of joblessness, hunger, and harsh living conditions.[11] This type of misrecognition is what gives neoliberal ideology its efficacy. Individuals struggling to secure their future in even the most insecure regions of this space help to reproduce existing power relations by tacitly accepting the neoliberal myth of the entrepreneurial self and forgetting the inherently social and interdependent nature of what it means to be an individual (Butler 2024, 2022).

Finally, the MCA presented in this chapter confirms the importance of economic and security capital as structuring elements in the US neoliberal capitalist space. The first principal axis accounts for nearly three quarters of the overall variance of the cloud, which indicates that the volume of economic and security capital is critical to understanding the space of US neoliberal capitalism. The second principal axis distinguishes a dominant pole in the space where energy and food security capital are concentrated, from a dominated pole where job security capital is concentrated. This reinforces the notion that neoliberalism is space governed by (in)security. Through the conceptualization and measurement of the neoliberal capitalist space, we have shown how neoliberalism functions as a space of insecurity. Objective probabilities of insecurity are internalized within the neoliberal habitus and transformed into expressions of uncertainty toward the future that are often misrecognized as ("subjective") individual phenomenon existing independently of a supposed ("objective") social reality. It is the simultaneous presence of neoliberal structures in the spaces of struggle, and in the spaces within the bodies of those engaged in the struggle, that allows for the myth of the entrepreneurial self to obscure the structural roots of insecurity and individualize failure within neoliberal competitions.

Notes

1 As Wacquant (2019:18) describes the field of power, we conceptualize the global field of neoliberal capitalism as a "multilayered kind of social space," consisting

of national spaces of neoliberal capitalism shaped by the general structure of the global field but varying to some extent based on national institutions and the historical trajectory of the country and its adoption of neoliberal policies.

2 MCA can have more than two dimensions. However, for ease of presentation, we limit our focus to the first two dimensions in the space, which account for the vast majority of the variance.

3 The attention-check question is: "The color test you are about to take part in is very simple. When asked your favorite color, you must select 'Green.' This is an attention check."

4 We considered including the count of the number of correct answers (0–3), but the reliability for an additive scale was low (alpha = 0.37). Financial literacy is an embodied form of what Fourcade and Healy (2024:121) refer to as "eigencapital," which is a resource associated with a well-situated position in terms of one's interactions in the digital economy. Reputation is one aspect of this privileged positioning, and financial literacy is a type of cultural capital (required by and) acquired in the process of building this reputation.

5 The alpha for the six-item index is 0.92.

6 The alpha for the six-item index is 0.76.

7 The alpha for the two-item index is 0.70.

8 Western (2006) addresses this type of "invisible inequality" in his study of mass incarceration and racial inequality in the US.

9 For a recent example of the approach we take, see Blasius and Friedrichs (2019). There are other techniques available in MCA as well, such as concentration ellipses (see LeRoux and Rouanet 2010:69–71).

10 We operationalize "high" insecurity as the two most insecure categories for job insecurity and the three most insecure categories for food insecurity, given the amount of clustering in the most secure category (64% are food secure). We chose to focus on cognitive energy insecurity, and we consider the three most insecure categories to be a "high" level of energy insecurity.

11 The consequences of a criminal record for the insecurity of one's position in the US neoliberal capitalist space are likely racialized (see Pager 2007). We leave this as an open question for future research to investigate, given that we have a relatively small sample size.

References

Benzécri, Jean Paul. 1992. *Correspondence Analysis Handbook*. New York: Dekker.

Blasius, Jörg and Jürgen Friedrichs. 2019. "Changes of Lifestyles in the Social Space: The Case of Gentrification." Pp. 61–79 in *Empirical Investigations of Social Space*, edited by Jörg Blasius, Frédéric Lebaron, Brigitte Le Roux, and Andreas Schmitz. Cham: Springer.

Bourdieu, Pierre. 2021. *Forms of Capital: General Sociology, Volume 3*. Cambridge: Polity Press.

Bourdieu, Pierre. 2020. *Habitus and Field: General Sociology, Volume 2*. Cambridge: Polity Press.

Bourdieu, Pierre. 2005. *The Social Structures of the Economy*. Cambridge: Polity Press.

Bourdieu, Pierre. 1996. *The State Nobility*. Stanford, CA: Stanford University Press.

Bourdieu, Pierre. 1990. *The Logic of Practice*. Stanford, CA: Stanford University Press.

Bourdieu, Pierre. 1988. *Homo Academicus*. Stanford, CA: Stanford University Press.

Bourdieu, Pierre. 1984. *Distinction: A Social Critique of the Judgement of Taste.* Cambridge, MA: Harvard University Press.

Bourdieu, Pierre. 1977. *Outline of a Theory of Practice.* Cambridge: Cambridge University Press.

Butler, Judith. 2024. *Who's Afraid of Gender?* New York: Farrar, Straus, and Giroux.

Butler, Judith. 2022. *What World Is This? A Pandemic Phenomenology.* New York: Columbia University Press.

Dardot, Pierre and Christian Laval. 2014. *The New Way of the World.* New York: Verso.

Fair, Helen and Roy Walmsley. 2024. *World Prison Population List, Fourteenth Edition.* https://www.prisonstudies.org/sites/default/files/resources/downloads/world_prison_population_list_14th_edition.pdf.

Foucault, Michel. 2008. *The Birth of Biopolitics: Lectures at the Collège de France, 1978–1979.* New York: Palgrave Macmillan.

Gwartney, James, Robert Lawson, and Ryan Murphy. 2023. *Economic Freedom of the World 2023 Annual Report.* https://www.fraserinstitute.org/sites/default/files/economic-freedom-of-the-world-2023.pdf.

Harvey, David. 2005. *A Brief History of Neoliberalism.* Oxford: Oxford University Press.

Hjellbrekke, Johs. 2019. *Multiple Correspondence Analysis for the Social Sciences.* Abingdon, Oxon: Routledge.

Kalleberg, Arne L., Barbara F. Reskin, and Kenneth Hudson. 2000. "Bad Jobs in America: Standard and Nonstandard Employment Relations and Job Quality in the United States." *American Sociological Review* 65: 256–278.

Le Roux, Brigitte and Henry Rouanet. 2010. *Multiple Correspondence Analysis.* Thousand Oaks, CA: Sage.

Le Roux, Brigitte, Henry Rouanet, Mike Savage, and Alan Warde. 2008. "Class and Cultural Division in the UK." *Sociology* 42: 1049–1071.

Lorey, Isabell. 2015. *State of Insecurity: Government of the Precarious.* New York: Verso.

Pager, Devah. 2007. *Marked: Race, Crime, and Finding Work in an Era of Mass Incarceration.* Chicago, IL: University of Chicago Press.

Rouanet, Henry, Werner Ackermann, and Brigitte Le Roux. 2000. "The Geometric Analysis of Questionnaires: The Lesson of Bourdieu's La Distinction." *Bulletin de Méthodologie Sociologique* 65: 5–18.

Stolper, Oscar A. and Andreas Walter. 2017. "Financial Literacy, Financial Advice, and Financial Behavior." *Journal of Business Economics* 87: 581–643.

Taylor, Astra. 2023. *The Age of Insecurity: Coming Together as Things Fall Apart.* Toronto: House of Anansi Press.

Wacquant, Loïc. 2009. *Punishing the Poor: The Neoliberal Government of Social Insecurity.* Durham, NC: Duke University Press.

Wacquant, Loïc. 2019. "Bourdieu's dyad: On the Primacy of Social Space and Symbolic Power." Pp. 15–21 in *Empirical Investigations of Social Space*, edited by Jorg Blasius, Frederic Lebaron, Brigitte Le Roux, and Andreas Schmitz. Cham: Springer.

Western, Bruce. 2006. *Punishment and Inequality in America.* New York: Russell Sage Foundation.

8

CONCLUSION

We began Chapter 1 by noting that this book is about two complex concepts, neoliberalism and insecurity, that help define the contemporary world. The previous seven chapters leave no doubt that neoliberalism and insecurity are complicated, multifaceted features of life in the late twentieth and early twenty-first centuries. It is also clear to us that neoliberalism and insecurity are intertwined with one another. Neoliberalism would not work without the constant threats of food, energy, job, housing, medical, water insecurities, and the like. There needs to be consequences for those who are losers of neoliberal competitions. Insecurities are those consequences. Further, for those individuals in the global neoliberal capitalist field who are successful at many of life's neoliberal competitions, the threat of many forms of insecurity is a specter that haunts these people, despite their successes. The threat of insecurity is pervasive. And it's that threat of insecurity which keeps almost all people in the neoliberal game of competition. In other words, even those who have successfully maneuvered themselves into the dominant region of the global neoliberal capitalist field are worried about some form(s) of insecurity. Recall that insecurity is about probabilities – being insecure is about lacking the ability to predict a stable and secure future. No individual can be certain that they will not fall victim to some type of insecurity at any time. Neoliberalism is happy to take advantage of the probabilistic nature of insecurity to help ensure that the competitions continue, and the insecure neoliberal subject is the main actor in the neoliberal capitalist field. Insecurity has become one of the main weapons wielded by neoliberalism to further the accumulation of capital throughout the world.

In this concluding chapter, we provide a summary of the first seven chapters of the book. We then delve into what we have learned, theoretically

DOI: 10.4324/9781003326892-8

and empirically, about the global neoliberal capitalist field from these seven chapters. We end with some concluding remarks on the theory of practice and how we envision the relationship between neoliberalism and insecurity playing out in the near future.

A Brief Recap

It is useful here to summarize what we have learned in Chapters 1–7. This will help us situate our forthcoming discussion of the global neoliberal capitalist field within the argument that we have constructed thus far. In Chapter 1, we began by delineating a time frame in which neoliberal ideas developed – post-WWII, or what we refer to, as others before us (e.g., Habermas 1988), as "advanced capitalism." We proceed to introduce neoliberalism and insecurity. In the case of insecurity, we begin with a discussion of three forms of insecurity: food insecurity, energy insecurity, and job insecurity. Scholars in many different disciplines have studied these three types of insecurity, typically examining each form of insecurity as a unique phenomenon. While the study of particular forms of insecurity is important for numerous reasons – chief among them to devise policy mechanisms to reduce that form of insecurity for as many people as possible – we also see value in studying the broader concept of insecurity. Building on the work of recent social critics (Lorey 2015; Taylor 2023), we arrive at a definition of insecurity (as noted above) as *the inability to successfully predict a stable and secure future*. Individuals, then, are driven by the desire for security – a high probability of a stable and secure future. However, as we have suggested, no one is completely out of insecurity's reach – though some are much more secure than others.

Early on, in Chapter 1, we note that there are both macro-level structural impacts and studies of neoliberalism and insecurity, as well as micro-level individual effects and related scholarship on the two main topics of this book. Both levels of analysis are important for a comprehensive understanding of the intersection of neoliberalism and insecurity. In fact, we argued that this literature needs to take a step forward by employing a theoretical and empirical perspective that can bridge (and perhaps transcend) the dualism of structural/individual-based explications of neoliberalism, insecurity, and their interrelation. To do this, we chose to conceptualize our project, its research design, and the empirical methodology based on Pierre Bourdieu's (1977, 1984, 1990) theory of practice. This approach has three main components – the field, capital, and the habitus. Fields are relatively autonomous spaces in which individuals compete against one another to reach more dominant positions within the field. Capital are resources. In much of Bourdieu's work, most famously in *Distinction* (1984), the two most important types of capital are economic and cultural. These two capitals – based on their composition and volume – are the structuring logics of the field he studied in *Distinction* (i.e., the social space of class relations). Bourdieu noted, however, that each field has its own structuring capitals, and all fields aren't necessarily structured by economic and cultural capital. The third and final element of the theory of practice is the habitus. The habitus operates unconsciously under the surface and guides the tastes, preferences, attitudes, and other manner of self-presentation. The habitus is the internalization of social structures and individual experiences. That habitus springs into action when it enters a field and perceives the structures of the world as natural when they are in tune with its own structures.

After reviewing the theory of practice generally, we explain how our study of neoliberalism and insecurity fits into the theory of practice framework. We posit the existence of a global neoliberal capitalist field that is structured by the volume and composition of economic and what we refer to as "security" capital. Security capital helps individuals insulate themselves from the negative effects of insecurity. We then conclude with a discussion of the existence of a "neoliberal habitus" that unconsciously governs the dispositions and actions of individuals in the global neoliberal capitalist field.

We spend most of Chapter 2 overviewing the history of neoliberal thought and policies in the Global North and South. The genesis for neoliberal ideas started, in earnest, in post-WWII Europe and the US. While neoliberal ideas were not in vogue during the beginning of the advanced capitalist period – strong State, Keynesian-influenced policies were – early proponents of neoliberalism, Ludwig von Mises, Fredrich Hayek, Milton Freeman, and the other members of the Mont Perlin Society regularly met to discuss the benefits of neoliberalism and to plan the neoliberal revolution when the opportunity presented itself. This happened in the late 1970s in the US and Western Europe, as national economies slid into recession and neoliberal policies were viewed by those in power, most notably President Ronald Reagan in the US and Prime Minister Margaret Thatcher in the UK, as the solution. While Reagan, Thatcher, and other Western European leaders began privatizing state-run industries, implementing austerity programs, and reorienting their economies to be congruent with global neoliberal capitalism in the Global North, the Bretton Woods institutions which these countries controlled began exporting neoliberalism to the Global South though structural adjustment loans and other mechanisms designed to create export-oriented economies dependent on global capitalism for economic growth (which often didn't follow).

Once we provided the background on neoliberalism in advanced capitalism, we shifted gears to a set of three chapters that examine the structural political economy of food insecurity (Chapter 3), energy insecurity (Chapter 4), and job insecurity (Chapter 5). We began our structural examination of insecurity with food insecurity, or the absence of food security. The UN FAO (2000:26) defines food security as a condition that is met "when all people, at all times, have physical, social and economic access to sufficient, safe and nutritious food that meets their dietary needs and food preferences for an active and healthy life." Chapter 3 begins with a discussion of how food insecurity arose around the world after WWII. We paid particular attention to the roles of food production, food aid, and food trade – structural conditions guided by neoliberal policies that increased food insecurity. We then discussed the ways food (in)security has been measured since the creation of the concept. This is followed by explanations on food insecurity in the Global South and the Global North, and how, in both cases, food insecurity is linked with global capitalism. Next, we highlight the role of large, global agrobusiness in the level and distribution of food insecurity throughout the world. Before concluding the chapter, we examined the association between the FIES and EFW index. We found that neoliberalism is positively associated with food insecurity in 2014, 2016, 2018 (in the Global North only), and 2021.

Chapter 4 covers the political economy of energy and energy insecurity. Energy insecurity can be defined as "an inability to adequately meet basic household energy needs" (Hernández 2016:2) or, a bit more specifically, when basic energy needs cannot be met for things like "cooking, boiling water, lighting and heating" (World Health Organization 2006:6). First, we reviewed the different ways energy insecurity is measured. Next, we examined energy insecurity, first in the Global North, followed by the Global South. We then highlighted the role of global corporate actors – and the related structural political economy – in the production of energy insecurity. Our analysis shows that in the case of unaffordable energy, energy insecurity in the Global South (measured by *Context Energy Survey* (CES)) is positively correlated with neoliberalism, as measured by the EFW index. However, we didn't find any indication that neoliberalism is positively related to other forms of energy security, such as too much reliance on foreign energy or the lack of clean energy.

In Chapter 5, we turned our attention to the structural political economy of work and job insecurity, and the role that neoliberalism plays at the macro level on job insecurity. Readers may recall that there are two main forms of job insecurity, cognitive and affective job insecurity. Anderson and Pontusson (2007:214) define cognitive job insecurity as "an individual's estimate of the probability that he or she will lose their job in the near future," while they go on to note that affective job insecurity "refers to worry or anxiety about losing one's job." Bourdieu, to our knowledge, never wrote or spoke specifically about food or energy insecurity – at least in any significant manner. The same is not true for job insecurity. As we noted, Bourdieu (1998) said that nonstandard employment arrangements and job insecurity are everywhere – and that was over 25 years ago. That statement is as true as ever today. After highlighting Bourdieu's contributions to the study of job insecurity and precarity in general, we provided an overview of existing empirical job insecurity research. We then discussed what we know about job insecurity in the Global North, followed by job insecurity in the Global South. At this juncture, we explicated how the global spread of neoliberalism impacted job insecurity, followed by a section dedicated to how precarious labor markets and constant worry over job insecurity created an entrepreneurial mindset, which some have referred to as "the entrepreneurial self" (Bröckling 2016) – foreshadowing some of our discussion in Chapter 6. In Chapter 5, we used linear modeling to predict the effects of a measure of neoliberalism (the EFW) on the ISSP's job insecurity variables. In many cases, we found a significant positive effect of neoliberalism on job insecurity, but the relationship between neoliberalism and job insecurity varies by time period, region, and measure (see Chapter 5).

We shifted gears in Chapter 6, turning our focus to the micro-level impacts of neoliberalism, insecurity, and their interaction. We began by noting that, along with the structural political economic changes brought on by neoliberalism, for it to work and become entrenched as a dominant ideology, individuals' norms and behaviors needed to change too. Individual responsibility and competition must be embraced by individuals in neoliberal societies – then the self-regulation preferred by neoliberalism can meaningfully take place (Dardot and Laval 2014). Next, we highlighted the role of Michel Foucault (2007, 2008) as the unofficial father of micro-level neoliberalism studies – focusing particular attention on his concepts of biopower and governmentality, which are used to unpack and understand how individuals are convinced to regulate themselves by Foucault and his contemporaries. This has led some social critics to suggest that there is a distinct "neoliberal governmentality" (Lorey 2015:34–35). We then moved onto a discussion about how neoliberal governmentality impacts insecurity broadly, and food, energy, and job insecurity in particular – at the micro, individual level of analysis. We conclude Chapter 6 with an introduction of what we refer to as the "insecure neoliberal subject," who are actors in the global neoliberal capitalist field.

Finally, in Chapter 7, we put it all together with an empirical example of the US neoliberal capitalist space. We collected survey data on a variety of neoliberal and insecurity-related topics from a representative sample of n = 1,013 US residents who were 18 years old or older. Using the data generated from the survey, we conducted a multiple correspondence analysis (MCA) (Hjellbrekke 2019; Le Roux and Rouanet 2010) on the data to provide us with a glimpse of the US neoliberal capitalist space.

Below, we attempt to bring it all together – what have we learned about neoliberalism, insecurity, their intersection, and, most importantly, the global neoliberal capitalist field over the course of this book? Let's dive in.

The Relationship between the Space of US Neoliberal Capitalism and the Global Neoliberal Capitalist Field

In this discussion, we want to make clear that we are discussing two different, yet related, social spaces. First, we have the "global neoliberal capitalist field," which is the larger field that we have been theorizing about in this book. Second, there is what we have been referring to as the "space of US neoliberal capitalism." This second social space is the one that we have empirically investigated in Chapter 7.

Ideally, an empirical investigation of individuals located in the global neoliberal capitalist field would entail collecting data from people across the world. This, of course, is almost impossible. Therefore, as a first step in understanding the structure of the global neoliberal capitalist field, we turn to an investigation of the space of US neoliberal capitalism using data collected from a survey administered to a representative sample of US adults. The space of US neoliberal capitalism is nested within the global neoliberal capitalist field.

Bourdieu suggested that some related social spaces and fields exhibit what he called "structural and functional homologies" (Bourdieu and Wacquant 1992:105–106). In other words, aspects of one social space or field can correspond with aspects of a second social space or field. For example, locations in the spaces of dominance and subordination align with one another (Swartz 1997), and the forms of capital that structure one space may also structure the related space. Clearly, we are arguing here that there are numerous homologies between the space of US neoliberal capitalism and the global neoliberal capitalist field. This enables us to empirically examine the US space but also apply some of our broad conclusions to the larger global field.

A complicating factor here is the level at which these spaces operate. In our case, we have the national-level space of US neoliberal capitalism and the global (or transnational) neoliberal capitalist field. Bourdieu himself worked almost exclusively with national-level fields – usually in France. It has been left to the next generation of Bourdieu scholars to theorize how national fields are nested within transnational (and global) fields. We will return to our discussion of how the space of US neoliberal capitalism in nested within the global neoliberal capitalist field a bit later in the chapter, after we first briefly review our MCA findings from Chapter 7 for context.

Structure of the Space of US Neoliberal Capitalism

The MCA of the space of US neoliberal capitalism that we undertook in Chapter 7 helps us understand the structure of that space. Recall that we suggested a combination of economic and security capital structured the global neoliberal capitalist field. In our empirical examination of the space of US neoliberal capitalism – which has numerous homologies with the global neoliberal capitalist field – the volume of economic capital, along with the volume and composition of security capital, delineates the space of US neoliberal capitalism. This national social space is then nested within the global field of neoliberal capitalism, which is a transnational meta-field (Atkinson 2020:252), connecting national spaces across the globe (see our discussion in Chapter 7).

The first dimension (horizontal axis) is the total volume of economic and security capital, and it accounts for the vast majority of the cloud variance (72.17%). Figures 1 through 2d, in Chapter 7, show that categories reflecting higher levels of both types of capital are located on the right side of the space. The second dimension (vertical axis), which accounts for 9.04% of the total cloud variance, is the composition of security capital. The second dimension ranges from the dominated pole at the top of the space, where security capital is primarily job-based, to the dominant pole at the bottom of the space, where security capital is rooted in food and energy rather than in jobs. We confirmed this particular interpretation of the axis with supplementary variables (e.g., age, father's education, and marital status) and the placement of key security capital variables, such as criminal record. Due to the stigma of a criminal record, formerly incarcerated individuals tend to suffer long-term effects of incarceration on their labor market opportunities (Western 2006; Pager 2007), which lends support to our assertion that the top left portion of this space (i.e., low volume of capital and security capital dominated by job-related capital) is the most insecure region.[1]

The location of individuals within the US space of neoliberal capitalism helps us understand the structure of the space and its implications for the experience of one or more forms of insecurity (see Figure 7.3 in Chapter 7). Among the three types of insecurity we consider in this book, food insecurity is most closely associated with the dominated region of the space in the top-left quadrant. For individuals only experiencing one form of insecurity, food insecurity is most likely to be associated with this type of marginality in the US space of neoliberal capitalism. One can experience job or energy insecurity in isolation and still occupy a more privileged position in space. The results also revealed that food insecurity is the least likely to be experienced in isolation, which is understandable, given that if you cannot afford to eat enough food, you probably can't afford to spend much to heat your home in the winter and you may be in a job that is unlikely to last very long. This highlights the connected nature of different forms of insecurity, which also has important policy implications. We can fight food insecurity directly by increasing access to food, but also indirectly by reducing other forms of insecurity, such as job insecurity. One of the benefits of MCA is that it allows us to see the connections between different forms of insecurity, which is reflected in the positioning of categories and individuals in space.

Moving from the US Space to the Global Meta-Field

In Chapter 1, we highlighted the work of Larissa Buchholz (2016), who provided a useful tool for theorizing transnational fields – the concept of "relative vertical autonomy." As she notes, "[a]s the 'relativity' of field autonomy suggest that national and global fields levels are only partially independent, we must approach them, by the same token, as still relatively interdependent" (Buchholz 2016:48). Taking the lead from Buchholz, we employ our empirical understanding of the space of US neoliberal capitalism to do two main things: understand the space of US neoliberal capitalism, and then use that national-level empirical analysis and our prior theorizing throughout the earlier chapters of the book to help understand the global neoliberal capitalist field. Here, we briefly discuss (1) how the emergence of the space of US neoliberal capitalism helps us understand the emergence of the global neoliberal capitalist field, (2) how the space of US neoliberal capitalism and the global neoliberal capitalist fields interact with one another, and (3) how national-level understandings of economic and security capital can be adapted to the transnational/global level.

It makes theoretical sense to begin with an understanding of the space of US neoliberal capitalism to help us begin to understand the global neoliberal capitalist field as the US (along with the UK) was the leader in embracing neoliberalism and related policies in the late 1970s and early 1980s. In other words, neoliberalism's emergence in the US created the space of US neoliberal capitalism, which then had tremendous influence on the global neoliberal capitalist field as the US began exporting neoliberalism (and the insecurities that come with it) to countries in the Global North, and then to countries in the Global South. The interaction of the space of US neoliberal capitalism and the global neoliberal capitalist field is important because, as noted above, these spaces/fields are somewhat interdependent. For example, even today, the US arguably is still the center of the neoliberal universe, housing, and/or having effective control over many of the powerful institutions of global capitalism. The space of US neoliberal capitalism is constantly shaping the global neoliberal capitalist field; however, the opposite is also true. The global neoliberal capitalist field is also shaped by the other national spaces of neoliberal capitalism. Finally, we must also consider the adaptation of capital. While Bourdieu noted that different fields are structured by different types of capital, we argue that the volume and composition of economic and security capital structure both the space of US neoliberal capitalism and the global neoliberal capitalist field. The adaptation takes place with the forms of security capital that are important in different national spaces of neoliberal capitalism. In our survey, we asked about forms of food, energy, and job security capital that would be relevant in the US case. We suspect that there will be some substantial differences in the forms of security capital that are important in countries at different levels of socioeconomic development, climates, and other variables.

We now turn to a summary of how we view the global neoliberal capitalist field now that our theoretical and empirical investigation of neoliberalism and insecurity have concluded.

The Global Neoliberal Capitalist Field

Our intent in the book was to demonstrate that not only are neoliberalism and insecurity linked, but to argue that insecurity is a fundamental part of neoliberalism and, more specifically, the global neoliberal capitalist field. We believe we accomplished this goal, first by highlighting the relationships between neoliberalism and food, energy, and job security at both the macro and micro levels of understanding. And, second, with our empirical analysis of the space of US neoliberal capitalism. Through this approach, shaped by a theory of practice framework, we have been able to avoid the dualism of structural vs. individual explanations of neoliberalism, insecurity, and their intersection.

We have located individuals with the space of US neoliberal capitalism with a combination of economic and security-related variables, including those which measure the extent and breadth to which an individual in the space has security capital. Although different forms of insecurity will undoubtedly matter more in some national social spaces than others, we believe the forms of capital structuring the national social spaces of neoliberal capitalism and the global neoliberal capitalist field are the same – economic and security capital. Neoliberal ideology has also transformed other social fields in the era of advanced capitalism, most notably the bureaucratic field (i.e., the State [Bourdieu 2014]) and the economic field (Bourdieu 2005). National bureaucratic and economic fields have become more neoliberal over time through their nesting within the global neoliberal capitalist field.

The concept of a global neoliberal capitalist field as a meta-field connecting national spaces of neoliberal capitalism allows us to move past misleading distinctions between objective and subjective forms of insecurity and instead highlight the interdependent nature of subjective experiences of insecurity taking place within the objective conditions operating within fields and social spaces. It is the "double life of the social" (Bourdieu 2020:24) connecting what we traditionally think of as "subjective" thoughts and feelings with "objective" conditions. The same social structures are embedded within objects and fields (i.e., "objective" conditions) and embodied or internalized within individuals in the form of the habitus (i.e., "subjective" expectations). Bourdieu (1984:126–127) conceptualized the habitus as a third layer in the social space, connecting the space of social positions with the space of lifestyles. In the global neoliberal capitalist field, we can think of the neoliberal habitus as the space connecting social positions with varying amounts of economic and security capital to everyday decisions at home and in the workplace in an effort to establish or sustain a stable future. Wacquant (2024:199) incorporates this connection between the embodied structures of the habitus and the objective structures of social space into his theory of group making and applies it to the concept of race.

As we discussed in Chapter 7, the US space of neoliberal capitalism is a space of objective probabilities of insecurity. We used the eight combinations of food, energy, and job insecurity in Chapter 7, not to suggest that there are distinct, bounded groups based on different combinations of insecurity but to show that these different configurations map onto the space in ways that support our claim that it is a space of insecurity. Each position in the space has a different probability of experiencing one or more forms of insecurity. Using a Bourdieusian perspective, we are suggesting that what scholars and policymakers think of as "insecure" or "secure" individuals with respect to food, energy, and jobs are different locations within the national space of neoliberal capitalism. This means that insecurity is ultimately rooted in economic and security capital. Individuals occupying a similar position in space should have a similar neoliberal habitus, which then leads to similar practices in the areas of food, energy use, and work. The empirical example focusing on the US space of neoliberal capitalism allowed us to illustrate our theoretical model, but there are a number of ways in which future studies of neoliberalism can extend our work and build on our findings. We consider some of these potential future directions in the concluding section.

Concluding Thoughts

Future Research on the Global Neoliberal Capitalist Field

In this book, we attempted to move the study of neoliberalism, insecurity, and their intersection forward by engaging in a theory of practice-based theoretical and empirical analysis of these topics. To our knowledge, no one has undertaken a study of these concepts using this framework. While we believe our approach provides a number of new insights into the study of neoliberalism and insecurity, we learned lessons along the way, which we believe provide fodder for future research.

One obvious suggestion for future research is to undertake similar studies, with a similar survey, in other countries. Although the space of US neoliberal capitalism is nested within the larger global neoliberal capitalist field, there is no doubt that the spaces of neoliberal capitalism will have some homologies with the US space; there will, we expect, be differences between countries' national spaces of neoliberal capitalism – in some cases, potentially quite substantial. Understanding other national spaces of neoliberal capitalism will broaden our understanding of the global neoliberal capitalist field.

Part of our theoretical argument is that the concept of "insecurity" should be engaged as a broad concept, in addition to the specific forms. For the purposes of this book, we chose three of the most frequently studied forms of insecurity – food, energy, and job insecurity. As we noted in several places throughout the book, there are a number of other types of insecurity that we did not include in this study. While we believe that our general definition of insecurity holds when other forms of insecurity are considered, our empirical analysis of the space of US neoliberal capitalist may have been somewhat different if we included other forms of insecurity, such as housing, water, or medical insecurity. That said, we believe the structuring capitals of the space would be the same. Additionally, the statistical toolkit available to map social spaces has expanded since Bourdieu's analyses of the French spaces of class, education, and the economy in the 1960s (Bourdieu 1984, 1988, 1996, and 2005), which will allow researchers to consider more advanced geometric data analysis techniques, such as methods designed for ordinal data (see Atkinson 2024) and methods based on combinatorial inference (see Le Roux, Bienaise, and Durand 2019).

Finally, some definitions of particular types of insecurity are based on the household level (rather than the individual level) – this is something that should be unpacked in further field analyses. This begs the question, could we do a field analysis of these topics using households as the actors/agents in the field, and can a Bourdieusian framework handle it? We believe the answer to this question is most likely yes, and it would require understanding the homologies and interaction with the family field, among other issues.

Before we conclude, we would be remiss without touching on a binary that we did not interrogate. It is clearly relevant to what our approach to the study of neoliberalism and insecurity can teach us. This, of course, is the security/insecurity binary.

Moving Past the Security/Insecurity Binary

Throughout the book, we have noted that one of the attractions of a theory of practice approach to the study of neoliberalism and insecurity (or any social science topic, really) is how it avoids dualistic thinking. Scholars use numerous words when discussing Bourdieu and dualism/dichotomy/binary, such as "avoid," "transcend," "bridge," and the like to highlight that the theory of practice wasn't beholden to binaries, such as structural/individual explanations of the effects of neoliberalism in which we focused on in this book. One binary we haven't problematized to the degree in which we did the structural/individual binary of neoliberalism is security/insecurity. In most cases, whether in research, policy, or the media, people are often characterized as either "secure" or "insecure."

Understanding (in)security from a Bourdieusian perspective necessitates that dualism be avoided. However, while the macro/micro dualism in neoliberalism studies is rather well established and recognized, research on insecurity (in general and its specific forms) has not problematized the categorization of individuals into "secure" and "insecure," to nearly the same degree. We waited until now to discuss this point. In our view, it was necessary to first establish a few things in the previous chapters to be able to adequately make this point and how we see the study of (in)security moving forward. First, we needed to define the general concept of insecurity before attempting to unpack the concept theoretically. Second, providing overviews of the political economy of three of the most common forms of insecurity, coupled with a review of how neoliberalism has ushered in the era of the "neoliberal insecure subject," highlights how there are different forms and amounts of (in)security. In Chapters 1–6, we were able to discuss and theorize the ways insecurity was linked with neoliberalism – however, we were constrained by two dualisms, structural/individual-level understandings of neoliberalism and security vs. insecurity. Indeed, those dualisms even structured how we organized this book, its chapters, and their contents. In Chapter 7, however, we were able to begin pushing past that dualistic thinking.

This is where our application of the theory of practice helps move us in the direction of (at least somewhat) avoiding dualism in the study and understanding of (in)security. The global (and US) neoliberal capitalist field, structured by security and economic capital, locates individuals in a two-dimensional space by their composition and volume of the structuring capitals. Rather than someone being labeled secure or insecure, individuals are now located in the neoliberal capitalist space, providing a much more fine-grained understanding of (in)security under neoliberalism. Insecurity is a matter of one's position in this two-dimensional social space, which does not lend itself to simple categorizations of individuals as secure or insecure.

What Does the Future Hold for the Global Neoliberal Capitalist Field

During the writing of this conclusion chapter, Donald Trump was reelected as the president of the US. The Republicans also won a majority of seats in the US Senate and the US House of Representatives as well. The US has made a profound shift to the political right. The sweeping Republican victory has to do with many issues; however, perhaps the biggest issue that brought together coalitions of voters who don't normally agree was the insecurities associated with neoliberal capitalism. And, that backlash against neoliberalism (even if the word neoliberalism is not specifically used) translated to votes for Trump and other Republicans who promised a more protectionist/isolationist approach to economic and foreign policy. Trump has mused that "tariff" is his favorite word as a way of signifying his desire to reshape the US economy away from neoliberal policies. Time will tell how successful Trump and his administration will be at making the US less neoliberal.

We will end by reminding the readers, once again, that social spaces and fields are typically nested within larger fields, while also intersecting with other fields in different ways. The space of US neoliberal capitalism, despite whatever changes the Trump administration does to it, will continue to be nested within (and therefore influenced by) the global neoliberal capitalist field. The bureaucratic field (Bourdieu 2014) operating within a national space will invariably help shape the national neoliberal capitalist space. However, the vast majority of the countries of the world are capitalist, and they also have to participate in the global capitalist economy, so homologies between the space of US neoliberal capitalism and the global neoliberal capitalist field will remain. One of the primary homologies – that we argue will remain – is the importance of security capital as a structuring mechanism for both the space of US neoliberal capitalism and the global neoliberal capitalist field. Neoliberalism and insecurity are inexorably linked, and will continue to be so into the near future.

Note

1 Incarceration is a phenomenon in the US that is highly gendered, classed, and racialized (Western 2006). We did not have a sufficient sample size to explore subgroup differences in the US neoliberal capitalist space. This is an important line of inquiry for future research.

References

Atkinson, Will. 2024. "Charting Fields and Spaces Quantitatively: From Multiple Correspondence Analysis to Categorical Principal Components Analysis." *Quality & Quantity* 58: 829–848.

Atkinson, Will. 2020. *Bourdieu and After: A Guide to Relational Phenomenology*. New York: Routledge.

Bourdieu, Pierre. 2020. *Habitus and Field: General Sociology, Volume 2*. Cambridge: Polity Press.

Bourdieu, Pierre. 2014. *On the State. Lectures at the Collège de France*. Cambridge: Polity Press.

Bourdieu, Pierre. 2005. *The Social Structures of the Economy*. Cambridge: Polity Press.

Bourdieu, Pierre. 1998. *Acts of Resistance: Against the Tyranny of the Market*. New York: The New Press.

Bourdieu, Pierre. 1996. *The State Nobility*. Stanford, CA: Stanford University Press.

Bourdieu, Pierre. 1990. *The Logic of Practice*. Stanford, CA: Stanford University Press.

Bourdieu, Pierre. 1988. *Homo Academicus*. Stanford, CA: Stanford University Press.

Bourdieu, Pierre. 1984. *Distinction: A Social Critique of the Judgement of Taste*. Cambridge, MA: Harvard University Press.

Bourdieu, Pierre. 1977. *Outline of a Theory of Practice*. Cambridge: Cambridge University Press.

Bourdieu, Pierre and Loïc J. D. Wacquant. 1992. *An Invitation to Reflexive Sociology*. Chicago, IL: University of Chicago Press.
Bröckling, Ulrich. 2016. *The Entrepreneurial Self: Fabricating a New Type of Subject*. Thousand Oaks, CA: Sage.
Buchholz, Larissa. 2016. "What is a Global Field" Theorizing Fields Beyond the Nation-State." *The Sociological Review* 64(2): 31–60.
Dardot, Pierre and Christian Laval. 2014. *The New Way of the World*. New York: Verso.
Food and Agriculture Organisation of the United Nations (FAO). 2000. *The State of Food Security and Nutrition in the World*. Rome, Italy: FAO. Available at https://www.fao.org/publications/home/fao-flagship-publications/the-state-of-food-security-and-nutrition-in-the-world/en.
Foucault, Michel. 2008. *The Birth of Biopolitics: Lectures at the Collège de France, 1978–1979*. New York: Palgrave Macmillan.
Foucault, Michel. 2007. *Security, Territory Population: Lectures at the Collège de France, 1977–1978*. New York: Palgrave Macmillan.
Habermas, Jürgen. 1988. *Theory and Practice*. Boston, MA: Beacon Press.
Hernández, Diana. 2016. "Understanding 'energy insecurity' and why it matters to health." *Social Science & Medicine* 167: 1–10. https://doi.org/10.1016/j.socscimed.2016.08.029.
Hjellbrekke, Johs. 2019. *Multiple Correspondence Analysis for the Social Sciences*. Abingdon: Routledge.
Le Roux, Brigitte, Solène Bienaise, and Jean-Luc Durand. 2019. *Combinatorial Inference in Geometric Data Analysis*. Boca Raton, FL: Chapman & Hall/CRC Press.
Le Roux, Brigitte and Henry Rouanet. 2010. *Multiple Correspondence Analysis*. Thousand Oaks, CA: Sage.
Lorey, Isabell. 2015. *State of Insecurity: Government of the Precarious*. New York: Verso.
Pager, Devah. 2007. *Marked: Race, Crime, and Finding Work in an Era of Mass Incarceration*. Chicago, IL: University of Chicago Press.
Swartz, David. 1997. *Culture & Power: The Sociology of Pierre Bourdieu*. Chicago, IL: University of Chicago Press.
Taylor, Astra. 2023. *The Age of Insecurity: Coming Together as Things Fall Apart*. Toronto: House of Anansi Press.
Wacquant, Loïc. 2024. *Racial Domination*. Cambridge: Polity Press.
Western, Bruce. 2006. *Punishment and Inequality in America*. New York: Russell Sage Foundation.
World Health Organization. 2006. *Fuel for Life: Household Energy and Health*. Geneva: World Health Organization. Available at https://iris.who.int/bitstream/handle/10665/43421/9241563168_eng.pdf.

APPENDIX A

Cross-National Incarceration Rates (Per 100,000 People) by Decade, 1950–Present

	Incarceration Rate								
Country	*1950*	*1960*	*1970*	*1980*	*1990*	*2000*	*2010*	*2020*	*Most recent*
Afghanistan						22	65	62	45
Albania					92	99	167	176	189
Algeria					122	108	161	151	217
American Samoa (USA)					148	241	337	350	538
Andorra					76	72	78	63	73
Angola					36	26	90	89	79
Anguilla (United Kingdom)						342	414	367	240
Antigua and Barbuda					327	218	339	280	400
Argentina			97	83	62	151	157	233	254
Armenia					161	236	162	75	79
Aruba (Netherlands)					242	253	232	165	288
Australia		72	82	66	84	114	135	160	158
Austria		116	121	107	83	86	102	94	98
Azerbaijan						317	241	214	244
Bahamas			1092	1823	485	470	372	460	409
Bahrain					56	57	89	281	234
Bangladesh			55	30	36	47	46	52	50
Barbados						527	322	296	258

(*Continued*)

(Continued)

	Incarceration Rate								
Country	*1950*	*1960*	*1970*	*1980*	*1990*	*2000*	*2010*	*2020*	*Most recent*
Belarus						566	418	370	345
Belgium	104	58	61	58	67	85	97	90	97
Belize			622	588	316	310	441	296	289
Benin					59	71	73	80	111
Bermuda (United Kingdom)				297	452	517	428	275	200
Bhutan							137	143	145
Bolivia				52	69	95	93	147	209
Bosnia and Herzegovina: Federation						45	77	78	83
Bosnia and Herzegovina: Republika Srpska					57	61	75	46	44
Botswana				259	378	381	256	162	161
Brazil	32	31	33	61	107	132	249	381	390
Brunei Darussalam				41	66	101	96	307	186
Bulgaria					156	124	131	106	101
Burkina Faso						19	33	35	39
Burundi					118	130	100	96	102
Cambodia			7		19	45	97	233	219
Cameroon					136	119	112	117	116
Canada	117	115	105	96	121	115	117	104	88
Cape Verde (Cabo Verde)					148	267	273	306	366
Cayman Islands (United Kingdom)				249	546	565	382	300	277
Central African Republic						25	19	26	40
Chad						29	41	59	59
Chile			142	136	171	215	320	215	281
China					107	111	121	121	119
Colombia				139	119	128	183	193	198
Comoros						39	22	26	46
Congo (Republic of)						44	33	33	27

(Continued)

(Continued)

	Incarceration Rate								
Country	*1950*	*1960*	*1970*	*1980*	*1990*	*2000*	*2010*	*2020*	*Most recent*
Cook Islands (New Zealand)						128	200	229	224
Costa Rica			81	100	127	193	259	395	298
Cote d'Ivoire					90	62	33	82	95
Croatia				82	32	45	110	87	106
Cuba							531	510	794
Curaçao (Netherlands)					346	431	365	236	261
Cyprus (Republic of)			42	35	37	45	108	73	103
Czech Republic	387	271	177	254	80	210	209	180	179
Democratic Republic of Congo						58	35	29	46
Denmark	88	71	70	63	67	63	71	70	69
Djibouti					100	27	89	67	71
Dominica			231	195	276	307	415	300	348
Dominican Republic				90	143	173	208	242	223
Ecuador			57	68	76	64	79	213	167
Egypt				68	58	84	83	114	116
El Salvador	254	294	166	73	112	132	399	572	1086
Equatorial Guinea								63	63
Estonia				404	284	343	267	184	132
Eswatini/ Swaziland					217	257	311	277	243
Ethiopia				85	55	85	136	127	99
Faeroe Islands (Denmark)					18	20	20	21	23
Fiji			123		110	146	127	276	248
Finland	187	154	111	106	69	55	61	51	51
France	88	59	57	66	78	82	99	119	109
French Guiana/ Guyane (France)					228	247	306	200	305
French Polynesia (France)					110	114	156	212	178
Gabon						195	210	241	228

(Continued)

(Continued)

	Incarceration Rate								
Country	*1950*	*1960*	*1970*	*1980*	*1990*	*2000*	*2010*	*2020*	*Most recent*
Gambia					40	34	53	29	22
Georgia					152	190	530	245	256
Germany					74	85	85	72	67
Ghana				42	46	51	56	43	45
Gibraltar (United Kingdom)			39	94	75	67	180	139	273
Greece		66	38	33	52	70	102	102	101
Greenland (Denmark)					165	157	302	233	241
Grenada					324	291	408	316	335
Guadeloupe (France)					169	147	174	172	197
Guam (USA)					258	440	352	318	475
Guatemala				61	58	62	78	142	123
Guernsey (United Kingdom)				53	69	94	114	131	125
Guinea (Republic of)					49	34	35	23	34
Guinea Bissau								31	31
Guyana			147	120	219	205	286	239	271
Haiti					21	49	53	94	99
Honduras				91	109	175	141	218	191
Hong Kong (China)			154	129	211	180	142	95	106
Hungary	200	137	178	164	119	152	163	172	203
Iceland				24	41	28	52	44	36
India			34		21	26	30	35	41
Indonesia			36		23	26	49	91	94
Iran				26	172	237	331	294	228
Iraq						26	125	145	179
Ireland, Republic of	18	16	25	36	60	77	94	74	88
Isle of Man (United Kingdom)				81	94	70	115	130	103
Israel			138	190	189	158	270	234	217
Italy	76	71	40	56	46	93	112	89	103
Jamaica			120	147	126	178	161	130	125
Japan	113	76	45	43	38	48	57	37	36

(Continued)

(Continued)

	Incarceration Rate								
Country	*1950*	*1960*	*1970*	*1980*	*1990*	*2000*	*2010*	*2020*	*Most recent*
Jersey (United Kingdom)					125	150	183	125	135
Jordan					87	107	82	198	185
Kazakhstan			466	539	336	520	393	157	184
Kenya			162		116	129	118	81	107
Kiribati					77	68	87	109	113
Kosovo/Kosova						11	81	101	99
Kuwait				96	106	162	131	117	103
Kyrgyzstan					203	402	183	171	117
Laos						70	94	119	166
Latvia				492	327	370	333	179	172
Lebanon					88	129	102	98	129
Lesotho					133	143	125	115	104
Liberia						29	39	54	55
Libya					135	178	220	139	269
Liechtenstein					59	50	39	31	15
Lithuania				326	232	410	275	220	177
Luxembourg	133	66	63	68	92	90	136	87	107
Macau (China)					207	196	172	227	197
Madagascar					180	121	89	99	98
Malawi					48	69	78	71	76
Malaysia			23	98	124	116	137	206	217
Maldives				1234	404	776	227	370	314
Mali					49	38	40	30	40
Malta	41	18	11	32	61	70	144	167	132
Marshall Islands					79	38	79	68	66
Martinique (France)				62	112	156	225	216	261
Mauritania					56	50	47	47	57
Mauritius			211	181	92	137	196	217	197
Mayotte (France)					88	98	99	158	186
Mexico			77	90	110	156	191	169	174
Micronesia, Federated States of					71	85	92	103	127
Moldova (Republic of)				353	253	260	183	254	236
Monaco					37	51	34	34	69
Mongolia					268	275	260	110	183
Montenegro						110	235	176	166

(Continued)

(Continued)

	Incarceration Rate								
Country	*1950*	*1960*	*1970*	*1980*	*1990*	*2000*	*2010*	*2020*	*Most recent*
Morocco		70	90	102	132	187	201	232	270
Mozambique					43	48	64	63	67
Myanmar (formerly Burma)					125	68	131	171	183
Namibia					176	254	191	157	318
Nauru						60	370	260	140
Nepal					30	25	40	87	90
Netherlands	54	45	30	27	45	87	92	60	65
New Caledonia (France)					149	154	171	180	201
New Zealand	54	74	83	83	116	148	198	186	173
Nicaragua					82	128	113	238	332
Niger					51	51	45	39	40
Nigeria				53	57	36	29	30	34
North Macedonia				95	83	59	122	102	138
Northern Mariana Islands (USA)					119	141	304	313	273
Norway	51	44	44	44	56	57	74	54	52
Oman						88	92	13	46
Pakistan					58	56	40	37	38
Palau						368	511	522	428
Panama			113	115	135	283	341	416	499
Papua New Guinea			153	75	74	65	61	60	54
Paraguay			59	44	51	60	99	194	233
Peru			80	100	82	107	155	277	272
Philippines					53	102	103	151	162
Poland	392	330	252	279	132	184	212	179	197
Portugal			64	56	92	126	110	111	116
Puerto Rico (USA)				130	315	384	294	285	221
Qatar				114	107	96	60	60	58
Republic of (South) Korea				130	124	136	97	105	103
Reunion (France)					143	144	129	132	137
Romania				132	112	215	140	113	124
Russian Federation					473	729	609	363	300

(Continued)

(Continued)

	Incarceration Rate								
Country	*1950*	*1960*	*1970*	*1980*	*1990*	*2000*	*2010*	*2020*	*Most recent*
Rwanda				126	99	227	547	545	637
Samoa					126	99	227	202	179
San Marino									9
Sao Tome e Principe					78	90	171	116	115
Saudi Arabia					120	116	176	161	207
Senegal					49	51	59	63	69
Serbia					37	82	155	153	162
Seychelles			653	494		205	462	345	413
Sierra Leone						26	34	47	57
Singapore				99	179	352	250	185	156
Sint Maarten (Netherlands)						396	405	179	196
Slovakia				244	87	129	186	192	179
Slovenia				73	42	58	64	56	84
Solomon Islands					91	28	51	77	79
South Africa		362	411	409	327	394	328	259	258
South Sudan							77	50	58
Spain	109	50	41	48	85	113	165	117	113
Sri Lanka			63	70	58	87	130	121	149
St. Kitts and Nevis				272	281	424	522	347	296
St. Lucia				134	203	291	301	184	308
St. Vincent and the Grenadines				151	297	280	379	369	353
Sudan					39	44	57	213	52
Suriname					120	163	194	197	185
Sweden	35	63	65	55	58	60	74	73	82
Switzerland				71	76	80	79	80	73
Syria					92	68			60
Taiwan					200	254	282	248	239
Tajikistan					74	175	121	118	141
Tanzania		113			138	135	81	52	50
Thailand		72	132	159	148	354	313	516	377
Timor-Leste (formerly East Timor)						35	23	53	55
Togo					78	61	64	50	59
Tonga			232	138	81	108	152	150	166

(Continued)

(Continued)

	Incarceration Rate								
Country	*1950*	*1960*	*1970*	*1980*	*1990*	*2000*	*2010*	*2020*	*Most recent*
Trinidad and Tobago		575	381	75	238	365	283	292	276
Tunisia					252	261	196	194	196
Turkey			161	156	81	73	164	319	340
Turkmenistan						410	488	552	576
Tuvalu						67	80	120	110
Uganda	51		93		98	92	91	133	150
Ukraine					225	443	338	126	123
United Arab Emirates					213	351	107		104
United Kingdom: England and Wales	47	59	80	87	90	124	153	133	145
United Kingdom: Northern Ireland			54	169	112	64	81	77	97
United Kingdom: Scotland	35	55	96	94	93	116	150	128	143
USA	176	193	161	220	457	683	731	505	531
Uruguay			80	64	95	135	257	372	424
Uzbekistan					258	258	143	68	85
Vanuatu					42	49	75	86	65
Venezuela		95	131	84	152	58	140	113	199
Vietnam					56	104	126	135	135
Virgin Islands (United Kingdom)					215	457	418	477	368
Virgin Islands (USA)					436	475	544	361	345
Yemen					84	84	42	48	35
Zambia					146	116	128	109	125
Zimbabwe					152	164	96	136	138

Source: World Prison Brief. 2024. "World Prison Brief Data." Institute for Crime & Justice Policy Research: Birkbeck University of London (accessed February 16, 2024). Available at: https://www.prisonstudies.org/world-prison-brief-data.

Note: In cases where incarceration values for the actual year were not available, we report the value for the closest year within that same decade.

APPENDIX B

Insecurity Survey

Q1

Please enter your unique Prolific ID.

The first set of questions concern your family growing up.

Q2

Were you living with both your own mother and father around the time you were 16?

1 Yes (mother and father together)
2 Yes (mother and father separately)
3 No
4 Don't know

Q2a

With whom were you living around that time?

1 Father and stepmother
2 Mother and stepfather
3 Father – no mother or stepmother
4 Mother – no father or stepfather
5 Some other male relative (no female head)
6 Some other female relative (no male head)

7 Other arrangement with both male and female relatives (e.g., aunt and uncle, grandparents)
8 Other (specify)
9 Don't know

Q3

What is the highest level of school your father (stepfather, or another adult male relative you lived with at age 16) completed or the highest degree he received?

1 Grade school or less (0-8 grades)
2 High school (12 grades or fewer)
3 Some college (13 grades or more but no degree)
4 College or advanced degree
5 Don't know

Q4

What is the highest level of school your mother (or another adult female relative you lived with at age 16) completed or the highest degree she received?

1 Grade school or less (0-8 grades)
2 High school (12 grades or fewer)
3 Some college (13 grades or more but no degree)
4 College or advanced degree
5 Don't know

Q5

What kind of work did your father (or stepfather, or another adult male relative you lived with at age 16) do for a living while you were growing up?

Open-ended response

Q6

What kind of work did your mother (or stepmother, or another adult female relative you lived with at age 16) do for a living while you were growing up?

Open-ended response

The next set of questions ask about your current employment situation.

Q7

At any time during the last ten years, have you been unemployed and looking for work for as long as a month?

1 Yes
2 No
3 Don't know

Q8

Last week were you working full time, part-time, going to school, keeping house, or what? Please provide one response only. If you were doing more than one of these last week, select the one closest to the top of the list.

1 Working full-time
2 Working part-time
3 With a job, but not at work because of temporary illness, vacation, strike
4 Unemployed, laid off, looking for work
5 Retired
6 In school
7 Keeping house
8 Other
9 Don't know

Responses 1, 2, or 3 ⟶ Continue on to Q9
Responses 4 through 9 ⟶ Skip to Q24

Q9

Are you self-employed or do you work for someone else?

1 Self-employed
2 Someone else
3 Don't know

Q10

On the whole, how satisfied are you with the work you do – would you say you are very satisfied, moderately satisfied, a little dissatisfied, or very dissatisfied?

1 Very satisfied
2 Moderately satisfied

3 A little dissatisfied
4 Very dissatisfied
5 Don't know

Q11

How many hours did you work last week, at all jobs?

Open-ended response

Q12

What is your occupation? I mean, what kind of work do you do?

Open-ended response

Q13

In what type of business or industry is your (or your employer's) company located?

Open-ended response

Q14

How long have you worked in your present job for your current employer or self-employed?

1 Less than one year
2 One to five years
3 Six to ten years
4 More than ten years
5 Don't know

Q15

Do you belong to a labor union?

1 Yes
2 No
3 Don't know

Q16

Would you say it is very true, somewhat true, not too true, or not at all true that your chances for promotion at work are good?

1 Very true
2 Somewhat true

3 Not too true
4 Not at all true
5 Don't know

Q17

As an official part of your main job, do you supervise the work of other employees or tell other employees what work to do?

1 Yes
2 No
3 Don't know

Q18

The next question concerns policymaking at your workplace, that is, making decisions about such things as the products or services delivered, the total number of people employed, and budgets. Do you participate in making these kinds of decisions, or even provide advice about them?

1 Yes
2 No
3 Don't know

Q19

Is yours a job in which you are required to design important aspects of your own work and to put your ideas into practice? Or is yours a job in which you are not required to design important aspects of your work or to put your ideas into practice, except perhaps in minor details?

1 Required to design work
2 Not required to design work
3 Don't know

Q20

Can you decide when to come to work and when to leave work, either officially or unofficially?

1 Yes
2 No
3 Don't know

Q21

Thinking about the next 12 months, how likely do you think it is that you will lose your job or be laid off – very likely, fairly likely, not too likely, or not at all likely?

1 Very likely
2 Fairly likely
3 Not too likely
4 Not at all likely
5 Don't know

Q22

How easy would it be for you to find a job with another employer with approximately the same income and fringe benefits you now have? Would you say very easy, somewhat easy, not too easy, or not easy at all.

1 Very easy
2 Somewhat easy
3 Not too easy
4 Not easy at all
5 Don't know

Q23

To what extent, if at all, do you worry about the possibility of losing your job? Would you say...

1 I worry a great deal
2 I worry to some extent
3 I worry a little
4 I don't worry at all
5 Don't know

The next few questions deal with energy use and bills in your house or apartment.

Q24

How much attention do you pay to the amount of energy you use to heat/cool your home?

1 None at all
2 Hardly any

3 A little
4 A fair amount
5 A lot
6 Don't know

Q25a

[Option 1] You said that you pay [a lot / a fair amount] of attention to the amount of energy you use to heat/cool your home. What is the main reason for this?

1 To minimize the money, spend on energy
2 To make sure my home is comfortable
3 To minimize the environmental impact of energy used for heating/cooling
4 To keep control over the amount of heat/cooling used
5 Other reason
6 Don't know

Q25b

[Option 2] You said that you pay [only a little/hardly any/no] attention to the amount of heat/cool your home. What is the main reason for this?

1 I use as much energy as needed to be comfortable
2 I set controls at a level I'm comfortable with then don't need to adjust
3 I don't feel I can control the amount of energy used to heat/cool my home
4 I'm just not interested in the amount of energy used to heat/cool my home
5 Other
6 Don't know

Q26

Over the last 12 months, how worried, if at all, have you been about paying for energy bills (gas/electricity)?

1 Very worried
2 Fairly worried
3 Not very worried
4 Not at all worried
5 Don't know

Q27a–Q27f

During the past 12 months, did your household cut back on fuel use at home in any of these ways listed below, because you could not afford the costs?

	Yes (1)	*No (2)*	*Prefer not to say (3)*
Turned heating/cooling down or off, even though it was uncomfortable in the house/flat	Checkbox	Checkbox	Checkbox
Only heated/cooled part of the house	Checkbox	Checkbox	Checkbox
Cut the number of hours that heating/cooling was on to reduce fuel costs	Checkbox	Checkbox	Checkbox
Used less hot water than I/we need to reduce fuel costs	Checkbox	Checkbox	Checkbox
Turned out more lights in my home than I/we needed to try and reduce the electricity bill	Checkbox	Checkbox	Checkbox
Had fewer hot meals or hot drinks that I/we needed to reduce fuel costs	Checkbox	Checkbox	Checkbox

Next, we would like to ask some questions about food and meals in your home.

For the following statements that people have made about their food situation, please indicate whether the statement was often true, sometimes true, hardly ever true, or never true for you in the last 12 months.

Q28

"The food that I bought just didn't last, and I didn't have money to get more." Was that often, sometimes, or never true for you in the last 12 months?

1 Often true
2 Sometimes true
3 Never true
4 Don't know

Q29

"I couldn't afford to eat balanced meals." Was that often, sometimes, or never true for you in the last 12 months?

1 Often true
2 Sometimes true
3 Never true
4 Don't know

Q30

"In the last 12 months, did you ever cut the size of your meals or skip meals because there wasn't enough money for food?"

1 Yes
2 No
3 Don't know

Q31

[IF YES ABOVE, ASK] "How often did this happen – almost every month, some months but not every month, or in only one or two months?"

1 Almost every month
2 Some months but not every month
3 Only one or two months
4 Don't know

Q32

"In the last 12 months, did you ever eat less than you felt you should because there wasn't enough money for food?"

1 Yes
2 No
3 Don't know

Q33

"In the last 12 months, were you ever hungry but didn't eat because there wasn't enough money for food?"

1 Yes
2 No
3 Don't know

Q34

The color test you are about to take part in is very simple. When asked your favorite color, you must select 'Green.' This is an attention check.

Based on the text you read above, what color have you been asked to enter?

1 Red
2 Blue

3 Green
4 Orange
5 Brown

The next set of questions deal with financial matters.

Q35

Suppose you had $100 in a savings account and the interest rate was 2% per year. After five years, how much do you think you would have in the account if you left the money to grow:

1 More than $102
2 Exactly $102
3 Less than $102
4 Don't know

Q36

Imagine that the interest rate on your savings account was 1% per year and inflation was 2% per year. After one year, would you be able to buy more than, exactly the same as, or less than today with the money in this account?

1 More than today
2 Exactly the same as today
3 Less than today
4 Don't know

Q37

Do you think that the following statement is true or false? "Buying a single company stock usually provides a safer return than a stock mutual fund."

1 True
2 False
3 Don't know

Q38

Do you currently have any retirement accounts such as a 401(k), 403(b), IRA, or other account designed specifically for retirement savings?

1 Yes
2 No
3 Don't know

Q39

In the past 12 months, have you invested money in a stock or mutual fund?

1 Yes
2 No
3 Don't know

Q40

Do you have money in an interest-earning checking account?

1 Yes
2 No
3 Don't know

Q41

Do you have money in a savings account?

1 Yes
2 No
3 Don't know

Q42

In the past 12 months, have you met with a financial advisor to discuss investments, planning for retirement, or other financial goals you may have?

1 Yes
2 No
3 Don't know

These next few questions have to do with your residence.

Q43

Do you grow any food at your residence to help supplement what you purchase to eat (e.g., have a fruit and/or vegetable garden)?

1 Yes
2 No
3 Don't know

Q44

Do you raise any animals at your residence in which you use to make food products to supplement what you purchase to eat (milk from cows, goats, etc., cheese made from the milk, chicken eggs, etc.)?

1 Yes
2 No
3 Don't know

Q45

Do you have a back-up electricity generator at your residence that keeps the electricity on in the event of a power outage?

1 Yes
2 No
3 Don't know

Q46

Do you have any alternative energy storage/supply mechanisms (e.g., solar panels) at your place of residence to supplement the electricity you pay for from a provider?

1 Yes
2 No
3 Don't know

Q47

Which category represents the total combined income of all members of this FAMILY during the past 12 months? This includes money from jobs, net income from business, farm or rent, pensions, dividends, interest, social security payments, and any other money income received by members of this family who are 15 years of age or older?

1 Less than $5,000
2 $5,000–$7,499
3 $7,500–$9,999
4 $10,000–$12,499
5 $12,500–$14,999
6 $15,000–$19,999

7 $20,000–$24,999
8 $25,000–$29,999
9 $30,000–$34,999
10 $35,000–$39,999
11 $40,000–$49,999
12 $50,000–$59,999
13 $60,000–$74,999
14 $75,000–$99,999
15 $100,000–$149,000
16 $150,000 or more
17 Don't know

The last set of questions deal with basic questions about your personal history and current situation.

Q48

In what year were you born?

Open-ended response

Q49

What is the highest level of school you have completed or the highest degree you have received?

1 Grade school or less (0–8 grades)
2 High school (12 grades or fewer)
3 Some college (13 grades or more but no degree)
4 College or advanced degree
5 Don't know

Q50

Are you currently married, widowed, divorced, separated, or have you never been married?

1 Married
2 Widowed
3 Divorced
4 Separated
5 Never married
6 Don't know

Q51

How many children have you ever had? Please count all that were born alive at any time (including any you had from a previous marriage).

Open-ended response

Q52

Currently, do you (or does your family) own your home, pay rent, or something else?

1 Own or is buying
2 Pays rent
3 Other
4 Don't know

Q53

Do you currently have health insurance coverage?

1 Yes
2 No
3 Don't know

Q54

If YES: What is the source of your health insurance?

1 Employer
2 Employer of my spouse or partner
3 Employer of another family member
4 Medicaid
5 Medicare
6 Individual plan from a private company
7 Other
8 Don't know

Q55

Do you currently have homeowner's or renter's insurance?

1 Yes, home-owner's insurance
2 Yes, renter's insurance

3 Yes, both
4 No
5 Don't know

Q56

Would you say your own health, in general, is excellent, good, fair, or poor?

1 Excellent
2 Good
3 Fair
4 Poor
5 Don't know

Q57

Do you describe yourself as male, female, or transgender?

1 Male
2 Female
3 Transgender
4 Something else
5 Don't know

Q58

What is your race and/or ethnicity?

1 American Indian or Alaska Native
2 Asian
3 Black or African American
4 Hispanic or Latino
5 Middle Eastern or North African
6 Native Hawaiian or Pacific Islander
7 White
8 Two or more races or ethnicities
9 None of these
10 Don't know

Q59

In what state or foreign country were you living when you were 16 years old?

Open-ended response

Q60

In what state do you currently live?

Open-ended response

Q61

Do you currently live in the same city or town you lived in when you were 16 years old?

1 Yes
2 No
3 Don't know

Q62

How many days per week do you exercise in a typical week?

Open-ended response

Q63

How would you rate your diet?

1 Excellent
2 Good
3 Fair
4 Poor
5 Don't know

Q64

Not counting minor traffic offenses, have you ever been convicted of a crime?

1 Yes
2 No
3 Don't know

Q65

Have you ever spent any time in prison or jail?

1 Yes
2 No
3 Don't know

Thank you for participating in this survey!

INDEX

Note: **Bold** page numbers refer to tables; *italic* page numbers refer to figures and page numbers followed by "n" denote endnotes.